Globalization, Development and the Mass Media

Globalization, Development and the Mass Media

Colin Sparks

SAGE Publications
Los Angeles • London • New Delhi • Singapore

SAGE Publications Ltd
1 Oliver's Yard
55 City Road
London EC1Y 1SP

SAGE Publications Inc.
2455 Teller Road
Thousand Oaks, California 91320

SAGE Publications India Pvt Ltd
B 1/I 1 Mohan Cooperative Industrial Area
Mathura Road
New Delhi 110 044

SAGE Publications Asia-Pacific Pte Ltd
33 Pekin Street #02-01
Far East Square
Singapore 048763

Library of Congress Control Number: 2007922075

British Library Cataloguing in Publication data

A catalogue record for this book is available from the British
Library

ISBN 0 978-0-7619-6161-1
ISBN 0 978-0-7619-6162-8 (pbk)

Typeset by CEPHA Imaging Pvt. Ltd., Bangalore, India
Printed in India at Replika Press Pvt Ltd
Printed on paper from sustainable resources

CONTENTS

ACKNOWLEDGEMENTS

Few books are written without the help of others, and this is no exception. I have benefited enormously from help by, and discussions with, a wide range of people and here I can only acknowledge very few of them. Needless to say, none of them is at all responsible for what appears here.

My first debt is a surprising one. The train of thought that led to this book was started by some casual remarks about the obsolescence of development made to me by Professor Adam Kuper of Brunel University. I am sure he does not remember them, and my thinking strayed a long way from his original point, but he nevertheless deserves the credit, or otherwise, for the genesis of this book.

The University of Westminster, and in particular the staff of the Communication and Media Research Institute, provided a relatively comfortable base from which to work on these problems. I am particularly indebted to the Dean of the School of Media, Art and Design, Sally Feldman, and her successive Research Directors, Professor Vincent Porter and Professor Annette Hill, for finding the resources to free some time for me. My colleagues Dr Naomi Sakr, Dr Tarik Sabry and Dr Winston Mano and Professor Daya Thussu have provided many valuable insights from their areas of expertise.

My research was helped enormously by the World Association for Christian Communication, and in particular by Dr Pradip Thomas, in allowing me to use their outstanding library and in giving me guidance on some of their more arcane holdings. Despite our philosophical differences, Dr Thomas and his colleagues were kindness and generosity personified.

A late version of the manuscript was read by Dr Peter Goodwin, Head of the Department of Journalism and Mass Communication at Westminster and by Dr Des Freedman of Goldsmiths College. They both made very valuable suggestions. Some of them I have followed, some it proved impossible to implement, and some I callously ignored. I thank them for all of the comments, whatever their fate.

I owe a completely different debt to my family, Susan and Katharine Sparks, and it is to them that I dedicate this book.

1

INTRODUCTION

This book is about the role that the media and other forms of communication can play in improving the conditions of life for the world's poorest people. The scale and depth of world poverty is perhaps too familiar, but some of the figures bear rehearsing once again. According to the World Bank, in 2002 there were 1,200,000,000 people who lived below its official poverty line, which is set at an income of $1 per day (World Bank, 2002a: 2). Many millions more live on incomes only a little higher. Roughly the same number of people has no access to safe drinking water and 2.4 billion lack adequate sanitation facilities (Schumacher, 2005). More than one billion have no access to electricity (World Energy Outlook, 2002). Worldwide in 2005, 771 million people, the majority of them women, were judged illiterate according to the most basic of definitions (UIS, 2005). 150,000,000 children under five years of age were malnourished in 2000 (World Bank, 2002b: 3). The litany of absolute deprivation goes on and on. The lives of these people are immeasurably remote from the experiences of the writer of this book, and from that of the vast majority of its readers, but common humanity must surely suggest to all of us that improving the lot of the world's poor is one of the most pressing collective tasks we face.

Poor and very poor people are to be found all over the world, even in the fabulously rich cities of Europe and North America, just as extremely rich people are to be found living in luxury surrounded by a sea of poverty in those countries where 23 per cent of the population exist below the World Bank's official poverty line. The vast majority of the poor, however, live in poor countries. Many live in Asia and make up a good proportion of the huge populations of India and China. Many more live in Africa and further millions are to be found in Latin America. There are even many who are very poor, in relative terms at least, living in the countries that have emerged from the collapse of Soviet communism.

The countries that are hosts to these oceans of human misery have been given various labels, many of which contain some derivative of the verb 'to develop': less-developed countries, under-developed countries, and developing countries. The very categories proclaim that changing the circumstances that blight the lives of millions is an urgent and present task. Literally millions of people – politicians, scholars, bankers, activists and very ordinary people – have for over more than half a century tried to find ways to end the conditions that produce poverty. These efforts have not been entirely fruitless. There has been change and progress, but it has been bitterly slow. The total number of people living on an income below $1 per day fell from 1.3 billion to 1.2 billion in the course of the 1990s. In some parts of the world, notably China, the fall in the numbers of the extremely poor was quite sharp, although the gap between rich and poor widened drastically and the destruction of existing social infrastructure has meant that while incomes rose marginally living standards remained static or even declined (Hart-Landsberg and Burkett, 2005: 67). Elsewhere, notably in the former communist countries of central Asia, poverty increased inexorably (World Bank, 2002a: 2).

Some of the people who have been concerned about development issues have been interested in the media. They have tried to find ways in which communication, and particularly the mass media of newspapers, radio and television, can be used to help countries 'develop' and thus to reduce the amount of poverty. Most recently, there has been enormous interest in the potential of the internet to aid in development. Many of those who have tried to use the media for development have been activists – journalists and broadcasters, development workers and politicians – but some have had a more theoretical role. There have been thousands of books and articles dedicated to trying to understand what role the media might play in development, and to finding ways in which it might play such a role more effectively. Unlike many areas of communication theory, these investigations have often been closely tied to practice: scholars have theorized about the best ways to use the media to help development, and activists have tried to implement their findings.

This book is concerned first with ideas about development and the media. It seeks to understand the theories that have more or less directly guided thousands of practical development projects, and it draws on the distilled experience of those projects – some of the most grandiose were even formally called 'experiments'– as one of the ways of judging the value of the theories themselves. These close links between the ideas discussed in the academy and their immediate practical utility are a relatively rare, and for this writer very attractive, feature of much of the writing about the role of the media in development. Here, however, the focus is on the theories that guided action rather than on the details of the practical implementation of development projects.

Not everyone who has written in this field has had a close concern with practical projects, and even many who did have such concerns based them explicitly on general theoretical propositions. More recently, and particularly in the last decade, writers about the international role of communication have tended to be influenced by theories of globalization, and have more or less consciously believed that the solution to poverty lay not in human agency but in the impersonal working of the market. For many of them, the only valid kind of practical project is that which leads to the opening of markets and the freeing of trade. Just as the World Bank, the IMF and the governments of the developed world came to agree on the 'Washington Consensus' that attempts at protection and the defence of local industries are obstacles to development, so there are those in the field of communication who hold similar views of the mass media. This book is also concerned with those theories, since they have, in the academy at least, replaced earlier interests in communication and development, although, as we shall see, ideas that are regarded as hopelessly outmoded in the best universities can retain a vigorous life outside their walls.

The historical dimension

The intellectual history of this field is conventionally divided into three, and sometimes four, distinct phases (Boyd-Barrett, 1997: 16–21; Sreberny-Mohammadi, 1991). The first concerns were with the effect of international propaganda, particularly in the context of the great wars of the twentieth century. Immediately after the Second World War, some of the people who had worked on propaganda issues began to think about the media and development. They believed that the mass media had a crucial role to play in fostering modern attitudes and beliefs, which were thought to be the primary conditions for any significant social changes. This was the period during which what came to be called the 'dominant paradigm' of development communication was elaborated. It was followed by a much more critical phase, in which two distinct emphases are discernable in the literature. On the one hand, attention was focused upon the structures of international communication, which were held to be at least partly responsible for the continued subordination of developing countries to the interests of the metropolitan powers. Media and cultural imperialism were the central theoretical concerns of what we may term the 'imperialism paradigm'. The other line of thought saw the key weakness of the dominant paradigm as residing in its top-down approach. It started from a belief that the experts know what is best for everyone else, and designed communication programmes to transmit the fruits of that expertise to the people who were to 'be developed'. The alternative was to find ways of allowing the objects of development to become its subjects, and to use the media to give them a voice of their own. This stress upon the needs of the communities in question in discussion of development we may term the 'participatory paradigm'.

In contrast to both of these approaches, more recent writing has stressed the extent of the global flow of media content, and seen in the variety of interpretations open to audiences evidence that the mass media could not possibly have the kinds of direct influence ascribed to them by earlier schools of thought. On the contrary, the products of the world's media industries often had a liberating effect, breaking down the habits and routines of obsolete social orders and promoting change and development. This domestication of the interests of grand social theory to the concerns of the media we should obviously term the 'globalization paradigm'. To this more or less conventional account, I will only add that most recently there have been some small signs of the emergence of a generation of writers who are advancing what may become another new paradigm, although this is as yet so underdeveloped that it is difficult to give it the same kind of snappy title as its predecessors (Hafez, 2007).

The general outline of this intellectual history is widely agreed by commentators on the field, and this book will not offer any radical departures from its main contours. We should note, however, that the different phases of this debate do not fit perfectly together. The concern with development communication, in all its variants, has a stress upon the local. The imperialism paradigm and the globalization paradigm, on the other hand, are concerned with very large scale issues. In practice, it is true, some of the later versions of development communication were quite closely associated with the imperialism paradigm, and more recently attempts have been made to associate them with globalization. As we shall see, these linkages have never been theorized, and indeed they rest on radically different foundations. The aim of making such a linkage was nevertheless entirely justified. The kinds of social change that are at stake in this book are ones that necessarily raise broader issues of power and property, and one of the aims here is to sketch how these two levels of analysis might be brought together more satisfactorily.

As a consequence, this book follows the established historical succession rather closely, but I would like at the outset to offer a disclaimer: this book does not pretend to be a formal history of the field. The study of intellectual history is as fascinating as any other kind of historical enquiry, but it imposes disciplines of completeness that are not appropriate to this project and it implies a greater dependence upon the written record than will be found here, where the focus is more on interpretation. There are large parts of what everyone would recognize as the 'history' of this field that are treated rather cursorily because they are not pertinent to the main focus of the book. A case in point is the detail of the progress of the New World Information and Communication Order through the various arms of UNESCO, which was one of the major sites of conflict about international communication for a decade in the 1970s and 1980s. As it happens, the succession of conferences, resolutions, amendments, victories and defeats, are well covered elsewhere, for example by Nordenstreng (1984, 1993), and I have very little to add to such scholarly endeavours. Many of the issues that were raised in that conflict, however, remain unresolved and the aim here is to address at least some of those rather than re-analyse the record. Of course, it is neither possible nor desirable to ignore the succession of events, since the relationship between theory and practice was, in this instance, both extremely close and very problematic, but the focus is on the guiding ideas rather than on the details of resolutions and votes.

Issues of redundancy and competence apart, the main reason there is no attempt here to produce a genuine history of the field because the aim is to present many of these ideas as contemporary concerns that continue to inform practice. Just as development, at least in the non-theoretical sense of people struggling to lift themselves out of poverty, remains the central existential concern for millions of people, so important parts of the legacy of thinking about the developmental role of the mass media remain in active use as practical guides around the world.

It is entirely true that very few people in the best academies in the USA or Europe are today much interested in development communication, in theoretical critiques of the dominant paradigm, or the implications of the distinction between media and cultural imperialism. At best, it is the province of specialists closely linked with practical concerns (Gumicio-Dagron and Tufte, 2006). This is partly for a very good reason: academics are trained to keep up to date, and to concentrate their energies on emerging issues and concerns. Intellectual historians apart, few people are concerned with material published forty or fifty years ago. There are, however, also some very bad reasons for the neglect of these ideas. One is the belief, which is emphatically not shared here, that change in the social sciences equates with progress in our understanding of the world. On this account, 'more recent' equals 'better'. Whatever may be the case in the physical sciences, social science is so bound up with interpretation that we cannot assume that date determines value. Max Weber, who figures largely in much of what follows, as he must in any account of communication theory, died eighty years ago, but he still remains an enormously interesting and stimulating author whose ideas were, in the 1990s, applied with great effect to very contemporary phenomena (Ritzer, 1993). The view taken here is that it is worth reading some of the texts of earlier phases of communication theory for the same reason: because we might learn something from them that will help us understand our present situation.

The second bad reason for not reading dated texts is that academics seldom look outside the world of scholarship. It is assumed that if an idea is disregarded in the best academies, then that is the end of the matter, and nobody anywhere could possibly be so foolish as to find it valuable or useful. This is a completely mistaken approach, at least for the issue of development and communication. Studies have shown that the founding texts of the dominant paradigm, despite a surprisingly long academic afterlife, have more or less vanished from the contemporary scene, at least as far as explicit citations in the scholarly literature are concerned (Fair, 1989; Fair and Shah, 1997). We shall see, however, that there are numerous contemporary large-scale social programmes that operate within the intellectual framework of the dominant paradigm, and even one or two academic studies that sneak it in, perhaps unconsciously. If one asks what currency many of the ideas discarded by academics decades ago still have, then in this case at least, the answer is: a great deal, amongst politicians, activists and development organizations.

Scholar militants

One of the reasons for the long life of the ideas under discussion is that, for the first two phases of thinking, the people who developed and advanced them were self-consciously concerned with implementing their ideas in social action. While the founders of the dominant paradigm taught in elite US universities (MIT, Stanford, Illinois), they did not consider themselves as privileged inhabitants of ivory towers cut off from the mundane activities of the world. They had a conception of the role of the academic that placed them in the centre of the great social conflicts of their age. The phrase they had to describe themselves was 'policy scientists', whom they defined as 'the man of knowledge as adviser, applying his special skills to current problems of public policy' (Merton and Lerner, 1951: 284). Programmatically, impartial scientific enquiry was one dimension of the work of policy intellectuals, but they willingly involved themselves in providing solutions to problems identified by their government, while remaining aware of, and avoiding the dangers of becoming, what they termed bureaucratic intellectuals for a garrison state.

In practice, however, the leading figures amongst them aligned themselves very closely indeed with the garrison state. If the policy scientist was 'concerned with bringing the findings of systematic research to bear upon current issues and process of policy' it was clear that 'one persistent issue of democratic policy in the last three decades has been: how to cope successfully with aggressive totalitarianism' (Lerner et al., 1951: 91). Any study of the published record shows a group of very prominent social scientists – Klapper, Lasswell, Lerner, Merton, Pye, Schramm, de Sola Pool – working together in different combinations on projects for various US government agencies. The historian of their efforts writes of 'the continuing, inbred relationship among a handful of leading mass communication scholars and the US military and intelligence community' (Simpson, 1994: 89). Simpson perhaps overstates the case that these scholars were attempting to develop a 'science of control', but a glance at two of the leading figures shows that the links he identifies were certainly significant in their careers. According to Daniel Lerner, 'The policy sciences of democracy face no more important task than to produce an accurate diagnosis of the Communization process as a guide to effective – in this case, usually preventive – therapy' (Lerner, 1967a: 467–8). He himself traced a path from the Psychological Warfare Division of the US Army, through the Hoover Institute, where he directed the programme on 'Revolution and the Development of International Relations' (Ithiel de Sola Pool was his assistant), to the Massachusetts Institute of Technology. Samarjiwa has persuasively argued that during that trajectory he established a relationship with the US Department of State that fundamentally influenced the intellectual framework of his major book, *The Passing of Traditional Society* (Samarjiwa, 1987: 7–10). The work at MIT, at least according to Mowlana, was funded by the Ford Foundation, allegedly acting as a conduit for the CIA and the US Air Force, and constituted an attempt to develop a systematic basis for government policy (Mowlana, 1996: 6ff). Wilbur Schramm was similarly engaged. He co-authored a US Air Force funded study about the North Korean takeover of Seoul (Riley and Schramm, 1951). The intellectual concern with anti-communism was a continuing one for Schramm. His influential volume on *The Processes and Effects of Mass Communication* (1961) displays a strong interest in propaganda and anti-communism: one of its chapters is a reprint from a USIA handbook (Bigman, 1952/61). Later in his career, Schramm founded the East–West Communications Institute, on the initiative of then Senator Lyndon B. Johnson, with funding from the US government (Keever, 1991: 7–8).

The later and very harsh critics of writers like Lerner and Schramm, coming from the imperialism paradigm, were at least as keen to involve themselves in political action, perhaps believing that philosophers had only interpreted the world differently but that the point was to change it. Among the key figures, Schiller, Smythe and Nordenstreng all identified themselves with leftist politics, although only Smythe acknowledged having joined a leftist party (Lent, 1995). Nordenstreng was for several years the President of the Prague-based International Organisation of Journalists, and as such played a very prominent role in UNESCO and other highly politicized fora in which media and cultural imperialism were hotly debated. Others, notably Colleen Roach, worked directly or indirectly for UNESCO itself, during the period when it was the key site of battles over a New World Information and Communication Order. As we shall see, the positions they took in these conflicts involved some very serious compromises, both in theory and in practice. The proponents of the participatory paradigm similarly contain many activists within their ranks, notably in non-governmental organizations oriented on development and communication, such as the World Association for Christian Communication.

It is only when we reach the period in which the globalization paradigm dominates academic discussion that we find a markedly lower level of involvement in direct social and political action. As we will see below, this detachment arises not from some scrupulous desire to retain scholarly independence but from a new assessment of the relationship between theories of communication and social change. The new paradigm more or less forecloses the possibility of the systematic use of the media for definite and intended social change, and thus there remain no grounds for the media theorist to contribute to practical projects.

The context of debate

These paradigm shifts did not take place in an historical vacuum. No ideas ever do evolve without reference to the times in which they are developed, and this general rule is doubly true in the case of ideas that attempt to make the sort of close link between theory and social action that characterizes those under discussion here. It is in fact very difficult to understand the emphases and implications of the different paradigms without at least some awareness of the historical conditions under which they were developed.

We can conveniently date the key moments in the evolution of these ideas to three pivotal dates: 1947 and the birth of the Cold War; 1968 and a global wave of radicalism; 1989 and the collapse of the Soviet Empire. We might, just possibly, add a fourth sometime around the start of the new millennium, although dating its precise origins remains problematic. In all of these cases, the fit will never be exact, but each of the periods inaugurated by those dates had characteristics that shaped the thinking of intellectuals who were engaged in work on the media. In order to better understand the detailed discussions in later chapters, we must here briefly review some of the key aspects of each of those periods.

The USA emerged from the Second World War overwhelmingly the world's strongest power. It dominated the world economically, politically and militarily. Fighting had wrecked many of its industrial competitors, while the USA had escaped direct damage and seen its economy shake off the Depression and grow explosively. Even after five years of peace and reconstruction, the total 1950 GNP of the USA was larger than that of the USSR, the UK, France, West Germany, Japan and Italy all added together (Kennedy, 1989: 475). The new political institutions of the peace, notably the United Nations but also the International Monetary Fund and the World Bank, were headquartered in the USA, which was by far their largest paymaster. US navies dominated the seas from the Mediterranean to the Formosa Strait, and US bombers alone carried the devastating new atomic weapons.

Like Britain a century earlier, the US translated this enormous economic superiority into a belief in international free trade. But France, Belgium, the Netherlands, Portugal and, particularly, the UK all had vast colonial empires that were anything but open to free trade. Despite being the victors in a 'war for democracy', the imperial powers showed no sign of being prepared to extend that system of government to their overseas subjects. Indeed, they had been prepared to use the soldiers of the defeated Japanese empire to help them restore their rule in Asia. The US had long devoted considerable efforts to trying to dismantle the barriers that surrounded these empires. During the Second World War, 'nearly all important leaders in Washington assumed and hoped that the United States would revive and reform capitalism everywhere in the world, but pre-eminently in the British Empire' (Kolko, 1990: 623). Within the field of communication, the US news agencies UPI and AP had long been in conflict with the British Reuters and the French Havas. They had even entered an alliance with the Soviet Union's TASS in order to break the hold of the imperial cartel (Rantanen, 1992, 1994).

The old colonial empires were now politically and economically enfeebled, but they were still prepared to fight to hold on to their possessions. True, never in their wildest dreams would they think of fighting the USA, but they were certainly prepared to fight their colonial subjects, and they did so, frequently and bloodily. It would have been logical for the USA, itself a nation borne out of armed revolt against an imperial master, to side with those who sought to establish their independence.

The reason why the USA was never prepared to do that openly and unequivocally, indeed why it very often found itself giving aid and comfort to the colonialists, and why in the most notorious case of Vietnam ended up taking over the role of occupier from one of them, was because it now faced a new and, its leaders believed, far more dangerous enemy than the tottering European empires. The real threat, Presidents from Truman onward believed, was the awful spectre of International Communism. The USSR was much weaker than the USA economically and politically, but everybody, friend and foe alike, believed it had a stronger economic model and was catching up with the west very rapidly. Ideologically, it was a very powerful pole of attraction indeed.

'Marxism–Leninism' as propagated by Moscow and its allies offered an ideology that stressed the struggle for national independence and which called for unity against the foreign exploiters and their allies. The 'socialist stage' would come later, long after the achievement of statehood (Harris, 1971: 130–203). These ideas found thousands, perhaps millions, of willing adherents around the world, particularly amongst those fighting colonialism and its legacies. In the struggle between the USA and the USSR, the latter's weakness in arms was compensated by its strength in ideas. As one US communication scholar noted, the local supporters of its ideas gave the USSR an additional channel of communication and 'this extra channel gives the Soviet Union an immense advantage' (Smith, 1952/1961: 173).

The USA thus faced a problem. The people with whom it might wish to ally in forcing open the markets of the old colonial empires were very often in thrall to the ideas, and sometimes the policies, of the new communist enemy. As the post-war world unfolded, in country after country, the USA found itself forced to abandon any democratizing ideas it had cherished during the struggle against fascism. Japan is an excellent example. Faced with mass support for 'overenthusiastic democratization', the US occupation forces reversed their policies and repaired relations with the Emperor and the old order. As a recent US historian of the occupation wrote: 'Initially, the Americans imposed a root-and-branch agenda of "demilitarisation and democratisation" that was in every sense a remarkable display of arrogant idealism – both self-righteous and genuinely visionary. Then, well before their departure, they reversed course and began rearming their erstwhile enemy as a subordinate Cold War partner in cooperation with the less liberal elements in society' (Dower, 1999: 23). Particularly after the victory of the Chinese communists, the US decided that anti-communism was more important than anti-colonialism and that it would at least tolerate the continuation of the old empires.

In the struggle against the reds, military power and economic leverage were important weapons, but the US needed an ideology as a counter to Marxism–Leninism as well. At home, the values of 'Americanism' could be redefined so that anyone with even moderately leftist views could be persecuted (Caute, 1978). Internationally, however, something else was needed. Communism offered a path out of dependence and poverty, and if the US was to counter that threat it needed an alternative that promised at least as much chance of success. As one proponent of development communication later wrote: 'If a nation was able to build a foundation of economic sufficiency ... the perils of a Communist revolution would be greatly reduced' (Chu, 1994: 35). 'Development' as a corpus of theories about communication and society arose directly out of these Cold War imperatives (Leys, 1996: 5–6). Within that general concern to provide a 'non-communist manifesto', as Rostow subtitled his famous book on economic growth, the dominant paradigm of development communication occupied a central place.

The critics of the dominant paradigm worked in the very different climate of 1968 and its aftermath. What one radical historian called the 'year that cast its spell on a generation' inaugurated a period when all of the contradictions of the post-war settlement came to a head (Harman, 1988: vii). The crisis of 1968 shook the developed West, the Stalinist East, the poorer countries of what was then called the Third World, and everywhere it had a profoundly radicalizing effect. A new generation of intellectuals developed, whose assumptions about the world did not automatically slot into the ready-made definitions provided by Washington and Moscow. True, the struggle between the 'Free World' and 'International Communism' remained the main feature of world politics, but in many ways its contours were changed. For one thing, the US was now clearly seen as the inheritor of the role of the former colonial powers. It might not have the same territorial ambitions as its predecessors, but it seemed, if anything, even more unwilling to allow the people of developing countries make their own choices about the future. What was more, as the US stumbled to defeat in Vietnam in the aftermath of the Tet offensive of 1968, it looked very much as though this new informal empire, too, was on the wane. Student unrest in the US, a general strike in France, several years of intense class struggle in other major European countries like Italy and the UK, all combined to make it look as though private capitalism had reached the end of its useful life.

But if the end of capitalism seemed nigh, it did not follow that all of its opponents looked any longer to Moscow for inspiration. The Soviet empire, too, faced an internal challenge, and it was the most serious since the Hungarian revolution of 1956. In Czechoslovakia, a group of reform communists won the leadership of the party in March 1968 and began to introduce some cautious market reforms, and to allow a small degree of political liberalization. The leadership of the USSR saw this as unacceptably threatening and invaded the country in August, in the name of 'proletarian internationalism'. They imposed their own leadership on the party and jailed, exiled or demoted the reformers. Popular opposition to their invasion was crushed. Although less bloody than the defeat of the Hungarian rising, with perhaps 100 opponents of the invasion killed in protests as opposed to the 20,000 or so in 1956, the outright conservatism of the Russian leadership was just as obvious (Harman, 1983: 187–211). The belief that communism could somehow be given a 'human face' and that it might somehow evolve into democratic socialism received a massive setback.

Resistance and repression echoed around the world. To name but a few, in Mexico, in Derry in Northern Ireland, in Bolivia, a few years later in Chile, and in the black ghettoes of the USA itself, there were outbreaks of popular opposition to the existing order. Everywhere, the established orthodoxies, political and intellectual, that sustained the ruling elites were subject to critical attack.

New thinking was clearly called for, in the field of development as much as anywhere else. The old recipes appeared to have failed. They had not brought much in the way of development, and what there was had ended up solidifying the power of the elites rather than helping the poor out of poverty. It was clear that the problem of development could not be explained entirely by the backwardness of the population. It seemed to be rooted either in the social structure of developing countries, or in the relationship between developing countries and the metropolitan centres, or perhaps in some combination of the two factors.

There were two main lines of thought in response to these reflections. The first concentrated on the fact that the domination of the rich countries over the poorer ones, of the developed over the underdeveloped, was obviously much more complex than the brutal simplicities of colonial dominance. The Portuguese empire collapsed in 1974 and the struggle for decolonialization was by then in the main victoriously completed. Nevertheless, the rich countries continued to dominate the economic and political life of the poorer ones. New mechanisms of domination, it was argued, had replaced the colonial governor and his military garrison. It was these external structures of dominance, articulated in the 'dependency thesis', that prevented the poorer countries from developing in the same way as the now-rich countries had done earlier. According to proponents of this view, 'development in the centre determined and maintained underdevelopment in the periphery' (Servaes and Malikhao, 1994: 9). It followed from this that the struggle for national independence implied an economic as well as political dimension. Just as it had been essential to kick out the viceroy and his soldiers and build an independent state, so it was necessary to separate the economy as far as possible from the tentacles of international capitalism, to protect the national industries and to try to build up a powerful economy out of one's own resources.

It was a simple further step from this stress upon breaking the economic ties that bound countries into a cycle of underdevelopment to arguing that it was necessary to break the cultural and media ties that had the same functions. The social and economic imbalance 'found itself reinforced by a no less important disequilibrum at the level of communication' (Masmoudi, 1986: 51). To proponents of this view, the model of the USSR, and even more of China, seemed attractive. In contrast with the stagnation and international impotence of the capitalist underdeveloped states, first the USSR and then China had managed to transform the structures of their societies. Starting from the most benighted backwardness, they had been able to construct modern industry and modern weapons, and thus build themselves into world powers. The USA, by contrast, had demonstrated that its differences with the old colonial powers were only secondary, and it appeared now as the main centre of economic, political and military domination (Tran van Dinh, 1987). It was out of that analysis of the nature of the world that the imperialism paradigm in media studies emerged.

It was, however, possible to make a different reading of the lessons of 1968, and to chart a different route for thinking about the role of the media in social change. Wherever one looked at that time, the old order was being challenged, whether it waved the Stars and Stripes or the Red Flag. The politicians and generals in Washington and Moscow alike found their plans opposed from below. US conscripts, French strikers, and Czech students all had in common the fact that they took initiatives of their own accord, developed their own ideas of what they wanted, and acted independently and decisively to realize them. They were not uniformly successful in achieving their aims, but they did suggest a powerful alternative to the elite-directed, planned and regimented theories of social change that inspired both the orthodox Communist Parties and the US proponents of development. It was one of the ironies of development theory in general, and of the dominant paradigm of development communication in particular, that it relied very heavily on the state as the main mechanism for achieving its goals (Stevenson, 1993: 27–8). In this account, in order to counter the threat of a statist ideology, it was necessary to rely on the state. The lessons of 1968 seemed directly to contradict this pervasive statism. It was from the perception that social change could, and perhaps should, be initiated from below, that the impetus to the participatory paradigm in development originated.

The third historical moment we need to consider is 1989. By that date, the whole world picture looked very different. The economies of the USSR and its allies no longer looked as though they would overtake those of the west. On the contrary, they were clearly riddled with crises. Popular discontent, particularly in Poland, had demonstrated that the regimes lacked any legitimacy with the working class whose interests they purported to represent. The USSR itself had been defeated in its very own colonial war in Afghanistan. The Chinese, for their part, had long since embraced the imperialist enemy and introduced large elements of capitalism into their economy. 1989 was the moment at which the Iron Curtain, which had metaphorically divided Europe since 1947, collapsed in a few breathtaking weeks. Communist parties lost power everywhere in the Soviet Empire, and by 1991 they were discredited even in the USSR itself. The 'other' pole that had sustained the Cold War simply collapsed under the strain.

These rapid transformations, however, were only the dramatic representations of a much deeper and wider change that had been going on for perhaps a decade. The 1980s saw a renewed wave of intellectual confidence in the market, and the collapse of the planned economies demonstrated the practical superiority of private capitalism. What was more, a number of countries, notably in East Asia, had succeeded in breaking out of the cycle of poverty and establishing themselves as genuinely developing countries. They all had vigorously capitalist economies with very strong export orientations. After the collapse of the USSR, the old recipe of the closed, autarchic economy no longer looked a viable alternative pathway for national development. The societies that stayed trapped in the Stalinist model, like Cuba and North Korea, were few and poor, and under constant siege from their richer and more powerful neighbours. Those that were prepared to enter the world market and carve out a niche for themselves, like South Korea and Taiwan, enjoyed economic growth and rising living standards. Other countries that had adopted much milder versions of national development than that propounded by the Stalinist regimes, based upon import substitution and substantial state direction of the economy, most notably Brazil and India, were also forced to accommodate to the power of the new global marketplace and seek to integrate more closely into international trade. For the Washington Consensus, 'the role of government is to provide ample room for entrepreneurs to invest in agriculture, industry, and services. That allows private firms … operating in competitive markets to be the engine of growth and job creation, providing opportunities' (World Bank, 2002c). The collapse of world communism simply confirmed in practice a theoretical conclusion that most had already reached.

Globalization, as a theory of an undirected, market driven, dynamic system, is clearly the intellectual product of these historical conditions. It was part of a more general shift in the intellectual climate away from Enlightenment-derived theories, as were both Marxism and its Cold War opponents like Positive Social Science, towards what is usually termed postmodernism. It shared with other theories in this school a scepticism towards the value of social and political action that was quite alien to the ideas of both of the sides in the preceding epoch. Marxists and anti-Marxists were agreed that something must be done, even if they could not agree as to what that was to be. Where the economic version of Globalization differed radically from the philosophical scepticism that characterizes many postmodern theories was in its absolute belief in the truth of the (characteristically Enlightenment) proposition that the market is the most beneficial form of social organization possible for humanity. The globalization paradigm in communication studies is clearly part of this more general re-alignment of thought towards an uncritical acceptance of the benign nature of capitalism.

It is possible that we are witnessing the beginning of another phase of thinking, although it is not yet quite clear whether we can easily ascribe a date to its origins. The later 1990s saw a series of international economic crises and a renewed interest in writing critical of the effects of globalization, and from Seattle 2000 onward the discontent that the workings of the market has provoked began to take organized form. It is also possible that, in a terrible and distorted way, the horrors of September 11 2001 and its continuing bloody aftermath have clarified the contours of the contemporary world. Its shape is far different from the rosy pictures of progress. Other writers in the same vein point to the extent to which the USA is the dominant world power, exceeding even the colossal imbalances of 1945 (Brooks and Wohlforth, 2002). In economics, politics, and particularly in military affairs, it is harder and harder to sustain the claims of polycentrism that underlay theories of globalization.

What precisely this new paradigm might be, and how it would differ from earlier attempts to understand the world, it is still difficult to say. There is as yet nowhere near the same clarity and unity of thought that allows us to identify the dominant paradigm, or the imperialist paradigm. This is partly because we can make those judgements with the benefit of a hindsight that is denied us with respect to debates through which we are now trying to thread our way. Another major factor, however, is the fact that while the various inadequacies of earlier paradigms are more or less apparent, at least to the critical observer if not the practical militant, there is as yet very little agreement as to what factors are of central importance in the new period, and no unified sense of where we should concentrate either our theoretical or practical energies. It is one of the aims of this book to help towards clarifying what the new paradigm might look like, and to suggest ways in which we need to think and act in order to develop it.

Issues of method

Throughout this introduction, and in the rest of the book, liberal use is made of the term 'paradigm'. This word is often used in the literature, for example by Servaes, (1989: 2–5). The term is, however, notoriously ill-defined, and some clarification is necessary as to how it is being used in this work. For the present writer, as for many intellectuals of a certain generation, including perhaps Jan Servaes, there is no mystery as to the origin of the term: it is derived from our youthful reading of Thomas S. Kuhn's brilliant book *The Structure of Scientific Revolutions*. Although it was later to be the subject of withering criticisms from a wide variety of viewpoints, the basic idea around which it was organized retains an enormous persuasive power (Easlea, 1973: 11–26). Kuhn did not offer much by way of a definition of the term 'paradigm', and according to later commentators he used it in a range of discrete senses, but what more or less stuck for a generation was the simple, non-philosophical sense that all 'scientific' enquiry rests on a common set of assumptions about the nature of the problem under investigation and the ways in which it was proper to investigate it. Kuhn argued that in choosing the term paradigm 'I mean to suggest that some of the accepted examples of actual scientific practice – examples which include law, theory, application, and instrumentation together – provide models from which spring particular coherent traditions of scientific research' (Kuhn, 1962: 10). What it is that a science will study is defined in a paradigm. Methods appropriate for scientific investigation are defined. What counts as evidence is defined. The nature of proof and disproof are defined. The criteria for satisfactory theory are defined. Within those definitions, science can be practised and will produce, not surprisingly, results that are recognized by other scientists as valid and legitimate, even true. This is what Kuhn called 'normal science' and it can endure for hundreds of years. This seems to be a convincing way of thinking about the historical record that was briefly described above, and it is in this sense that the concept of paradigm is used in this book.

There is a further step to Kuhn's account which is followed less closely in this book. In his account, it is the pressure of internal factors, the accumulation of contradictory evidence which he calls an 'anomaly', that lead to a crisis of normal science, and eventually the abandonment of one paradigm and the construction of a new one: this the nature of his concept of a 'scientific revolution' (Kuhn, 1962: 91ff). This is one of the most interesting parts of his thinking, but it is of doubtful utility in this context. In all of the cases examined in more detail below, parts of the problems they have encountered are certainly due to the obstinate refusal of the evidence to fit neatly into the required theoretical moulds, just as Kuhn claimed that experimental science problematized the Newtonian paradigm. The failure of development was a reality and it was upon that evidence that many critics of the dominant paradigm rested. On the other hand, one of the paradigms, that of imperialism, that replaced the dominant paradigm, had certainly been around for longer than development theory and was definitely not a response to a crisis in development theory. It was not so much that people working inside one paradigm came up against accumulating obstacles, but that they were replaced in the centre of intellectual attention by an older alternative. The idea of a shift from one paradigm to another resulting from an accumulation of evidence and a sharp re-orientation of fundamental scientific principles being required to begin to provide a more adequate account does not seem to fit the examples considered here.

The historical sociology I have sketched above seems to me a necessary element in explaining intellectual crises and revolutions, in the social sciences at least. Different paradigms co-exist and it is moments of sharp social change that make one or another seem for a time more attractive to large numbers of people, social scientists and activists. So, in the above account, it is fairly clear that it was the relative decline and eventual collapse of the Soviet Union and its empire that made state-oriented theories of national development very much less attractive, rather than anything internal to the theory of dependency.

In arguing for the primacy of historical events in explaining the perceived relevance of different theoretical systems, I do not think I am thereby simply endorsing relativism. It is perfectly possible to argue that in some periods some ideas are less attractive to many people than others, without at the same time arguing that they are all of equal value. We can most certainly retain the view that a paradigm is more internally coherent and has greater explanatory power than its competitors while at the same time recognizing that it is not widely as accepted or influential as they are. We can acknowledge that there is an important distinction between the claim that something is true and the fact of people accepting that it is true.

The term paradigm is used here in what is not, admittedly, a very precise way. It does not rest upon a clear formal definition, and it is shorn of some of its important original constituents. It is useful, however, because it does very clearly indicate the ways in which groups of thinkers, and indeed activists, who differ on many aspects of their thinking, can be grouped together as a class of people who share certain basic, underlying assumptions. We use it in much the same general way as the term 'discourse' was used by Tomlinson to discuss 'the discourse of cultural imperialism' (1991: 8–11).

The evidence reviewed in this book seems to support the view that there are relatively coherent sets of ideas and practices that we are justified in considering as 'paradigms', but of course there are major differences between different writers, even when they more or less consciously share a common project. There is still a problem of how to classify work that shares much of the framework that informs a particular paradigm but nevertheless makes a significant departure from its main trajectory. For us, this is a problem that is present most acutely in the later work of Rogers, and others who have followed his critical self-evaluation. However one assesses these developments, it is difficult to see either the concepts or the practical outcomes as being straightforwardly a development of the dominant paradigm, but nor do they really seem to constitute sufficient of a break to mark the establishment of a new paradigm. The way around that dilemma adopted here is to introduce the concept of the 'variant', by which is meant a position that is derived from the original paradigm but nevertheless displays a sufficient degree of difference to warrant being separately considered.

There is one methodological consequence of the above discussion that requires comment. If one is to discuss the ideas of other authors, and particularly if one is intending to be extremely critical of some of the things they say, then it is very difficult to avoid quotation. The present author had his initial training in literature, long before the rise of critical theory, and was taught the absolute value of the text. That is apparently now considered a naïve approach, but old habits die hard and the belief in the primacy of the original text lingers on. The current author likes to quote, and quote extensively, because this is fairer to the writer under discussion, clearer for the reader, and usually gives a better account of the issues than any attempt at reshaping the original. Earlier versions of this text contained very extensive quotations, most of which were later excized. For one thing, they make an already long text so very much longer. For another, while the agglomeration of vast unedited quotations linked by a few lines of pithy commentary may have worked very well in *The Gutenberg Galaxy*, it does not meet the expectations of contemporary scholars and their students. This text, therefore, does contain quotations but they have been pared to the barest tolerable minimum.

The structure of this book

The shape of this volume follows the methodological principles and the historical succession outlined above. It is argued, non-contentiously it is to be believed, that there have been a number of distinct ways of thinking about the role of communication in solving the problems of world poverty, which are sketched at the start of this chapter. It is claimed, again hardly contentiously, that these can be meaningfully called paradigms. More contentiously, four distinct paradigms are identified and the outline of an emergent fifth paradigm is discussed. An attempt is made to give as fair and complete account as is possible of the theoretical underpinnings of the different paradigms, and to explore their implications. The book examines the main reasons critical writers have given for questioning and rejecting particular paradigms. At the same time, it is shown how the earlier paradigms, which have seemed obsolete to many academic observers, have continued to have a vigorous life in shaping practical communication projects right up to the present day.

The overall organization of the book is into three sections. In the first of these, the classical dominant paradigm is outlined and set in its intellectual context, its main shortcomings and critiques are considered and one of its main contemporary developments is introduced. In the second section, the strengths and weaknesses of two new paradigms that resulted from the breakdown of the original dominant paradigm are discussed. The third section looks at more contemporary issues, notably the globalization paradigm, its strengths and limitations, and tries to bring the argument more or less up to date in the light of developments in the twenty-first century.

Chapter 2 therefore examines the emergence of the dominant paradigm and its theoretical origins in the work of Max Weber. Particular stress is placed upon the concept of modernity, and its place in the social structure of development. The third chapter considers the critiques that were made of the dominant paradigm and looks at the ways in which some of its proponents attempted to modify certain aspects in order to retain the fundamental framework. The chapter concludes with an examination of the contemporary practical survivals of this apparently discredited theory, and of the reasons why that may have occurred. It is proposed that these contemporary survivals do not constitute a new paradigm but rather a 'continuity variant' of the old dominant paradigm.

The fourth chapter examines one of the attempts at a new paradigm that emerged from the critiques of the dominant paradigm. The various ways in which the concept of 'participation' has been used to question some of the central features of the dominant paradigm are reviewed. Given that there are such a wide range of meanings that have been invested in the term, the different versions of what is here called the 'participatory paradigm' are discussed in some detail.

Chapter 5 looks at the other new paradigm that emerged from the critique of the dominant paradigm: that of media and cultural imperialism. The theoretical underpinnings of this new paradigm are considered, as are the political implications that it had in practice. Chapter 6 looks at the critics of the paradigm, particularly those that stress the inadequate accounts of media effects and the complexity of international programme flows.

Chapter 7 outlines the globalization paradigm and examines the ways in which it differs radically from all three of the earlier paradigms. The eighth chapter considers how far the globalization paradigm fits the evidence from the contemporary world. It is argued not only that there is a very poor fit indeed but that the blind adhesion to its precepts has blinded even well-intentioned scholars to some of the central social phenomena of the contemporary epoch.

The final chapter considers whether there is, sufficient evidence for us to claim that we are living in a new historical epoch in which it is reasonable to expect a new theoretical paradigm. The earlier paradigms are reviewed, and their most important flaws are considered alongside the insights that they have given. All of the earlier paradigms, it is argued, have made some contribution to our understanding of the ways in which the media can and do play a role in the attempt to improve the world. However, it is the participatory paradigm that provides the most promising platform for the construction of a new paradigm that can address the distinctive features of world poverty today.

It must be reiterated that this book is not a practical manual for using the mass media to change the world. On the contrary, it is an academic work that attempts to follow the logic of ideas, and it takes account of their practical consequences only from a theoretical point of view. At times, the nature of the material that is addressed is rather remote from the real and pressing problems that we briefly reviewed at the start of this chapter. The fact that the ideas discussed are rather remote from the difficult task of actually using the media is not something that should be celebrated, but it must be recognized as inevitable. The world is not transparent, and the right course of action does not immediately present itself to people of goodwill and good sense. On the contrary, opacity and obscurity are more important elements in sustaining the existing inequitable and destructive world order than are mendacity and crime, and if the world is to be changed for the better then there is an inevitable task of clarification and analysis to be carried out. That task necessarily involves examining and critically reflecting upon the dominant ways of thinking about a problem, in our case the problem of what kinds of communicative action might improve the world. Perhaps another writer could have done this job more clearly and directly, but anyone embarking on such an undertaking is obliged to follow the paths defined by others and to engage with them on terms that others have set. Sometimes those terms are wilfully obscure, but sometimes it is reality itself that is difficult and complex, and no-one can hope to understand it even in part without some degree of difficulty. Only if we have a pretty clear idea of the way in which the world works today that is even approximately accurate will we know what kinds of action on our part might make it work a bit differently and a bit better.

2

COMMUNICATING MODERNITY

The basic ideas of the dominant paradigm of development communication were developed by US policy scientists who saw themselves more or less unequivocally as participating in efforts to provide different answers to the problems of poverty than those advanced by their Communist alter egos (Flor, 1991). The impetus for the elaboration of this paradigm was proclaimed by its own most influential figures as coming from the 1947 Truman doctrine and the Four Point Programme of 1949, which made it quite explicit that the USA would offer its own model of the path to development for the poorer countries of the world (Hernández-Ramos and Schramm, 1989: 9). It is important to recognize this provenance if we want to understand what the strengths and the weaknesses of the dominant paradigm were and are, but it should not lead us into misconceptions about the aims that the proponents of these ideas set themselves. The aim of the dominant paradigm was not to freeze the unequal relations between the rich countries and the poor countries, or the rich and the poor within countries, but to provoke social change. While advancing the interests of the USA was the strategic goal of policy science as a whole, the dominant paradigm was developed expressly to help improve the lot of the poor. The need for social change was to be found in the misery that poverty and underdevelopment caused for those unfortunate enough to be its victims. Schramm wrote eloquently about conditions under which his emblematic underdeveloped families, the 'Ifes and Bvanis', lived. He recorded their inadequate calorific intake, the lack of available medical care, the fact that their life expectancy was half that of people living in the developed world, and he charted their exclusion from schooling, literacy, democratic participation and so on (Schramm, 1964: 18).

The aim of development communication was to assist in changing the situation of the Ifes and the Bvanis, in increasing the productivity of their labour and the size of the national economies in order that these citizens of developing countries could enjoy a better life. Countries would be helped to shift from subsistence agriculture based on obsolete technologies to up-to-date scientific agriculture directed at the production of marketable products. Handicraft industries would be replaced by modern industrial processes with large-scale plants and factories. Rural life would give way to urban life and an oral culture be replaced by a literate one. What is striking in retrospect is how close the goals of this programme were to those of Stalinist Marxism, which promised more or less the same things when it spoke of national development (Servaes, 1989: 10–11; Mowlana, 2001: 180).

The origins of the dominant paradigm

The inspiration for the dominant paradigm was the work of Max Weber (Hernández-Ramos and Schramm, 1989: 10–11; Servaes and Malikhao, 1994: 5). Quite apart from its other considerable merits, the work of Weber provided a congenial starting point since he had formed many of his ideas more or less explicitly as a critique of Marxism (Weber, 1968: 277–8). Weber saw capitalism as more than simply a system of property relations and often he used the broader term 'modern' for the system he was analysing: for example, in his influential analysis of bureaucracy he termed it 'modern officialdom' (Gerth and Mills, 1958: 196ff). For Weber, the modern, properly capitalist, outlook preceded the actual establishment of capitalist social relations, as he argued in his famous example of Benjamin Franklin. The modern mental type, which was the necessary precursor and accompaniment of capitalism, was the opposite of the routinized, superstitious, inflexible, uncalculating, non-scientific traditional outlook. Weber argued that the development of capitalism depended primarily on its victory in an ideological battle over other ideas: 'The most important opponent with which the spirit of capitalism has had to struggle was that type of attitude and reaction to new situations which we may designate as traditionalism' (Weber, 1968: 59). The establishment of the modern outlook and thus the acceleration of social development had been one of the consequences of the dissemination of Protestant ideas, and from this had arisen the edifice of capitalist development (Eisenstadt, 1973: 241ff).

These ideas were very widespread in US social science during the 1950s and 1960s (Moore, 1963; Eisenstadt, 1966; Inkeles, 1966). The emphasis was taken over directly into the dominant paradigm. One of its leading proponents wrote that 'Development is a type of social change in which new ideas are introduced into a social system in order to produce higher per capita incomes and levels of living through more modern production methods and improved social organization' (Rogers, 1969: 9). In the field of media and communication the central intellectual force in developing the dominant paradigm as a theoretical system was Daniel Lerner, particularly through his major book *The Passing of Traditional Society* (1958). This study of social change in the Middle East operated with a clear opposition between traditional and modern societies. The people of the Middle East wanted social change, development, and a better standard of living. These desirable goals were embedded in the living example of the USA: 'What America is ... the modernizing Middle East seeks to become' (Lerner, 1958: 79).

In practice, this identification of modernity with the west proved contentious. There were those who were unequivocal in their views: 'Historically, modernization is the process of change towards those types of social, economic and political systems that have developed in Western Europe and North America' (Eisenstadt, 1966: 1). The consequence of such a view was that social change would have to be very drastic indeed: 'What is involved in modernization is a "total" transformation of a traditional or pre-modern society into the types of technology and associated social organizations that characterize the ... nations of the Western World' (Moore, 1963: 89–90). Lerner himself was slightly more cautious and recognized that there were currents in the developing world that were not altogether happy with the bald statement that the best they could hope for was to emulate the USA. In this respect, 'modernity', a category free of the obloquy that attached to capitalism and socialism, had a special value: 'For the Middle Easteners more than ever want the modern package, but reject the label "made in the USA" (or, for that matter, "made in the USSR"). We speak, nowadays, of modernization' (Lerner, 1958: 45). Others were even more hesitant about generalising one model of the future. Writing a decade later, Rogers stressed that: 'Modernization, then, is a multi-dimensional concept which is not to be equated with Europeanization or Westernization and which implies no value judgement as to its desirability' (Rogers, 1969: 15).

Lerner, basing himself on fieldwork conducted in several countries in the Middle East, identified two basic types of mental structures. One, the traditional, was essentially illiterate, and was fixed and oriented towards stability and the past. It was embedded in a set of skills and a pattern of emotions, which excluded the ability to imagine oneself as being in a different position from where one was now. Such societies were unable to develop because the population lacked not only the technical skills but also the future-oriented perspective that could lead them to work, save and plan for a different and better life. Instead, they were satisfied to continue in the ways of their fathers and grandfathers. Like their forefathers, the inhabitants of such societies were content with various forms of dictatorial and traditional government. Contrasting with this was the modern personality, which was literate, fluid, and open to change. It was 'mobile', in that it desired change, betterment and self-advancement (Lerner, 1958: 47). Above all, the modern personality was capable of 'empathy', by which Lerner meant that it could imagine itself in different circumstances, so it had a future orientation that was unavailable to the traditional personality. This category of empathy was one of the keys to development: 'It is a major hypothesis of this study that high empathic capacity is the predominant personal style in a modern society, which is distinctively industrial, urban, literate and *participant*. Traditional society is non-participant' (Lerner, 1958: 50). Societies in which this modern personality type dominated, Lerner argued, were capable of change and development, and tended towards democratic forms of government, which was itself one of the forms of participation (Lerner, 1958: 48ff). Modernity did not essentially lie in a set of techniques or knowledge but in a 'state of mind, a psychological disposition, an inner readiness' which made the 'modern man ... [open] to innovation and change' (Inkeles, 1966: 141).

If the problem of under development was primarily a consequence of the static ways in which people thought about the world, and the traditional knowledge that they brought to their contemporary problems, then it followed that the road to development led through changing those beliefs and making scientific knowledge available to them. The formal education system was one of the ways in which people could be encouraged to adopt new ideas and beliefs: it was through education that mass literacy could be achieved, for example. But education was slow and very expensive, and the mass media seemed to offer a much more efficient way disseminating modernity than any other available technology. They were, in Lerner's phrase, a 'mobility multiplier'(Lerner, 1958: 52). They could transmit some of the central aspects of the modern personality type, notably the ability to imagine different ways of living, extremely efficiently. As he put it later, 'The multiplicative property of communication lies in its power to raise and spread empathy among its audiences' (Lerner, 1967b). They had this potential because they were a major mechanism by which other life situations could be represented. People could read, could hear and perhaps see, that things were done differently elsewhere, and thus the possibilities of them developing empathic personalities were enhanced: 'The media teach people participation by depicting for them new and strange situations and familiarizing them with a range of opinions among which they can choose ... empathy ... is the basic communication skill required of modern man' (Lerner, 1958: 412).

What was more, the mass media offered a much less costly way of propagating new ideas in remote regions than through the recruitment and training of large numbers of people who would go into the field and act as teachers or 'extension workers' charged with the task of changing people's minds through face-to-face contact. The scale of the audience that mass media could produce meant that they could reach into the minds of vast numbers of people at the same time and for vastly less cost. Radio, in particular, was relatively cheap and had a very large potential audience (Schramm, 1977: 106–39). The technologies of production and distribution were relatively affordable and the medium could be grasped even by those without any formal education, which is a pre-requisite for newspaper readership. So seductive was the power and cost-efficiency of radio that the early emphasis upon the centrality of literacy in making the modern personality more or less disappears from the later literature, even the work of Lerner.

Radio apparently worked and it did indeed produce evidence of the modern personality. A later study, dedicated to Daniel Lerner, claimed the characteristics of modernity could indeed be found empirically amongst the population of developing countries (Inkeles and Smith, 1974: 290). It was through the mass media that the 'people in villages and impoverished cities everywhere have discovered a land of their heart's desire and have come to know that there is a different way of life from their inherited rut' (de Sola Pool, 1966: 105).

The place of mass communication

The use of mass communication to affect, and if possible accelerate, the process of social change was theorized as depending upon a number of key factors that were thought to be of more general relevance to mass communication processes. Consistent with the methodological individualism inherited from Max Weber, the dominant paradigm laid stress upon the effect of change at the individual level. According to Lerner, 'Only insofar as individual persons can change their places in the world, their position in society, their own self-image, does social change occur. Social change in this sense is the sum of mobilities acquired by individual persons' (1963: 331). Change in individual social attitudes would lead more or less automatically, and without any serious conflict, directly to the transformation of the social structure and the patterns of life experienced by the whole population. As Rogers put it, 'Modernization at the individual level corresponds to development at the societal level. *Modernization* is the process by which individuals change from a traditional way of life to a more complex, technologically advanced, and rapidly changing style of life' (Rogers, 1969: 14).

If modernity was primarily a state of mind, then the main task of development communication was to alter states of mind. From the start, however, theorists recognized that these mental changes were complex. There were gaps between knowing about something, having a positive attitude towards it, and changing behaviour in accordance with those beliefs. It was, however, assumed that a well-designed programme of development communication would be able to overcome these gaps, and that new knowledge would lead more or less directly to changed practice. Transfer of knowledge was central to the project. One study, *Farmers' Ignorance and the Role of Television*, defined knowledge and ignorance in the following unequivocal terms: 'Knowledge is considered as possession of full, accurate, in-depth information; ignorance is defined as the lack of knowledge' (Shingi and Mody, 1974: 8). The role of the mass media in development was to help to create specific kinds of social change such as 'the transition to new customs and practices and, in some cases, to different social relationships. Behind such changes in behavior must necessarily lie substantial changes in attitudes, beliefs, skills and social norms' (Schramm, 1964: 114). The rise in productivity and the shift towards the gross material manifestations of development would result from these mental changes.

The state played a major role in effecting the individual changes that the dominant paradigm was concerned to promote. It is one of the many ironies of the dominant paradigm that an ideology designed to counter the state-worshipping Communists should itself place such a stress upon the state as a primary agency of social change. The stress upon state action was, of course, unthinkable inside the USA, and was strictly for export only (Stevenson, 1993: 27–8). The states in question were mostly very new ones, which had emerged from the struggle against the colonial empires, and whose shape and structure very often reflected the arbitrary decisions of their former rulers. Many of these states lacked any well-developed links, physical or symbolic, with the majority of their populations, and they frequently suffered crises of legitimacy as a consequence. One major task in development was to give these new states a sense of a direction in which they could move that would strengthen their internal cohesion, and another was to win the population over to accepting them as the natural leaders of society.

Schramm elaborated a six-point plan for action designed both to stabilize the new states and to use them for social development. According to him, communication must first be used to 'contribute to the feeling of nation-ness'. Second, it had a role as the voice of national planning. Third, it needed to play a role in teaching 'necessary skills'. Fourth, it had a role to play in the extension of the market. Fifth, it needed to help people adjust to the social changes brought about by the very success of the plan. Finally, it had the task of 'preparing people to play their role as a nation among nations', presumably by being ready to exercise the sovereign rights of nations (Schramm, 1963: 30–57). State control and direction of even the details of the communication message was thus a programmatic requirement of the dominant paradigm.

Communication orthodoxy, in the period when the dominant paradigm was being elaborated, believed in the indirect influence of the media upon the mass of the population. The theory of 'two step flow' argued, based on studies of electoral choices in the USA, that the population was not an undifferentiated mass, all of whom were equally susceptible to the influence of messages transmitted by the mass media. On the contrary, the bulk of the population gained information and formed its views as the result of the actions of opinion leaders. If one wished to achieve an overall change, as the proponents of development communication most certainly did, then the key groups upon whom to concentrate were these opinion leaders. The key thinkers of the dominant paradigm, many of whom had worked on elites in other circumstances, identified local elites as the key groups of opinion formers because they were the people who produced and disseminated ideas about the world (Lerner and Gorden, 1969). What elites thought and did was likely to form the raw material upon which the mass of the population worked in order to form their own views of the world. Concentrating upon the elites, who tended to be richer and better educated than the mass of the population, and thus to have a stake in the existing order, improved the chances of promoting change while at the same time retaining intact the social structures of developing countries.

The task of development communication was to identify and empower those sections of the elite who were oriented towards change, so that they could articulate a new vision for the whole of society. Lerner identified the 'spokesman' who 'defines new identities for changing persons, reshapes old expectations and formulates new demands to fit new lifeways'. Finding the persons who could be a 'functional new elite' was one of the main problems in the Middle East because it was to them that the mass of the population looked for a workable account of the emerging society (Lerner, 1958: 407).

The consequence of a concentration on elite-oriented communication directed attention to the ways in which innovations spread throughout society. If one succeeds in convincing the elite about a particular idea or belief in advance of the mass of the population, then it becomes a matter of some importance to understand the nature of the process by which other people come also to hold them. This process, known as the diffusion of innovations, was one that had already been well studied in the USA itself. The diffusion of, particularly, agricultural innovations amongst farmers, had revealed, amongst other things, that there was a characteristic pattern to the spread of new practices and that the early adopters would tend to come from elite groups (Rogers, 1992). The micro-sociology of change thus appeared to show that if one wanted to introduce a novelty, then the efforts of the change agent (either an individual or the mass media) should be concentrated upon the social elite who were most likely to adopt it. Since they would also have local prestige, their adoption of an innovation would ensure that their example would prove a desirable one to the bulk of the population. There was, then, a fortuitous congruence between what was understood to be the key to successful communication and what was known about how new ideas spread through society; in both cases, the best thing to do was to focus one's attentions first of all upon the elite.

Development communication, in its pristine phase at least, thus had a coherent programme that apparently rested on the firm foundations of studies in propaganda, the sociology of elites, the effects of mass communication, and the science of diffusion. The findings of each of these separate branches of the social sciences came together to provide a detailed account of how non-systemic change took place, and guidance on how it could be assisted and accelerated. The tasks of the policy scientists was relatively clear. They had a scientific knowledge of the nature of modernity and the pre-requisites for its attainments. They knew the processes by which those pre-requisites could be implanted and nurtured. They needed to advise the local governments to set up programmes whose objective would be to introduce modern ideas to the population. That introduction could be through various aspects of the formal and informal education system, but it would be at least powerfully aided by the fact that the mass media, radio in particular, could reach very large audiences quite easily and cheaply. These change agents would convince individual members of local elites of the superiority of particular ideas or techniques, let us say agricultural techniques or fertility control practices, and they in turn would act as early adopters and opinion leaders who would persuade the mass of the population to follow them in changing their ways. The cumulative effect of all of those changes would be empathy, modernity, development and, eventually, democratic capitalism.

Presented thus, the programme of development communication is elegant, coherent, and apparently uncontentious. It has, it is reasonable to say, the clear characteristics of a paradigm. Its outlines are illustrated in Figure 2.1. One can readily understand that such a paradigm would have considerable appeal even to people who did not share the particular ideological framework of its originators. Indeed, if one neglected the context within which it had been developed, and ignored the fact that it accepted existing social relations as a given, then it could easily be reduced to a purely technical project. The fact that it could be made into a 'cookbook' of techniques that could be employed to achieve particular, discrete, objectives without raising any awkward questions about social power meant that it

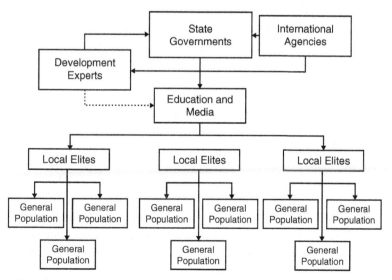

Figure 2.1   The Development Communication Model

was available to people of a variety of different ideological positions. Even if one did not believe in 'modernity', the techniques of attitude change still seemed extremely persuasive and practically useful. No matter what their ideological viewpoint, governments and other powerful agencies could be expected to find attractive a theory that promised to help them alter the undesirable habits of their subjects while not provoking them into disorder. Funding bodies, whether national agencies or international donors, could support particular projects secure in the knowledge that they were not likely to be accused of fomenting discord, whatever the social structure at which the programme was directed. Once the desirable attitudinal and behavioural changes had been identified, then it was simply a question of the identification of the target audience and the design of a message in the appropriate form.

Consolidating the paradigm

The intellectual power of the dominant paradigm of development communication, and the material resources available for its articulation and practical deployment, were so substantial that it almost immediately commanded a wide international following, which it retained for decades. As research has shown, scholarly writing about mass communication and development between 1958 and the mid 1980s was very strongly influenced by the leading thinkers of this paradigm, and in particular by Lerner (Fair, 1989). Many prominent theorists whose later work was in other paradigms began their intellectual careers speaking of Lerner's ideas about 'empathy', and praising Schramm for 'summing up all we have been trying to say' (Terhanian et al., 1977: 9; Moemeka, 1981: 104). As we shall see later, there is evidence that the essential structure of the paradigm remains active and influential even today. The wide acceptance of the paradigm, and the fact that it was extensively applied to practical problems of development communication, meant that it was rapidly extended and elaborated to take account of problems that were given new prominence as a result of experience.

One major impetus for elaboration was the recognition of the pressing circumstances under which programmes of development were taking place. Weber's Protestant Ethic had matured over centuries and worked its way through the main European societies at a very leisurely pace before it gave rise to anything recognizably like modernity and capitalist development. The circumstances of the mid-twentieth century, in which different and incompatible, but nevertheless fully elaborated, models of modernity and of development, were contesting fiercely as part of a global conflict between different ideologies, did not permit such an unhurried development. Development, if it was to take place at all, needed to provide rapid results: 'developing countries are societies-in-a-hurry' (Joseph, 1997: 25).

This sense of urgency raised two acute problems: where do modernising ideas come from, and how to ensure that the changes provoked were of the desired kind? In the classical Weberian case, the elements of the modern personality had matured within the religious culture and social structures of Western Europe and had been articulated in the course of a stubborn and bitter struggle against alternative, traditional views of the world. There was no time, nor indeed the opportunity, to allow the normal process of historical development to produce indigenous versions of 'modernity' within the cultures of developing countries. Even if the natural development of other cultures would eventually lead to some mental state that had the recognizable features of modernity, and that was by no means a certainty, to wait passively for such a change to occur was not an acceptable option. Positively, it would condemn the masses to an indefinite period of avoidable misery; negatively, it would surrender the ideological terrain to the Communist enemy.

There was already in existence a fully-elaborated version of modernity. It was understood and taught in the universities of the developed world, and these institutions produced a flood of experts hailing from all around the world who could bring change to the pre-modern parts of the world from outside. The proponents of the dominant paradigm specifically rejected the notion that the population of a developing country might spontaneously think independently, identify a problem, decide upon a solution and implement it themselves. Both the definition of the problem and the correct solution would come from the outside expert: 'The present era is certainly one of *directed contact change* caused by outsiders who, on their own or as representatives of planned change, seek to introduce new ideas to achieve definite goals' (Rogers, 1969: 6). The static, traditional, personality was unable either to identify what was wrong with the existing situation or to comprehend the possibility of changed circumstances, or to understand the techniques that might be used to improve the situation. The flexible, modern, scientific expert, on the other hand, had all of the tools needed to see the problem and to implement the solution. In this model of change, the common people were the objects of history. The subject was the modern outsider. As Joseph put it, 'The masses in the countryside have to be urged to adopt scientific culture' (1997: 24).

The fact that change had to come from the outside, that it would have to be imposed upon the bulk of the population, and that it would be a very rapid business, raised acute problems of social order. The autochthonous Weberian version of modernity had evolved through a series of major crises: wars of religion, popular revolts, the peremptory removal of crowned heads from royal bodies, and so on. Such difficulties and disorders were not likely to be lessened if the pace of change was very much greater than it had been in Europe. One of the observed results of 'development-in-a-hurry' was that the process of development itself produced a desire for the material benefits of modernity that outstripped the actual changes in living conditions. Lerner labelled this as a deterioration in the 'Want: Get Ratio', in which people's wants rose relative to what they were able to obtain. In turn, this led to a 'revolution of rising frustrations' and either a regressive stress upon tradition or a turn to 'aggressive violence' (Lerner, 1967b: 105). In other words, the attempt to find a route to development that would undercut social unrest, and thus the dangers of communism, could actually produce conditions that were much more favourable to subversion.

Part of the solution to this problem, which Lerner elsewhere characterized as the question of 'how to develop a participant public without unleashing an unruly mob?' lay in the already noted stress upon the role of the local elite and their ability to act as spokesmen and formulate what one can only term a hegemonic vision for the whole of the nation (Lerner, 1958: 397). If they could produce convincing accounts of why the disruptions caused by change were necessary, and how enduring the temporary indignities and deprivations that they entailed, were essential steps on the road to a generally much better future, then the local elite would be able to control the process of modernization and ensure that it ran according to plan.

The elites of developing countries, however, were not necessarily homogenous groups all dedicated to the project of modernization. They were usually themselves divided between modernizing and traditional elements (Schramm, 1967: 16). It was the modernizing element of the elite that was the key to transition, but they were often ill-equipped to play this role since they were the group most likely to have been 'educated abroad and who share little but the national identity and (perhaps) a common language with the peasant masses' (Rogers, 1969: 362). They were therefore likely to have a different set of values and beliefs from the masses, and more likely to find their natural home in the city rather than the countryside where the mass of the population who needed changing tended to reside. There were, in addition, limits to the extent they could rely upon foreign experts, of whatever nationality, to help them in development tasks, since not only was there often a general attitude of suspicion towards westerners as relics of the struggle against the colonial past, but such experts were often suspected of being engaged in a 'battle, on behalf of his own country, for the mind of the country he is assisting' (Dube, 1967: 97). The 'outsiders' who would decide upon the need for change and guide its course, were extremely isolated, intellectually, culturally and socially, from the very people whom they wished to change. No matter how good their intentions, they faced major problems in making themselves understood.

The potential isolation of the change-oriented sector of the elite and their expert advisors meant that the mass media had an important responsibility for the way in which they presented the programme of modernization. While the media were central to the task of motivating change, it was essential that development communication be deployed in ways that did not raise unrealistic expectations of the rewards for change. If transitional societies have failed 'to maintain the balance of psychic supply-and-demand', then it was one of the main jobs of the mass media to teach the population that there were limits on what they could expect to acquire (Lerner, 1963: 333).

In Lerner's original account, this need to moderate expectations primarily referred to the material dimension of development: the media needed to tell people that life would be better if they accepted change, while making sure they did not all believe that the world would be perfect by tomorrow. There was also, however, an important sense in which a confrontation with the reality of developing societies led to the adoption of very modest goals for political change as well. In its original form, the developmental paradigm had stressed the close links between development, literacy, participation and democracy. Experience suggested, however, that the pressures of breakneck development were so great that it might be essential to stress one element, material progress, at the expense of others: press freedom and political liberties, for example. Schramm wrote that one would normally expect to find government control of radio in a modernizing society, and that in the case of the press: 'A developing country, even the most democratically inclined one, is in a more or less constant condition of crisis …. In that situation a country is perhaps justified in asking its press to enlist in the national effort' (1967: 10). The task of the expert was to manage communication policy so that it would be possible to 'maintain public aspiration at a healthy level of discontent, in order to prevent complete political and social disorganisation' (Rogers, 1969: 13). Without some discontent, of course, there would be little incentive for change, but with too much there would be the danger of revolution. This, of course, is another of those striking parallels between the two camps in the Cold War. The Communists said that national development, socialist construction, and whatever, were all goals that overrode democratic niceties. Faced with the upheavals generated by modernization, Schramm and company said more or less the same thing.

The culture of the peasantry

The theory of development communication was operationalized in countries where the vast majority of the population were peasant farmers or agricultural labourers of a distinctly traditional cast of mind, which was why it appeared a particularly appropriate solution in the first place. Rogers claimed that peasants form 'the most frustrating audience for international, national and local programs of planned social change' (1969: ix). They did not respond immediately and positively to the influx of new ideas and methods that were intended to lift them out of their immemorial misery and lead them to a better life. The primary reason for this was that they inhabited what Rogers variously called 'the subculture of peasantry' and the 'subculture of tradition' (1969: 24, 39). The main features of this obstacle to development were ten in number: mutual distrust in personal relations (they thought everyone they met wanted to swindle them); perceived limited good (they did not believe that things could really get much better for everyone); dependence on, and hostility to, government authority (they both expected the state to boss them around and resented it for so doing); familism (they only trusted people who were blood relations); lack of innovativeness (they did not always look for better ways of doing things); fatalism (they did not believe circumstances could be any different); limited aspiration (they did not want to rise very far in the world); lack of deferred gratification (they did not save for the future); a limited view of the world (they had little conception of how things were outside of their village); and ,very much in the Lerner tradition, low empathy (they could not imagine themselves in another's situation) (Rogers, 1969: 25). While the governing elite might, as Lerner claimed, want to emulate the USA and change their country from top to bottom, the evidence seemed to suggest that the peasants simply did not want to change their ways. As a later writer put it: '[Nigeria's] very large rural population has rightly been seen as a drag on national development' (Moemeka, 1981: 1).

The very people in whose interest development communication was being conducted refused to see the value of what it preached. Schramm, in a passage that would have major implications for later developments, suggested there might be reasons for this peasant suspicion of, and hostility to, the government: 'I have been in villages where for many months the only real contact with the government and its development program has been the tax collector. In others I have observed communication come down to the village by media or sometimes by community workers, but great frustration has existed because there seemed to be no channel by which the needs and wishes of the villagers could be expressed to the government' (1967: 23). In order for there to be progress 'Peasant attitudes towards government must change in order for the national governments of less developed countries to attain a relative degree of political stability. Only when a government feels relatively secure can it turn its full attention to development plans' (Rogers, 1969: 23). The task of development communication was therefore not only to tell peasants that there were better ways of raising crops but also that they should trust the experts who introduced these innovations and not ostracize them on suspicion of being spies for the tax collector or the recruiting sergeant.

Given this social distance between the elite and the mass of the population, and the fact that 'change agents' generally came from outside of the communities that they were attempting to influence, there was an obvious danger that the content of development communication would be misleading or downright incomprehensible to its intended audience. The development communicator faced a problem in common with every other propagandist: how to put a message in a form that would be recognizable and acceptable to the intended audience, and to ensure that the meanings that they took from the message were the ones intended. When the expert communicators spoke a different native language (say, Spanish) from that of the peasants they were trying to influence (who spoke, say, Quechua), and those very same communicators had received their education in development in yet another language (say, English), then the possibilities of ineffective communication, or communication that produced unintended results, were obviously legion.

The general difficulty facing development communication was that 'the source is usually quite heterophilous [different] to the receiver' (Rogers, 1973: 54). The condition for creating a developmental message that would be comprehensible to its audience was that producers and audience were 'homophilous', sharing the same language, assumptions, belief systems and so on. This was not normally the case. While steps could be taken to recruit so far as possible staff who were the same as the people to whom the programme was directed, this would inevitably be only a partial solution. If one had a development programme directed at changing the dietary practices of illiterate peasants, it might indeed be possible to recruit some of them to be the local change agents, but having a scientific knowledge of dietetics in order to see the need for change, and producing the radio programmes that constituted the mass communication component, were both predicated on literacy and formal education. It was recognized that 'there is a limit to the extent to which even the most talented producer can create programmes which are meaningful to people who differ greatly from himself' (de Sola Pool, 1977: 136). The social and cultural gap between source and receiver was built into the underlying conception of the dominant paradigm.

One way that this gap could be minimised was through research into, or experience of, the audience's prior beliefs and values. Rogers noted that 'an effective communication message must be planned in terms of accurate knowledge of an audience ... One must know his audience ...' (Rogers, 1973: 31). If the necessary research were undertaken systematically and sympathetically, it would be possible to design effective messages that would be properly understood by the peasant. One of the major roles of social science research in developing countries was therefore to provide the kind of data that would permit 'more effective communication between top government officials and the people' (Rogers, 1969: 380). In overcoming the problems created by the gap between modernity and tradition, it was the tools of modernity as exemplified in the methods of scientific social research that were the natural choice.

Exploring this gap between the modern change agents and the traditional societies that they sought to transform led the dominant paradigm to the verge of a new insight. As we saw above, in his classic book Schramm recognized it as a problem that villagers often had very good reason to be suspicious of outsiders, particularly when they came with the authority of the state. In order to overcome this problem, he argued that communication plans must be developed with a recognition of this perceived isolation, and he proposed that they should be 'as local as possible' in order to avoid the dangers of the remote modernising centre deciding upon unrealistic objectives and methods (1964: 123). The kind of communication that might work involved some form of participation by the mass of the population, and 'horizontal' communication between different groups of them in order to supplement the 'vertical' communication from the modernising centre (ibid. 36–37). Examples of such communication might involve 'advisory committees, local origination and feedback programming' (de Sola Pool, 1977: 136). In this way it was intended to maximize feedback or, in a more developed form '*participation* by both parties to the suggested changes … the villagers' needs, wishes, ideas, and knowledge should enter into the transaction equally with those of the change agent' (Schramm, 1967: 24). The changes to the classical model of development communication that followed from consideration of the social realities of attempting rapid modernization in a society with sharp divisions, if not hostility, between elite and peasant masses we may schematically represent as in Figure 2.2.

In Schramm's account, this introduction of 'feedback' was never examined in more than immediate practical terms. Consulting with villagers, and even allowing them to express their own views, seemed an eminently sensible

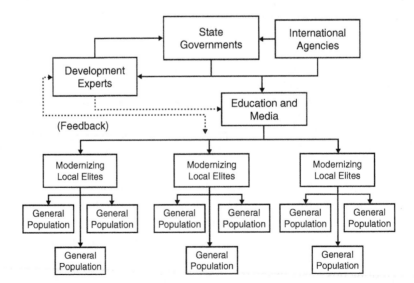

Figure 2.2   The Modified Development Communication Model

practical measure. The issue that he did not confront was the extent to which such practices fitted in with the stark opposition between the modern and the traditional posed by theory, and how it could do anything more than give an unwarranted voice to the most obstinately immovable aspects of the culture of the peasantry. If development communication was simply a practical toolkit which allowed one to identify and resolve problems that prevented people living better lives, then simply adding another tool to the technical arsenal at one's disposal was a logical step to take. But the dominant paradigm made much greater claims than merely to practical utility; it claimed to be a theory of how social change took place in developing societies. Theories demand consistency and internal logic. In this case, consistency and internal logic did not admit any voice to the traditional, the ignorant, and the superstitious. Why listen to what the obstacle to development had to say? At the theoretical level, the modest introduction of feedback contained within it the potential of a development that could be deeply disturbing to the dominant paradigm.

Conclusion

The founders of the dominant paradigm had a very clear theoretical framework. Whatever sense one ultimately makes of these ideas, it must be allowed that the people who developed them were engaged in a serious intellectual exercise and were motivated by what they believed to be the best interests of the people of the developing world.

It is for these reasons that it is necessary to depart from the conclusions drawn by Simpson that these ideas were simply concerned with 'managing change' (1994: 81–85). Managing change was certainly one of the objectives of development communication, but this was not the major inspiration of the paradigm. On the contrary, the main objective was to produce change in order to shift from the traditional to the modern personality, and thus from the traditional to the modern society. Certainly, there was never any idea that this change would, or even could, be spontaneous and unorganized. Change always emanated from the modern change agents, who were interlopers into the traditional world and it was they who identified the problems and decided upon the appropriate course of change. In this, the underlying philosophy was as 'planned' as anything its Stalinist opponents ever dreamed up, and to this extent it was indeed promoting controlled change. The logic of the social circumstances in which change was to be conducted, and the pace of change forced upon societies by the nature of the modern world, were such as to reinforce this drive to manage and control. The intention to change people and change societies was limited by the desire to maintain stability and bolster the authority of ruling elites, and this of course meant the careful delimitation of the kinds of change that were to be encouraged and the kinds of action that were to be endorsed.

Against Simpson's wholly pessimistic conclusions that the sole aim was to manage change, it seems fairer to view the dominant paradigm as one that promoted managed change.

If the contemporary reader discards intellectual fashion and political distaste, it is possible to recognize the dominant paradigm as an example of a powerful and well-constructed social theory. It had very considerable successes with scholars and politicians around the world. This was neither a simple product of the wealth and power of its US proponents, nor a simple accident of time and place. It arose from the fact that the dominant paradigm identified an important problem and proposed a coherent set of remedies. This coherence and power was in large measure drawn from the conviction with which some of the central concepts were defined. If one's reading of Weber led one to the conclusion that a particular psychic structure was the key to social development, and this is very far from being an untenably eccentric reading, then all of the rest follows logically. As a matter of historical fact, only European and North American societies had produced 'modern' personality types, and there was no guarantee that the cultures of other societies contained the raw material out of which a Benjamin Franklin could arise unaided. It was also clearly the case that in many contemporary societies the majority of the population experienced very severe material deprivation and that there were those within them who were looking for a solution to the problems of underdevelopment with considerable urgency. The presence of the Soviet communist alternative path to development was a palpable reality and if one held that it was a task of the first importance to challenge that ideology, then developing an alternative was an urgent task. In those circumstances, the introduction of modernity from outside and the promotion of modernity through the mass media were both rational responses to the situation. And if modernity came from outside, the people most susceptible to it were the elite, and if the people to be changed were so resolutely wedded to their traditional views, then it followed that change would always be problematic and likely to lead to social conflicts between the modern elite and the traditional peasants. Therefore, the kinds of material used in promoting change would need to be carefully designed so that it did not negate itself by provoking some kind of revolt. In order to make sure that change-oriented media did indeed contain the correct kinds of messages, it was essential to know as much about the intended recipient as was possible, and to this end research and consultation were invaluable tools.

The coherence and elegance of a theory, however, is only one measure of its value. The other test is its practical efficacy in resolving problems. In the case of the dominant paradigm, this latter was by far the most important test of the theory's value, since it not only claimed to interpret an important part of human experience but also to have produced techniques that could materially alter it in ways that were both predictable and would lead to a bettering of social conditions. What was more, by common consent, the conditions it promised to better were agreed to be in urgent need of thoroughgoing improvement, and there were simple indices by which outcomes could be measured. The dominant paradigm asked to be judged by its results, and it is to that judgement and its consequences that we turn to in the next chapter.

3

THE PASSING OF MODERNITY

The dominant paradigm had considerable appeal, both as an intellectual landmark for scholars and as a guide to practical action for experts and politicians. If Lerner produced the most elegant theoretical statement, Schramm's definitive book, *Mass Media and National Development* which was first published in 1964, was the work that extended the reach of the paradigm beyond the academy. It was very quickly adopted as a canonical text by UNESCO, by development workers, and by many national governments. It provided a clear statement of the main ideas of development communication in an approachable style and it lent itself readily to practical application.

Despite this enormous success, within a decade of its publication the theory and practice of the dominant paradigm were under systematic attack. In 1976, the leading thinker of the second generation of the school, Everett Rogers, published a detailed and very self-critical account of the paradigm and his own part in elaborating it. The title of his definitive article made clear the extent to which a retreat was under way: it proclaimed 'the passing of the dominant paradigm' (Rogers, 1976).

This remarkable reversal of fortune had its roots in a number of connected developments. One was the changed intellectual climate as the depths of the first Cold War gave way to the flowering of the late 1960s. Closely related to that was a gathering suspicion of the efficacy of development, and of development communication as its handmaiden. These external factors were complemented by a reconsideration of the theoretical foundations of the dominant paradigm, and a growing conviction of their inadequacy as an account of communication processes themselves.

By the mid 1970s, only about a decade after its most forceful formulations, the dominant paradigm seemed discredited. It was dismissed even by many of those who had been its militant proponents. In its place, there was no new dominant paradigm. Rather than a single orthodoxy to which the vast majority of theorists and practitioners adhered, there was a range of views, each of which highlighted different issues and proposed different practical solutions to what it saw as the most pressing problems of the developing world.

In this chapter, we will examine the major criticisms of the dominant paradigm and consider the responses of its adherents. We will then look in some detail at one of the new sets of ideas that were advanced in its place, and examine what contribution they have made to development communication.

The failure to achieve development

The first and most withering criticism of the dominant paradigm was that it did not work. As one of its most prominent critics observed, two UN development decades had failed to lead to very much real development. Despite systematic efforts, large areas of the world did not appear to be reaching the take-off phase and the gap between the most developed and the less developed worlds was widening (Beltrán, 1989: 12). Development communication had been actively applied to the problems of social change and it had followed the prescriptions of the dominant paradigm. Development was understood explicitly as the consequence of the spread of the modern personality. A UNESCO conference in Bangkok, for example, concluded in terms that exactly articulated the orthodoxy of the dominant paradigm: 'appropriate programmes are those that will lead to a change in the traditional attitudes of the rural people, make them accept the necessary changes in attitudes, and enable them to acquire the necessary skills that are implied in progress' (Anon, 1967: 41). Programs designed to achieve such changes had been widely implemented, but the behavioural alterations that were supposed to follow did not take place. In the African case, one author wrote: 'After many decades of employing the modern mass media as tools for development, the records in many African countries show that very little has been achieved in such critical areas as political mobilization, national unity, civic education, and the diffusion of new agricultural techniques and products' (Okigbo, 1995: 4).

The grandest example of the thousands of attempts to use the technology of mass communication to achieve changes in attitude and behaviour was 1975–76 Satellite Instructional Television Experiment (SITE) in India, which employed the then revolutionary technology of satellite transmission to reach specially installed television receivers in rural villages across the sub-continent. The initiative for this came in large part from the government of India, which retained strong control over the project (Eapen, 1986). They decreed that 'television must be utilized in the developmental process as an instrument of social change and national cohesion by unhesitatingly upholding progressive values' (cited in Chander and Karnik, 1976: 24).

To this end, the experiment aimed to help rural areas through improving education, diffusing new ideas about family planning and agriculture and generally disseminating modernity. The results of this enormous effort were much studied, but the research evidence yielded only the most uncertain results: 'Communication media ... may have a relatively modest and supportive role to play and by themselves they cannot be used to engineer social change. More legitimately, they can be expected to serve as media for bringing about increased general awareness and only gradually to bring about a change in long-held attitudes' (Gore, 1983: 55). If, as Rogers had maintained, 'modernization is essentially a communication process', then the failure of modernization must inevitably also be a failure of communication (Rogers, 1969: 42–43).

Even where carefully designed programmes had been mounted, people did not necessarily modify their behaviour. The dominant paradigm had noted, and puzzled long over, what it termed the 'KAP gap'. By this was meant the differences between knowledge (K), attitude (A) and practice (P). It was very often the case that there was a contradiction between the positive scores on the first two measures and reality of no discernable shift on the third (Rogers, 1973: 366–96). People who knew about, for example, modern techniques of family planning, and were favourably disposed towards them, nevertheless resolutely refused to change their behaviour and adopt them in practice. According to the dominant paradigm, this was not what should take place: 'the implicit theoretical premise is [that] when given relevant information about a new practice ... the audience will likely abandon the old in favor of the new, provided that the new practice is seen to be more rewarding' (Chu, 1994: 39). In reality, knowing about modernity and its benefits did not seem to be enough to make people behave as moderns.

This observation, however, led to the possibility that the entire theory and practice of development through the dissemination of western modernity was alien to the developing world, and that its promoters, whether they were foreign experts or local officials, were distant from the realities and values of the mass of the population. The local modernizers sought to impose their programme on their societies in order to secure their own positions, not to improve the lot of the poor: 'The political and bureaucratic elite, forcibly modernized (Westernized) earlier by the colonial regimes and alienated from the traditional society ... comfort their guilty consciences and seek legitimacy for their newly acquired power in transforming their societies into powerful and respectable ones' (Inayatullah, 1967: 100). This charge went to the root of the whole edifice of development and development communication as a project of modernization. Its founding theoretical claim was that social change was the sum of individual change, but according to critics like Inayatullah there were issues of social structure which profoundly limited the possibilities of individual change. The fact that certain personality attributes might have worked to produce change in the west, but seemed not to alter behaviour elsewhere, suggested that the concept of modernity might not be universal.

The rediscovery of social structures

The view that there was a fundamental problem with the ideas of modernity and development was most famously articulated by Luis Ramiro Beltrán in 1974, in an article whose title reveals very clearly the nature of his views: 'Alien Premises, Objects, and Methods in Latin American Communication Research' (Beltran, 1976). Beltrán pointed out that the definition of modernity at stake was one elaborated in the USA and implemented by experts trained in the USA (as Beltrán himself had been). Although he did not advance any view as to whether the US methods would be appropriate in the USA itself, Beltrán certainly took the view that they were inadequate for the study of realities in Latin America. In particular, he was concerned to understand 'the blindness to social-structural determinants transpiring from diffusion research' (Beltrán, 1976: 22). According to him, the central reality that critical studies of diffusion had discovered in the Latin American context was that the overall social structure had a decisive influence on the widespread adoption or otherwise of a particular innovation. In this, Beltrán obviously echoed other practical critiques we have already examined. In order to respond to that problem, it was necessary to construct a new, specifically Latin American theory of social change that would begin from the analysis of the social structure and to fit the issues of communication into that framework. As he put it, 'questioning the present structures of Latin American society is an attitude shared by all researchers using this new approach' (Beltrán, 1976: 36).

Attention to social structures revealed that there was much more at issue than the opposition between knowledge and ignorance, and the concept of the 'sub-culture of peasantry' concealed important differences in both attitude and potential for behavioural change. Developing countries contained within them widely differing social groups with different material and psychic resources, and the development communication effort was inserted not into an homogenous mass of traditional people but into a social structure in which some were better equipped to understand, accept and implement its messages than were others. Studies found that 'in general, the data indicate quite clearly the inequality in the distribution of mass media in the developing countries. The stratification of distribution occurs not only between urban and rural areas ... the distribution of mass media and development information availability in rural areas mirrors the unequal distribution of other resources' (Shore, 1980: 44–5). In a situation of unequal resources, information 'tends not to trickle randomly but flow along established channels defined by the social structure' (Hartmann et al., 1989: 259). As a result of this 'the members of the upper segments [of an Indian village] have better access to the mass media [and] they utilize the knowledge received for their further development' (Ashok Kumar, 1999: 144). Even the 'successes' of development thus tended to reinforce the positions of dominant groups rather than reach the very poor. So, for example, the result of the Green Revolution in agriculture in India was certainly change, but it was noted that 'the main gainers have been the rich influential farmers in regions endowed with water and fertilizer facilities' (Sondhi, 1983: 130).

The real picture of the effects of development communication was thus similar to that portrayed in Figure 3.1. The wholly-modern experts, who were very often a more or less direct representative of the state, took the initiative in a programme of development communication (Rao, 1997: 33). Whatever their intentions, the natural audience for the messages about modernity were those who already had one foot in that camp, who tended overwhelmingly to be from the elite layers of richer, more privileged and, usually, more educated people. They were more likely to receive the messages, better equipped to interpret them, possessed of more resources that would enable them to implement changes based on this knowledge, and thus they were more likely to modify their behaviour in the intended, more 'modern', direction. One study, designed strictly according to the prescriptions of the dominant paradigm in order to test the hypothesis that 'There exists a strong positive correlation between exposure to mass media and socio-economic development of the rural people', came to the conclusion that: 'media communication is a better promoter of development for those sections of the rural population who have attained a certain level of socio-economic advancement. That is, the less advanced categories are benefiting less by development communication' (Joseph, 1997: 218).

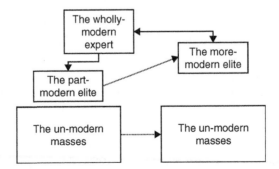

Figure 3.1   The effects of differential modernity

Up to a point, of course, this was exactly what the dominant theories of indirect influence and the diffusion of innovations predicted. The first to take up innovations were indeed those from elite groups. What did not occur, however, was the spread of those innovations throughout the rest of the population according to the smooth S-curve predicted by theory. As one prominent student of development communication wrote: 'Even with the addition of the mass media and literacy, the expected diffusion of innovations in the third world did not eventuate as it had done in the developed countries' (Melkote, 1991: 25). Normally, the innovation only diffused to a few, and when it followed the curve of theory, it ended with very many less than the whole population adopting the novelty. For the majority of the population 'their absorption of the communications can be increased only if they are brought to the take-off stage on the socio-economic front' (Joseph, 1997: 218). In other words, the rural poor needed to reach a certain level of development before they were in a position to respond to the messages of modernity (Sinha, 1983). Clearly, the social structures of the developing world contained differences of a kind that were much more intractable than those which separated the innovative and laggard grain farmers of Iowa. The consequence was that the modern section of the population benefited from innovation and became 'more modern', whilst the mass of the very poor remained bound up in tradition (Kumar, 1995: 83).

Economic development was a pre-condition for the acceptance of development messages, rather than the other way around. Instead of raising the standards of the entire population, the effect of the dominant paradigm was to increase social divisions within the countryside. In sum, as one writer put it: 'By the mid-1970s it had become apparent that the mass media have no special power to accelerate change in society and that communication cannot alter an unfair social and economic structure on its own' (Beltrán, 1989: 14).

Challenges to modernity

In its neglect of the importance of the social structure, the dominant paradigm not only failed to grasp the real obstacles to change and development, but also tended to undermine possible alternative paths to change and to pose the stark opposition between radical modernity and invariant tradition as the sole alternatives facing developing societies. The relentless pursuit of modernity in disregard of social structures had another, and more dangerous side, since it could lead to the destruction of alternative paths of social change, and thus to the remergence of resolutely anti-modern and anti-developmental forces as the sole viable alternatives to continued uncontrollable change. The example of Iran, where the Shah had followed a radical project of modernity that had involved the destruction of existing social organizations and the persecution of all political opponents, particularly those on the left who offered a different version of modernity, appeared to offer an awful warning of the dangers of this path. Part of the Shah's project of modernization had been the construction of modern media of mass communication, notably television, under the close supervision of the regime. These were consciously pitted against the existing, traditional, networks of communication, which were primarily religious in nature and personnel. The result, of course, was a mounting crisis and the victory, in 1989, of the religious forces that overthrew the Shah and established a state that, whatever its virtues or vices, operated with a different set of values from those of western modernity. One prominent analyst of this process wrote that 'When modernity is understood as a discrete concept, and set against tradition … the chain of empathy is tragically broken. Modernization from above, accompanied by a good measure of cognitive tyranny, treats its objects of manipulation (man, nature) as things to be molded into a new and different case, against their will and against their sense of history and well-being' (Terhanian, 1984: 166). The main lesson of the Iranian modernization debacle was that programmes of developmental change needed to take full and proper account of the traditional customs and beliefs, including the religious and superstitious beliefs, of the population that was to experience change. Otherwise, the result would be the brutalization of the population and their rejection of the positive elements of reason and modernity that could otherwise have been incorporated into a new belief system that synthesized the best elements of the old and new.

There were, it was claimed, other ways to think about development and social change. Inayatullah, in his sharp early critique of the dominant paradigm, did not reject the idea of development in itself. On the contrary, he saw it as something quite distinct from modernization, and offered an interestingly contrasting definition to that outlined by writers like Lerner and Rogers: 'One possible definition of development could be that it is a process through which a society achieves increased control over its environment, increased control over its own political destiny, and enables its component individuals to gain increased control over themselves' (Inayatullah, 1967: 101). A stress upon 'control', in contrast to the orthodox emphasis on 'growth', suggested a different system of values whereby the outcomes of social action would be judged. If modernity was inextricably and fatally linked with the 'West', then non-western societies would need to seek their values elsewhere.

Many writers have rejected the idea of modernity, at least as embodied in the west, as the motor for a single process of development. There were other possible versions of development, and of the role of communication in development, which did not depend upon Lerner's ideas about modernity. If anything, they appeared to work very much better. Countries such as

China, Cuba and Tanzania had all rejected the straightforward prescriptions of US theory and, in different ways, managed to find alternative paths towards what then appeared to be successful and equitable national development (Hedebro, 1982: 8). In another of those ironic parallels, it was very often the case that these alternative models laid even more stress on the role of the mass media than did the dominant paradigm. Rogers himself had noted, rather wistfully, that 'Only in less developed communist nations such as mainland China and Cuba, have national planners viewed mass media development as a central factor in propelling their country forward' (1969: 100).

The Communist states had always provided the major alternative model of national development, but they were clearly within the 'western' camp in terms of the origins of their ideas. Japan, however, provided the clearest case of a country that had most certainly achieved a triumphant level of development while at the same time remaining resolutely distant from the western version of modernity. In one influential version, the argument about Japan as an alternative model of modernity was articulated in terms that Lerner himself would undoubtedly have recognized (Ito, 1993, 1997). If it was possible to achieve the astonishing transformation of Japan from underdeveloped introversion to global economic giant, while retaining so many of the old ways, then something similar might be possible elsewhere.

Although they certainly provided an alternative view of how development might be achieved, both the communist and Japanese examples amounted only to the replacement of the USA as the exemplar of modernity with some other national manifestation, and thus while they alter the preferred outcomes of the process, they were set within a pattern of thought that retained the same essential structure as did the dominant paradigm. In fact, of course, these alternative versions of modernity tended, as we have seen, to have many points in common with the dominant paradigm. In particular the communist stress upon experts (cadres and commissars) and government initiatives (five-year plans) as the key agents in setting the goals of development and initiating the changes in popular behaviour that followed from those goals bore a marked similarity to the more programmatic statements of writers like Schramm. They are therefore open to many of the same objections, except that the dominant paradigm had the advantage that its own vision of modernity was, in theory at least, more open and democratic than either the communist or Japanese versions, and in practice it was very much richer than the communist alternative.

Other writers attempted to construct programmes of 'development' independently of established examples. Very often they have based themselves upon non-western value systems. So, for example, Sondhi has long argued for a specifically Indian theory of communication and tried to elaborate it on the basis of Indian religious philosophy (Sondhi, 1980, 1985: 19–25). Others have taken Islam as an inspiration for a 'monistic/emancipatory model of communication and development' (Mowlana and Wilson, 1990: 73). Still others have looked to the Sarvodaya Shramadana Movement as the source of 'a development strategy springing from the deepest currents of the culture that permeates [Sri Lankan] society' (Dissanayake, 1984: 39). What these attempts have in common is a stress upon what we may broadly call 'cultural' as opposed to 'material' values in judging the criteria of development. The intention is to reject the 'old [western] bifurcation of culture and technology, tradition and modernity, and traditionalism and technology' in favour of 'cultural authenticity as a necessary precondition to the development process' (Wang and Dissanayake, 1984: 18). Because of this stress upon the importance of culture, usually defined more or less as a 'whole way of life', these versions of development give more much weight to popular agency in the process of change than any version of the dominant paradigm, and thus fall more properly into the participatory paradigm that we will examine in a later chapter. Here we need only note that unless one has a single and definite notion of the constituents of modernity, be it the US, the Communist or the Japanese, and a belief that this knowledge resides in the hands of an expert elite who need to enlighten the masses, then the dominant paradigm cannot be sustained. Once one admits the traditional, the popular, the irrational, as a source of value, then the whole edifice becomes unworkable.

Lerner, for one, was not prepared to admit the force of this critique. The obvious polar opposite of the 'West' was the 'East', and it was this implied juxtaposition that Inayatullah claimed was mapped on to a conception of western values as 'materialistic' and eastern values as 'spiritual'. Lerner reacted strongly against this interpretation. He recognized there was, in any such debate, what he termed an 'ethnocentric predicament', but he claimed that the 'West' was a recent artefact with no genuine substance: supposedly 'western' nations differed as much between themselves as they did with their equally differentiated 'eastern' cousins (Lerner, 1967a: 110ff). He did not deny that the 'East' had its own long traditions, and that these included several great spiritual dimensions, but 'what I reject is the equation of spirituality with poverty, disease, ignorance and apathy among the helpless people of Asia' (113). He was confident that '... many Asian people *do* want materialism in the sense of better homes, better food, better hygiene, better education, better lives for their children' (114). It was in this sense that the USA could provide a model that he believed could legitimately be offered and accepted internationally without any taint of domination or insensitivity (Lerner, 1967a: 110). There is an undoubted note of arrogance in Lerner's litany of necessary lessons to which the East must submit, and it has a curious, and rather alarming, contemporary ring to it, but we should not allow our concern with the form of his discourse to obscure an understanding of what was at stake in this debate. Essentially, the issue was the fundamental theoretical foundation of development communication: whether there was any such thing as a universal set of values and beliefs called 'modernity' that could be generalized beyond the USA and communicated to others. Depending upon the answer to that question, the dominant paradigm must stand or fall.

Responses to the critique

The attack on the dominant paradigm was thus fairly comprehensive. Critics questioned its efficacy in achieving its proclaimed objective of raising the living standards of the people of developing countries. They suggested that the model of social change was based purely upon the dissemination through the mass media of the psychic attributes of the modern personality as defined in the developed western countries, and particularly in the USA. The model did not achieve its grand aim of changing personalities, thus of changing social conditions, or even in its more modest interim goals of changing particular localized patterns of belief, attitude and behaviour. Similar criticisms of the inadequacy of the theory of the modern personality, of the role of the mass media as multiplier, and of the need for a radical reconsideration of the objectives and methods of development came from a variety of sources, many of them inside 'the west' (for example: Golding, 1974; Hedebro, 1982: 13–22; Servaes, 1989: 9–11; Bessette, 1995: 111–16; and many others).

The criticisms were so wide ranging and devastating that they could not be ignored. Even the most determined exponents of the dominant paradigm had to reconsider their position and most shifted the ground of their arguments significantly. One major response to the criticisms was to restate the basic principles of the old model, and to seek to modify it only in order to make it work more effectively. This minor revision left intact the basic theoretical structure and it is therefore difficult to suggest that it represents something as distinct as a new paradigm. It was, rather, a variant of the dominant paradigm, which we here term the continuity variant. This approach continued to believe in the superiority of modern over traditional ideas, and continued to seek change at the level of the individual rather than the social structure.

The second possible response was to change the basic model of the diffusion of a new personality type and abandon the idea of the superiority of the modern, western expert who sought to achieve change. Change remained desirable, but it was to be promoted from a quite different starting point in the ideas and desires of the population of under-developed countries themselves. This approach thus differed from the dominant paradigm in seeking to discover the needs of the population, rather than assuming that they required an external stimulus in order to achieve change. It was also prepared at least to consider that change might involve some alterations to the social structure in order to succeed. Its guiding light was no longer modernization but the expressed needs of the population. This response, which strongly echoed the new stress upon popular self-activity current in the 1970s, represents such a significant break with the old ways of thinking that it is justified in saying that it constitutes a new paradigm. We will call it the 'participatory paradigm', since its distinguishing feature is precisely the stress upon the decisive role of the population determining the nature and direction of social change.

The third alternative shared the emphasis upon the role of structural factors in social change that occurred in the same decade. External constraints upon developing countries were taken as the decisive factors impeding social change and better living conditions for the mass of the population. In this account, attempting to change people without recognizing that they lived in circumstances that constrained their freedom of action was a hopeless project that served, at best, to obscure the real solutions to social problems. This view is again so different from the old way of thinking that we must consider it an overall alternative, which we can term the 'imperialism paradigm.'

The lines of division between the approaches of people involved in development activities have perhaps never corresponded exactly to these different theoretical approaches. Many individuals have worked in two of the paradigms outlined above. In the practical business of attempting to better the conditions of the world's poor, some have occupied a shifting ground between the continuity variant and the participatory paradigm. Even more, perhaps, have seen the participatory and imperialism paradigms not only as compatible but as complementary. It is possible that some people have inhabited all three positions, although it is hard to cite concrete examples of such versatility. From the relatively comfortable position of the theoretical investigator, however, the approaches are clearly distinct and incommensurate. In the remainder of this chapter and in the two following, we will look at each of these developments in turn.

The enduring power of the dominant paradigm

It is tempting to think that the dominant paradigm had indeed passed entirely. Few people today would be so bold as to make the same claims for modernity, or dismiss the peasant masses as utterly benighted, as did Lerner and Rogers. After all, even Rogers himself was not prepared to follow the robust lead from Daniel Lerner. He responded to criticism with the acknowledgement that 'the old conception of development' was no longer adequate and now needed to be understood as a historically and intellectually limited construction (Rogers, 1976: 122ff). He identified four main influences that had shaped the original idea of development: a stress on industrialization; a related concern with the deployment of capital-intensive technology; an obsession with economic growth: a definition of growth in terms of quantifiable measures of aggregate increases. The shortcomings of this approach had led to three different responses. The first was a critique of the basic assumptions of the classical idea of development. As Rogers argued, that model was now recognized as an ideological construction: 'Continuing underdevelopment was attributed to "traditional" ways of thinking and acting of the mass of individuals in developing nations. The route to modernization was to transform the people, to implant new values and beliefs' (Rogers, 1976: 126). The second critique shifted the focus from the internal structures of the developing countries to their relations with the outside world – most notably to their continuing relationships of subordination to the developed countries and in particular to the USA, and this led to a line of thinking that we will examine in a later chapter. The third strand of criticism led to a stress on the inadequacy of technological solutions to what were, ultimately, human problems of social relations.

As a response to these criticisms and the shock of world events in the 1970s, Rogers detected a major shift in the definition of development. Instead of a single model of a developed nation, exemplified in the USA, it was now necessary to recognize that there could be different and contradictory definitions of development. The new paradigm was marked by four emphases: on equality of distribution; on popular participation; on self-reliance; and on a preservation of elements of the old order, for example the integration of western scientific medicine with Chinese traditional medicine (Rogers, 1976: 130–31).

These shifts in the definition of development produced, he claimed, changes in the understanding of the nature and effects of development communication. In particular, recognition of the structural constraints on development led to a new modesty about the possible role and achievements of development communication. Development communication now needed to be located much more centrally within conceptions of social change as a whole, rather than being seen as something that could substitute for, or at least accelerate, change in other parts of society.

In response to these problems that he identified with the dominant paradigm, Rogers proposed a much revised alternative. The most important innovation he proposed was to shift the focus of development communication efforts from 'what the government does to (and for) the people' towards 'self development' (Rogers, 1976: 138). This meant dropping the old 'top down' model of communication and finding new ways of using the media to provide people with the information that they determined as useful to the problems they faced. Instead of the central government employing experts who diagnosed the problem, framed the response and implemented a campaign of persuasion, the aim now was to create a situation in which government agencies responded with technical information in answer to developmental initiatives originated locally. The role of the mass media was now 'to feed local groups with information of a background nature about their expressed needs, and to disseminate innovations that may meet certain of these needs' (Rogers, 1976: 139). In this new framework, the mass media were only one of a matrix of communication mechanisms, including very importantly the traditional media of pre-modern societies, but at the same time it was important to explore the possibilities given by the then new technologies like satellites and computing.

It might seem, then, that even its most fervent and systematic adherent had abandoned the dominant paradigm in favour of what was recognizably a version of the participatory paradigm. Bibliographic studies tell us that, despite a life extending to the mid 1980s, 'in the 1987–1996 period, Lerner's modernization model completely disappears' (Fair and Shah, 1997: 10).

The reality is rather more complex. As we saw in the last chapter, the dominant paradigm had always advocated a form of 'participation', albeit one so weak as to constitute mere 'feedback', in order the better to understand the situation of the people who were going to be exposed to modern ideas via the mass media. We have also seen, in the discussion of the nature and evolution of the dominant paradigm, that there were people operating with the basic set of ideas expounded by Lerner throughout the 1970s and 1980s, and we can cite other work that employs unrevised versions of the dominant paradigm as recently as 1999 (Melkote and Mudpidi, 1999). What the bibliographic study tells us is that there are few direct citations of Lerner after about 1987, but nevertheless the ideas that he elaborated have clearly remained influential in their pristine state (Mowlana, 2001: 181–82). One more qualitative study of development scholarship found that, whatever their explicit theoretical citations, 54 per cent of studies still used the old development measures and 'scholars from Asian developing countries were even less likely to follow [the alternative paradigm] than their western counterparts' (Wei, 1998: 37). He concluded that 'the dominant paradigm is far from "passing" in Asia', although it is fair to note that only 3 per cent of the respondents had been wholly educated in Asia, as opposed to the 54 per cent who had some education in the USA. Other studies have found the dominant paradigm alive and well in Africa (Mezzana, 1996: 184–9). Rogers himself also came to the conclusion in the years after he proclaimed its demise that, while far less dominant, the dominant paradigm had most certainly not 'passed' and was still an important compass in understanding development issues (Rogers, 1989).

The continuity variant

This continued use of the basic intellectual structures elaborated by Lerner and his co-thinkers nearly half a century ago constitutes one of the major current ways of thinking about development communication. In some important respects this approach is markedly different, at least in its emphases, from the classical form of the dominant paradigm, but it is not sufficiently differentiated as to constitute a new paradigm in itself. For that reason, we consider it here a clearly differentiated body of work that remains within the fundamental paradigm but offers an important alternative account of some key features. It is this kind of relationship that we have argued constitutes a 'variant.' The new approach is a variant of the dominant paradigm, but it is one that inherits so many of its values, goals and methods that the title it is given here stresses the extent to which it carries on from the work of the original: hence the term 'continuity variant'.

One key to understanding why it remains so enormously influential can be found in Rogers's 1989 re-statement of the dominant paradigm. He defined development as 'a type of directed social change that provides individuals with increased control over nature' and went on to list examples that gave heavy emphasis to the natural, and particularly the medical sciences (Rogers, 1989: 72). However unfashionable 'western modernity' may have become around the world, the concrete achievements of the scientific methods developed by western modernity remain extremely persuasive, and employing those methods remains a powerful development goal. Even those who loudly reject 'western values' are very far from rejecting physics, chemistry, biology and so on, particularly in their practical and applied versions. On the contrary, they are very often the most enthusiastic proponents of the technical advances produced by 'the west'.

The clearest examples of the continuity variant are thus very often to be found in the field of health communication. This arises from the status of medicine in the world today. Health, as the outcome of practices identified by the discoveries of scientific medicine, is one of the central, although perhaps least contentious, aspects of modernity. The distinct shape of scientific medicine, a child of the Enlightenment, has been overwhelmingly the product of first European and then North American research and clinical practice (Porter, 1997). Its export to other parts of the world, particularly the former colonial empires, was one of the direct legacies of western rule. It was the colonial rulers who established hospitals, trained doctors and nurses, instituted programmes of public health, and so on. Most often, modern, western, scientific medicine sees itself still today as the opposite of, and inimical with, the beliefs and practices of traditional medicine. It often fights bitter battles against the lingering vestiges of pre-modern health care, which it attempts to de-legitimize and if possible criminalize. As it happens, while scientific medicine struggles against ignorance and superstition in developing countries, it also does this in the heart of the west itself. The governments of developed nations, no less than undeveloped ones, listen to the scientific advice that informs them of the shortcomings of traditional practices from the point of view of health. And the governments of both kinds of societies seek to change popular practices to those believed to produce more desirable health outcomes. If one wishes to find a pristine example of the struggle between modernity and tradition, one need look no further than medical practice.

This enthusiastic adoption of the programme of modernization is accompanied by a very orthodox theory of the role of the mass media. Programmes of health communication anywhere in the world, in New York as much as New Caledonia, are necessarily predicated on the idea that a scientific elite has access to knowledge that they wish to spread to the mass of population, in order to improve life expectancy, well-being, infant mortality rates, and so on. They usually involve an engagement with, if not an actual struggle against, the traditional beliefs and habits of the population. Even within developed countries, then, there is a strong sense that health communication is part of the process of the bringing the light of modernity to the non-modern darkness of popular practices (Apfel, 1999: 2; Institute of Medicine, 2002).

Health communication represents the strongest case for theories of development communication based on a theory of modernity. While we might want to criticize the building of a steel works, or a telecommunications infrastructure, or a nuclear power station, few critics of modernity are so bold as to argue against technologies that can reduce infant mortality, eliminate crippling diseases and prolong life expectancy. While it is certainly possible to find fault with this or that campaign's ability to realize its objectives, it is hard to find fault with what we might term 'vital modernity' as a project in itself. Of course it is possible to criticize the arrogance and stupidity of medical professionals, to point to their neglect of the insights of traditional medicines, and to show how their ignorance has led to human suffering. It is quite true that human health is not only, perhaps not even primarily, a matter of the proper functioning of a human biology that is identical throughout the species, and that social and psychic factors that vary from place to place are central to well-being: poverty, for example, has clearly been central to the impact of HIV/AIDS in Africa (Schutte, 2003). These, really, are all ways of saying that scientific medicine is not good enough at doing what it sets out to do, and is allowing prejudice to blind it to the truth, or is operating within limits it cannot influence. It is, however, a different and harder thing to say that the project of reducing human suffering through the application of scientific knowledge is fundamentally a mistaken one. Perhaps there are such resolute critics of modernity, but they do not appear to be well represented in the study of culture and communication.

Health communication is, and has always been, a central dimension of development communication. Schramm and Rogers both wrote extensively on the subject. Thousands of programmes have been implemented to improve popular knowledge of modern medical techniques, to make people less hostile to them, and to change their behaviour in line with the prescriptions of science. There is still a vigorous programme of research and practice in precisely this area. Nowhere is the project communicating modernity more strongly represented today than in the worldwide attempts to improve people's lives through spreading the findings and the applications of scientific medicine.

The starting point of much health communication is, essentially 'we know and they need to know'. The major contemporary textbook on communication in family planning programmes, produced by staff at the Johns Hopkins School of Public Health in the USA, who are clearly world leaders in this field, and whose model of health communication is widely imitated, explicitly starts from the revisions to the dominant paradigm proposed by Rogers in the 1970s. The authors accept that early efforts were stymied by their limited conception of communication, which saw the expert as constructing a pre-designed message that would provide everything that the audience needed to know, think and feel. In place of that, the new paradigm starts from a recognition of the two-way nature of communication, and gives the audience a much more central place in the construction of the programme. As the authors put it, it is only after extensive pre-testing that 'the program managers have any degree of confidence that audience members will interpret family planning messages in the way that they were intended'. (Piotrow et al., 1997: 18).

This passage is a very stark statement of the minimal adjustments made to the old dominant paradigm in order to achieve the thoroughly contemporary continuity variant. In this account, the experts are different from their audience in almost every respect. The experts have intentions as to what sense the audience should make of their messages. The experts set the goals of the programme and design the material it will use. True, these experts need to take into account the nature of the audience, and they need to test that they have correctly understood that audience, in order to achieve the results that they themselves have defined even before they came in to contact with such a strange and alien group of people. The experts are communicating something, here the fruits of modern medicine, of which they are in possession, to people who are ignorant of these insights. The experts need to know about their audience in order to make sure that they really do get the message. There are numerous other contemporary examples that operate within exactly the same framework (Salmon and Atkin, 2003; Muturi 2005; Farn et al., 2005; Pilsbury and Mayer, 2005; Thomas, 2006).

Although some writers on health communication are clearly aware of the notions of participation discussed in the next chapter, they at best give them a supporting role in the design of projects (Knight, Lapinski and Witte, 1998: 157–60; Kar et al., 2001). The predominant basic structure of this model of communication, and the underlying model of development, is that there is a pre-defined modernity, embedded in certain medical technologies and the accompanying practices of their use, which is known to the experts and unknown to the audience. The experts will find the best way of transferring their knowledge and the desired attitudes to the audience, and to the extent that they need to do that efficiently they will research the peculiarities

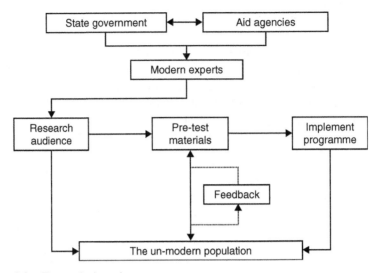

Figure 3.2   The continuity variant

of the different audience segments and design campaign communications accordingly. This model of communication is illustrated in Figure 3.2. It differs from the earlier models only in that it now has a dimension of research and pre-testing, which involves a 'feedback loop'.

This model of communication clearly differs only in the tiniest details from the original classical model. The extent of the modification concerns only the fact that the need for the modern expert to understand the world of the non-modern objects of the communication strategy is made quite explicit, although in fact we saw above that recognition of this was actually present in Schramm's canonical text itself. This change is accommodated only in order to permit the more effective transmission of an already established set of new ideas. The success or otherwise of the particular example can be measured through the extent to which change in attitudes and behaviour towards the desired norm have taken place, and there is considerable uncertainty as to whether health communication campaigns have actually achieved their desired effects (Hornik, 2002).

There have certainly been new departures within health communication, or at least new emphases, which mark contemporary practice out from the simple repetition of the dominant paradigm. One good example is the use of pro-social entertainment programming. These are not entirely new: the British radio 'soap', *The Archers*, which recently marked its 15,000th episode, was originally aimed at changing farming practices. Their use has, however, been much more directly assimilated in contemporary discussion of health communication. One much cited example is the Tanzanian radio soap *Twende na Wakati* (a literal translation of the title is *Let's be Modern*), whose impact has been widely studied (Singhal and Law, 1997; *The Drum*

Beat, October 31 1999). The use of serial dramatic television fiction for the promotion of development objectives is also quite widespread (Brown et al., 2003: 91–98). Despite the general adoption of this form, not everyone is so convinced of their efficacy and some writers in the developing world have queried whether the development of more commercialized media will mean the end of such efforts in their own context (Sherry, 1997; Gupta, 1999: 93).

The dominant currents in contemporary health communication are, despite their slight adjustments, clearly deeply indebted to the dominant paradigm. In the place of its all-embracing conception of modernity, it has the more modest scope of 'vital modernity'. It does not have, at least explicitly, such a grandiose conception of how it can effect social change through the spread of knowledge, but it retains a belief that it can effect change through exactly that. It further differs in that it does not have such an explicit view of the problematic nature of its audience as did the dominant paradigm, but it retains the distinction between knowing expert and ignorant audience. It has, certainly, developed and embellished the original insight of the dominant paradigm as to the need to understand the world within which the audience lives and thinks in order to influence it, and it has adopted new media forms, but it retains the belief that this is necessary in order to carry out its task of disseminating scientific knowledge efficiently and accurately. In its fundamental conception of human relations and the place of communication and media within them, it is recognizably the same paradigm.

4

VARIETIES OF PARTICIPATION

The dominant paradigm entered a major theoretical crisis in the 1970s. Much later, it became clear that it had proved sufficiently robust to survive its critics, at least in terms of its practical applications through the continuity variant. It survives to this day in a barely modified form that continues to provide the framework for numerous programmes of communication. The strength and resilience of the dominant paradigm was not, however, sufficient to restore it to an unchallenged place at the centre of all thinking about the role of communication in assisting people to improve their lives. Alongside the continuity variant of the dominant paradigm, several other versions of development communication have been elaborated. Whatever its practical persistence, it was no longer possible to speak of a 'dominant' paradigm at the level of theory. The alternatives that were developed are sufficiently different in their underlying assumptions and theoretical frameworks as to merit description as an alternative paradigm.

A decade after Schramm's definitive statement of the dominant paradigm, the general intellectual landscape looked entirely different. While the theory and practice of development communication continued to attract a substantial amount of interest, the main stress was now on 'participation' as the key to successful projects. One index of how far the debate had shifted can be found in the words of Robert McNamara, speaking as President of the World Bank in Nairobi in 1973. He pointed to the fact that development projects were decided centrally and imposed upon a population, with or without their consent. From now onward, he said, the views and wishes of the 'recipients' of development projects would be canvassed in advance and would play a part in shaping the nature of those projects (Ascroft, 1995: 266–7).

As we have seen, the recognition of the need for participation was open to reinterpretation and recuperation into a barely modified version of the dominant paradigm. It could simply be a new term applied to an unchanged reality of centralized decision making and top-down implementation. It was also, however, open to much more challenging interpretations.

Thinking through the consequences led many writers and activists to seek a new, participatory, paradigm.

The participatory paradigm

The starting point of this new paradigm was radically different from that of its predecessor, and even from that of some of the more outspoken critics of the dominant paradigm like Beltrán. For the participatory paradigm, there was no self-evident category of modernity, whether embodied in a western society or elsewhere, and therefore no single goal towards which every nation should aspire: 'Development is not a series of known steps through which each country passes towards pre-defined goals' (Berrigan, 1981: 12). The stress upon industrialization and urbanization as the essential stepping-stones of development were replaced by an acceptance of a broad range of technologies and social structures as providing valuable ways of living (Narula and Barnett Pearce, 1986: 33). The new paradigm recognized wide cultural differences between different parts of the world, notably between the 'West' and the 'East'. This meant that societies were likely to have different trajectories and to have 'their own normative goals and standards, which may or may not coincide with those of the post-industrial West' (Jacobson, 1994: 65). To the extent that these trajectories could be considered as 'development', it was as processes that had no necessary unity or singular direction: 'the central idea is that there is no universal development model, that development is an integral, multi-dimensional, and dialectic process that can differ from society to society' (Servaes, 1989: 32).

Because of these differences between the social meanings of development, each of which was local and specific to different societies, the needs that any development project might seek to meet must be defined by the people involved in the situation, rather than being identified by distant, expert elites. These needs and desires could be discovered in the local community, since 'it is at the local community level that the problems of living conditions are discussed and interactions with other communities elicited' (Servaes, 1996a: 10). It was from the community that communication projects should therefore emanate. Only by allowing the people who experience the projected social transformation to define the goals, scope, pace and nature of the projected changes was it possible to ensure that they are fully engaged with the project. Imposed, top-down development projects are likely to fail precisely because they do not command the enthusiastic support of the population, and indeed might well meet determined popular resistance. The reason for such obstacles was because elite definitions of the problem are likely to misconstrue aspects of the situation that are of central importance to the population, and thus to propose solutions that are either mistaken in their intentions or objectionable in their methods: 'Experience shows that the point of departure for development communication is not the dissemination of an innovation or a new idea that is full of promise, but the grassroots expression of its needs' (Bessette, 1995: 123).

If local communities were to identify their central problems, to articulate and define the goals of development projects, and to decide upon the appropriate measures to improve their condition, then communication was a necessary component of any developmental effort. In the dominant paradigm, communication was from the knowledgeable, westernized elites to the peasantry: 'In the use of media for development, emphasis has been on telling and teaching, rather than an exchange of requests and ideas between the centre and outlying areas' (Berrigan, 1981: 7). The aim of communication in the new paradigm was to allow the members of a community to exchange ideas, beliefs and proposals, and to facilitate the emergence of agreed objectives and methods. The new methods were based on the principle of dialogue, and media became 'the means of expression *of* the community, rather than *for* the community' (Berrigan, 1981: 8). The primary aim was no longer the dissemination of information but to 'encourage exchange among the various parties concerned with any given development problem' (Bessette, 1999: 5). In short, vertical communication was replaced by horizontal communication, monologic communication by dialogic communication (Rahim, 1994).

Only such development projects as meet these criteria could genuinely expect to be 'sustainable' in the sense of effecting a genuine and long lasting change in the lives of the population, and of establishing structures and practices that they were able to maintain independently once the resources mobilized for the initiative itself have been exhausted. The aim was not simply to 'transfer information' from scientific experts to ignorant peasants but to share ideas and experience between equals, 'on the one hand, technical specialists learn about people's needs and their techniques of production; on the other, the people learn of the techniques and proposals of the specialists' (Balit, 1999: 4). Projects that depended upon the continued input of knowledge, or materials, from outside the community itself could not genuinely be considered to represent a form of development. On the contrary, they constituted a new and intensified form of dependency. If the outside inputs were removed, then the changes would vanish and, at best, the population would revert to its old ways. At worst, the destruction of the old social structure would be so complete that the community would collapse. The model of sustainable development recognized that, while everybody requires some help at certain crucial points of change, only when a population itself was determined to change its own ways of living, and found the resources within itself that permitted such new ways of life to continue in the longer term, could anything of substance actually be achieved.

Articulated in these terms, the participatory paradigm had the same kind of intellectual coherence and elegance as did the original dominant paradigm. True, it proposed more modest goals, both for development and for the role of communication in development, but the methods it proposed were, potentially at least, far more democratic than those of the older model. The stress upon participation, upon horizontal communication, and upon the valuation of the beliefs and experiences of the mass of the population all had, and continue to have, a much broader contemporary appeal than does a rhetoric that stresses the roles of experts, of science and of elites. It is little wonder that, in the democratic enthusiasms of the 1970s, such a theory came to command instant and widespread support, nor that it should have an enduring attraction for writers concerned with alleviating human misery.

The appeal of the participatory paradigm was certainly sufficiently great that it replaced the dominant paradigm in scholarly studies, so that in the period between 1987 and 1996 'the most frequently-used theoretical framework is participatory development' (Fair and Shah, 1997: 10). Developing the paradigm, and implementing it in practice, proved a much more difficult task. In particular, despite the extensive lip service paid to the idea of participation by international organizations, national government agencies, non-governmental organizations, and development theorists and practitioners, the number of development programmes that demonstrated a manifest commitment to participation was very small. Two experienced writers observed that they 'had yet to come across more than a small handful of projects which pay more than lip service to the participatory involvement of their intended beneficiaries in the conduct of any part of the project' (Ascroft and Masilela, 1995: 289). This scepticism as to the practical impact of the participatory paradigm is not restricted to those who might be thought hostile or indifferent to its implications. The leading theorist of participatory communication wrote modestly that 'participation in communication hardly exists, except in a very limited way, in a number of small localized experiments' (Servaes, 1997: 99). This apparent disjuncture between theoretical exploration and the practice of development is remarkable, and it leads to a paradox that requires detailed examination: the dominant paradigm passed in theory, but retained a very extensive appeal in practice; the participatory paradigm, on the other hand, triumphed in development theory, but has failed to command any substantial support in practice.

The theory of participatory communication, despite its strong and immediate appeal to anyone of a democratic cast of mind, in fact rests upon what turn out upon investigation to be very contentious claims, and the problems that it poses have been resolved in a number of different, indeed contradictory, ways. Depending upon the kinds of answers given to some of the underlying problems, radically different prescriptions for studies and practical projects have been developed. In practice, as we shall see, there is not one 'participatory paradigm' in the same way as there was one 'dominant paradigm'. On the contrary, there are at least two major variants that provide different theoretical and practical answers to the problems involved.

Modern science and traditional knowledge

The starting point of the participatory paradigm is the critique of modernity and modernization as the motors of development. However conservative it may have been in practice, the early programme of development communication was intellectually a very radical one. It rested on the assumption that the methods of modernity, and most notably those of modern science, yielded knowledge of the natural and social worlds that were different not only in content but also in epistemological status to the knowledge held by 'pre-modern' peoples. So the scientific study of the components of agricultural practice yielded different and better methods of producing crops than did the results of the practical experiences of generations of peasant farmers. The scientific study of human behaviour yielded more rational patterns of belief and behaviour, for example with regard to childcare, than did the experiences of generations of peasant mothers. There was little role in this model of development for anything more than the most limited 'feedback'. The only real interest that the scientist might have in what a peasant thought would be in designing a persuasive piece of communication to embody modern ideas, measuring just how far they had absorbed the chosen modern ideas, and whether these new ideas had led to any changes in practical activity.

This naive faith in 'science', and the contempt for the variety of human experience it rests upon, is easy both to see and to critique. In subjecting the dominant version of modernity to a critical examination, the new paradigm was forced to reconsider the status of traditional knowledge and beliefs and to question the epistemological gulf that separated them from modern science. If science does not provide all of the answers, and if there might be times when science is shown to be wrong, and when traditional knowledge gives a better guide to action, then the relationship between the two systems of thought becomes extremely problematic. In its radical form, the new paradigm argues that 'The largely unquestioned assumption that *scientific* knowledge is more valid or valuable than other knowledge is erroneous. The traditional or *indigenous* knowledge is simply *different* knowledge formulated in response to differing environments, conditions and cultures' (Arnst, 1996: 113).

There are, however, two separate steps that follow from this proposition. It is a contemporary commonplace to point to the ethnocentrism and other limitations of western thought and western experts, who have most certainly been guilty of arrogance and ignorance in their handling of 'traditional' people and their knowledge (Sondhi, 1983: 21). It is, however, a further step to argue that this traditional knowledge provides at least the basis of an answer to the problems of development (Sondhi, 1983: 118–30; 1985: 19–25). That, however, is the consequence of taking seriously the statement that the knowledge held by traditional peoples is simply different from that deposited by scientific enquiry and can make exactly the same claims as a guide to effective action.

If science can claim no universal status for its answers, nor that it is necessarily a superior mode of knowing about the world, then logically, both the findings of science and the beliefs of traditional knowledge can be equally valid, even though they contradict each other on essential points of practice and theory. Few writers concerned with the participatory paradigm appear to be prepared to carry through the critique of modernity to this logical conclusion. Those who do, notably Jacobson, make the obvious link with post-modern theories of knowledge (Jacobson, 1996a: 270–71). For him, there are many interpretive paradigms, none of which, especially not western science, deserves any special epistemological privileges (Jacobson, 1996b). Enlightenment and 'reason', as exemplified for example in the work of Habermas, make unreasonable claims to universality that obstruct the recognition of the relativity of any system of thought (Jacobson and Kolluri, 1999).

Most theorists of the participatory paradigm have rather more difficulty in resolving this problem. A good example concerns the relationship between scientific and traditional agriculture. According to one writer, while the participatory approach believes that 'indigenous agriculturalists', far from being the repository of ignorance, know a great number of very useful things about agriculture in their own area, it still believes that 'their productivity and general well-being could be improved by learning from the outside, from other people's indigenous knowledge systems (IKSs), and from the (Western, formal) scientific knowledge system (SKS)' (Awa, 1996: 127). Only the most inflexible proponent of modern science could possibly disagree with this statement, but at the same time it fails to resolve the problem. In cases where the two knowledge systems give similar answers as to what to do in a given context, or if they address different but complementary areas, then there is no problem to resolve. But in those circumstances where they give contradictory advice about the same issue, there is no clear way for anyone to determine what aspects of the different knowledge systems might be useful in any particular situation. The pragmatic solution to the dilemma is to say that the issue of determining the value and utility of different kinds of knowledge is a matter of judgement, to be reached on a case by case basis, taking into account all of the relevant factors, and allowing proper attention to all possible ways of thinking about the particular issue under consideration.

This pluralistic approach would apparently allow for full participation by the indigenous agriculturalists in determining what course of action to pursue, since no prior choice is being made between the claims of the SKS and those of the IKS, but a closer examination reveals that this is not at all the case. The only people who are able to determine whether the SKS contains material that would benefit the people are those who have mastered its complexities, and these are by definition those who have already fully internalized one of the most substantial components of western modernity. In practice, too, it is these experts, rather than the 'indigenous agriculturalists' who will sift other IKSs, determine whether they contain anything of value, and decide whether it should be introduced into a particular context. In other words, the practical outcome of this apparently participatory and pragmatic approach to the problem is to leave all of the decision-making power in the hands of elites who possess scientific knowledge of the recognized western kind.

The same author in fact later comes very close to recognizing precisely these implications of his position when he argues that while 'the value of indigenous people's knowledge has been underestimated and undervalued, yet it would be a mistake to take all indigenous beliefs and practices as the absolute truth … romanticising indigenous belief systems can be inappropriate, for example, when some mythical beliefs lead to irrational behavior' (Awa, 1996: 143). 'Romanticising' beliefs, and judging their 'irrationality' are, of course, things that can only be done by people who do not share them. The extent of the intellectual disagreement between this version of the participatory paradigm and the dominant paradigm is, here, very difficult to discern. One may be less arrogant in the expression of its pretensions but, in the end, both rest upon the judgement of the scientific expert thoroughly trained in the ways of western modernity.

This same equivocation about the value of tradition repeats itself in context after context. We can observe it in discussions of the contradictory nature of traditional media. Thomas, for example, generalizes from his own practical experience to argue that while traditional media (in this case, Indian popular theatre) can be an important means by which societies can come to a better understanding of themselves, they are also potentially conservative forces acting to preserve age-old inequalities and repressions (Thomas, 1995a: 148).

Writers critical of the participatory paradigm have been quick to note this problem with regard to the kinds of social change that it privileges. According to two contemporary authors, the participatory paradigm 'calls for structural transformations along with the preservation of tradition. Anyone familiar with the Third World realities realizes that these are inherently antithetical goals'. As an example, they consider an issue, the empowerment of women, which is today widely recognized as the key to achieving a range of classical development objectives: 'in India there exists a complex network of traditions and rituals – from arranged marriages to socially acceptable attire – that serves to keep women in their subservient place. Any structural transformation would necessarily involve abandoning these traditions' (Ang and Dalmia, 2000: 25–6). For these two adherents to the dominant paradigm, the solution to the contradiction is clear: an unequivocal commitment to the methods and ideas of modernity is the only way that these problems, and all the other egregious evils that afflict the world, can be combated.

This solution, is, of course, not available to the participatory communication approach, since it begins by arguing that the setting of goals and the determination of means are the tasks of the people who constitute the community that is developing: 'the participatory model incorporates the concepts in the emerging framework of multiplicity/another development ... It points to a strategy that is not merely inclusive of, but largely emanates from the traditional 'receivers' (Servaes, 1999: 88). Taken literally, this view would lead to the conclusions drawn by Jacobson, which at least have the (modernist) virtue of consistency, but most writers modify their community centred relativism with an appeal to a set of common, indeed universal, values. Servaes argues that the participatory paradigm 'stresses the importance of the cultural identity of local communities and of democratization and participation at all levels – international, national, local and individual' (ibid.). These values of democratization and participation recur again and again, and are supplemented by other cognate ones, for example that the concept of cultural renewal incorporates 'a universal value framework which is egalitarian, equalitarian, less repressive and adapted to the local ecosystem' and 'the role of communication in participatory development needs to reinforce the purposes of liberation, freedom, justice and egalitarian ideologies' (Nair and White, 1995: 140, 187).

These lists of values sound universal, and extremely appealing, at least to the ears of the modern western expert, but it is not at all self-evident that everybody shares this judgement, in the west or anywhere else. There are certainly plenty of people in the west who reject egalitarianism, for example. Equally, there is little evidence that pre-modern human communities are naturally endowed with a sense of liberation and freedom. In reality, however attractive they may be, the fact is that these 'universal' values have the same function for the participatory paradigm as does 'modernity' for the dominant paradigm. They form an absolute standard against which the value of other ways of thinking and feeling can be measured and judged. Those expressions of local community sentiment that fit into the universal standard are valuable as the levers of development. The paradigm is silent on the fate of those sentiments that contradict the universal standards, but this silence solves nothing. After all, unless one has a standard for making such judgements, how is one to answer Rao's elegantly-phrased question: 'The idea of development communication ... is to bring about a *change* for the *better* ... but this is difficult because who knows what is better?' (Rao, 1997: 2).

Who initiates change?

It might be tempting to dismiss these abstract questions as being of purely theoretical interest. After all, a similar temptation has certainly overcome the contemporary adherents of the dominant paradigm. Never mind the theoretical contradictions, they effectively say, our concern is with what works in practice: anything that helps in, for example, the struggle against the spread of HIV, is worth doing however shaky its theoretical foundations. Similarly, proponents of the participatory paradigm can argue that while there might be an epistemological ambiguity at the root of their views, it does not stop them using the paradigm to better people's lives. The problem, as we have seen, is that these theoretical matters strongly influence what happens in practical activity. The adherents of the participatory paradigm who wish to concentrate on the pressing matters in hand and leave abstractions to the comfortable professors are no more insulated from the consequences of theory than are the followers of the dominant paradigm.

We can see this clearly if we consider the status of the 'change agent', which is the technical term for the individual who brings knowledge, or experience, or perhaps simply labour power, to the business of development. Except in very rare cases, this is an outsider to the particular situation and there is always likely to be a gap in knowledge, belief and understanding between the community and the agent (White and Nair, 1999: 49). In the case of foreign experts, even if they have the best of intentions, their everyday behaviour and language can set them apart from the local population, many of whose beliefs and attitudes they do not and cannot share (Tsatsoulis-Bonnekessen, 1995). Even 'local' experts, however, can also have a sense of their distance from the people they are working with. Despite sharing many things, for example linguistic resources, with their fellows, they are distanced as a necessary result of the very education and knowledge that makes them an expert in the first place (James, 1995). The resulting attitude is one that considers that: 'the rural population is always tradition bound, characterized by a high illiteracy rate and is highly suspicious of new ideas, in addition to being very deeply superstitious' (Moemeka, 1995: 336). The people who are going to provide the knowledge and expertise that can lead to development inhabit, at least in part, the world of the SKS. The people they will help develop inhabit the IKS.

This social and cultural distance is integral to the position of the change agent. It is not simply a matter of personal attitudes but of the project of development itself. In its most acute form, it is experienced by those altruistic individuals who move from the comforts of modernity to try to help in the difficult process of development. Their personal motives are beyond question admirable and their sacrifices often very considerable, but they must act within a history and a structure that assigns them a very specific social place. Karen White, a former aid worker in Africa, wrote a quite agonizing self-analysis that concludes: 'What they [development workers] need to recognize is how they create a dominant role over the people they seek to help based on their own experience' (White, K., 1999: 25).

But if an identity of knowledge, interest and experience between change agent and local population is effectively impossible, then there must always be a serious question mark over the extent to which a local community has autonomously arrived at a particular proposal for development. If the change agent is 'dominant', then they are more or less certain to dominate the choice of project and the methods used to conduct it.

The contradictions of communities

The necessary cultural distance between the change agents and the people they are trying to help is not merely an issue concerning feelings of discomfort or the mutual incomprehension between two parties, although for a project based upon communication these latter would be difficult enough. The change agent always faces a problem of choice. The change agent does not, and cannot in practice, come to a community and help it solve its agreed problems but is forced to intervene in it, to support one group, and its values and aspirations, against another. This is inevitable because the term 'community' does not designate a simple, homogenous grouping with common interests and intentions. On the contrary, 'the concept of the small community as a cohesive and integrated entity fighting for justice against powerful external forces is inspired by the romanticism of populist thought rather than a serious analysis of community life and its complex characteristics and dynamics' (Midgley, 1986: 35). Real life communities almost invariably contain conflicts, and sometimes these can be murderous (Lusi and Batundi, 2002).

The very process of arriving at the kind of participation that is required by the paradigm is one that mobilizes conflicts which otherwise might have been latent or invisible. Communication is a particularly sensitive matter in a situation of conflicting interests. The right to speak is always embedded in social relations and these generally give priority to one group and discourage another: 'Within the community, there are several reasons why people might be reluctant to participate. *Communities might be socially stratified, conservative, and may contain a range of conflicting and competing groups and interests*' (Cohen, 1996: 229). Obvious examples include differences based upon wealth, gender and age, those between employers and employees, and a legion of others based on relationships, religion, locality, ethnicity, and so on. Very often the problems that one group identify as serious and pressing, and the solutions they believe are appropriate and effective, are bitterly opposed by other groups who believe, rightly or wrongly, that they stand to lose from that particular form of development. In other words, arriving at a common and agreed set of objectives for development is not a simple matter of allowing everybody to have their say and then reaching a consensus but may well involve quite sharp conflict (Arnst, 1996: 113).

Without a conscious effort to overcome it, the weight of established social relations tends to ensure that the people who dominate the discussions, set the goals, act as mediators, and to determine generally the nature of the development activity will be the existing elites. Even when a conscious effort is made to reach out to the poor, it is often the privileged strata in the community who eventually come to dominate projects and emerge as the chief beneficiaries of the development process (Ngidang, 1994).

Advocates of the participatory paradigm quite rightly reject an outcome that simply perpetuates existing inequalities, and make an exemplary and conscious effort to reach the poorest and most oppressed sections of society. They seek to find ways of changing the balance of power in a community. They try to construct 'a dialogue between power holders and the powerless [that] it is both empowering and disempowering i.e. the dominance of power holders is reduced' (White and Nair, 1999: 37). In order to have any hope of being effective, the change agents regularly have to attempt to change the balance of power inside the 'community' they are trying to assist. They need to assist those who are normally excluded, and to reduce the influence of those who have always controlled what is said and done. Changing the balance of power, however, is necessarily a 'political activity' and therefore implies at least the possibility of conflict (Thomas, 1995b: 54).

Small scale power and large scale power

The potential for political conflict lies both within the community and in its relations to the macro-structures of social power. In practice, the two are often very closely linked in terms of personnel, interests and values. Any stress upon empowering those who do not have power runs the risk of challenging those who currently hold power and enjoy its fruits: 'according to many authors, genuine participation directly addresses power and its distribution in society' (Servaes, 1996b: 15). The attempt to shift the balance of power necessitates a political perspective and risks conflict (Chin, 2000: 33).

A clear example of how this works relates to gender relations, which are today widely recognized as one of the keys to any development project. The empowering of women can lead to a pained reaction on the part of men whose traditional position of domination is thereby challenged. One report of a project that involved women developing a successful dairy industry noted that as the women began to become more active and independent, and as they started to have a bigger say in how the community was run 'the shift from a passive (server) to an active role began to unbalance cultural and social roles' and led to friction between the women and the rest of the community: 'they have been accused of abandoning their husbands and children as well as being bad women in general' (Guevara, 1995: 270). One can imagine, although it is more difficult to find them documented in the development literature, that projects that addressed other central power relations within a community – for example between landlords and labourers – would be likely to lead to similar kinds of reaction. Certainly, the general history of developing countries is everywhere deeply marked by struggles, often horribly bloody struggles, between peasants and landlords over precisely the power relations within communities.

A similar problem of the relationship between the community and the wider power structures of society has also frequently been noted. The existing structures of power tend to marginalize the majority (Mody, 1991: 20). The structure of the state, and in particular the bureaucracy, is not concerned with the welfare of the subject population. They tend to be more concerned with preserving their own privileges and power. As a result, 'authentic governmental promotion of popular participation is quite unlikely' (Servaes, 1996b: 23–4).

The participatory paradigm thus faces an unavoidable dilemma. Either it accepts that what it wants to achieve is likely to involve a confrontation with those who hold power locally and nationally, or it seeks to strike some kind of compromise with them. Taking participation seriously has very radical consequences indeed. As one writer put it: 'All in all, it is difficult to imagine a participative society in which the means of production are owned by a few people who have the capital and who reserve the right to make important decisions themselves. The organisation of the economy is, then, the crucial difference between a non-participative society and a participative one' (Bordenave, 1995: 41). Following this line of thought leads very far beyond the simple question of how to improve this or that local situation and raises issues about the structure of power and wealth not only within a country but also between countries. It enters territory that has, historically, been populated not by the protagonists of development but by the opponents of capitalism. Articulating a Latin American experience, there are those who argue that it is only to the extent that the project manages to realize an aggressive grass roots organization against power-holders that it led even to the few examples of genuinely popular participatory communication and successful implementation of development initiatives that have improved the lot of the poor: 'there are even cases where mass, popular movements using alternative "people's media" have been a major influence in historic national political change' (White, R., 1995a: 110).

Not all of those who adhere to the idea of participatory communication have been prepared to follow this logic. They have preferred to agree with Hornik that 'communication technology projects, as with most development projects will rarely succeed without prior commitment to change in the sector by substantial political forces' (Hornik, 1988: 24). In this context, the political forces that are at stake are elements within the existing order, and 'technical' interpretations of development communication address 'political and economic constraints by lowering their sights and choosing targets achievable within these limits' (Hornik, 1989: 22). This apparently sane and rational strategy has much to recommend it, in that it accepts that it is not possible to change everything at once and that the resources needed for concrete projects are today held by the wealthy. To put it very crudely, in order to get the money needed for a project, it has to be cast in terms that the rich and powerful will not see as threatening. After all 'challenging entrenched groups in the design of an information program is a risky path' (Hornik, 1988: 161). In this approach it is recognized that while in origin the stress on popular participation, or 'power to the people', was threatening and 'connoted a revolution', it has been possible to generate new concepts of 'generative power' that do not generally lead to social conflicts (White, S., 1994: 22–3). Those that do still occur can be overcome by the exercise of 'transformational leadership' (Lozare, 1995).

This strategy rests upon a clear division of the world. On the one hand 'politicisation through the use of community media ... is appropriate in those countries where a high level of development has been achieved' (Berrigan, 1981: 43). In the west, where something approaching democracy and freedom of speech is well established, then it is entirely possible to pursue fully the project of popular empowerment and allow the voice of the poor and oppressed to be heard in the media. In the developing world, on the other hand, 'political action would lead to the overthrow of the governing elite without providing the means for changing conditions and the confrontations that follow would commonly lead to repression and regression where democratic rights are concerned' (Bessette, 1995: 119). For these writers, it is, apparently, precisely the lack of development that prevents the systematic deployment of the technologies of development communication that could actually address the problems faced by the population. In their place, experts should concentrate on the problems of 'reconciling the value dissonance' between the various parties to a development project (Nwafo Nwanko, 1995: 101).

This is recognizing difference with a vengeance: the proponents of this position are arguing that, because of existing hierarchies and distributions of power in the developing world, it is necessary to abandon the stress upon inclusivity and autonomy that legitimized the project in the first place. The difference between the west and the rest is as sharp in this version of the participatory paradigm as it ever was in the dominant paradigm.

True, the opposition is not between modernity and tradition, but between the advanced (and democratic) in which participation can be fully realized, and the backward (and dictatorial), where it is necessary to keep a tight rein on the means of communication lest they should be misused by the people to pursue ends outside of the limits set by the development communicators and their powerful allies. Because these latter are likely to respond to any proposals for substantial change with violence, it is necessary for the development communicator to make sure that none of the proposals that get aired challenge the powerful.

What is participation?

Very wide differences in strategy go under the label of 'participatory communication', and indeed even publish in the same volume under that title. This suggests that the concept of 'participation' is rather more complex, not to say contradictory, than it appears to be in some of the presentations of the participatory paradigm. Given the centrality of this category to the entire paradigm, it is quite surprising to discover how rarely it is analysed at all, let alone subject to a rigorous critique.

Once examined in detail, participation turns out to be a category capable of meaning very different things (Hewavitharana, 1995). At one extreme, the concept is invested with many of the characteristics of a revolutionary programme: 'the demand for a participatory structure of communication arises as part of the logic of a popular social movement, not from the logic in the mind of a planner, no matter how perfect this might be' (White, R., 1995b: 235). At the other extreme, one of the pioneers of participation in development communication, Orlando Fals Borda, told his interlocutor that while it had appeared to be a radical alternative to the kinds of development strategies propagated by institutions like the World Bank, in practice it had turned out that it was 'a lifesaver to institutions that need to justify themselves and their enormous budgets' (Gomez, 1999: 152). 'Participation' at this end of the spectrum is little more than a way of phrasing a strategy that is almost as determined by experts as was that of the dominant paradigm (Chin, 1996).

Peruzzo is one of the very few writers who has attempted to systematize the different senses of the term 'participation' and her analysis is extremely illuminating. Her categorization is presented in Figure 4.1. She argued that it is possible to distinguish between the general areas of non-participation, controlled participation and power-participation (Peruzzo, 1996: 169–73). Of these, non-participation is fairly self-evident, since it is only too familiar from the authoritarian structure of most social institutions, whether they are located in developed or underdeveloped countries. In this model, the director of an organization, let us say the vice-chancellor of a British university, decides what policies will be followed (perhaps in consultation

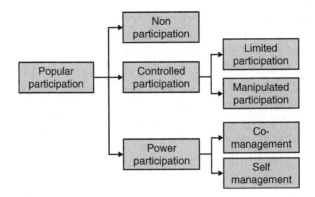

Figure 4.1   Peruzzo's typology of participation

with a few of their close cronies) and then imposes it upon the academic and technical staff and students. There is no room for discussion, for the collective formulation of aspirations or policies, or for anything other than simple obedience.

The category of controlled participation is more complex, and breaks down into two sub-categories: limited participation and manipulated participation. The first of these involves social structures in which those in dominant positions determine the overall goals of an organization but permit some discussion of elements of their proposals, for example the details of implementation. More generally, this is a model of social organization in which the fundamental parameters are set by the elite, who go on to determine the nature and scope of participation and the topics about which discussion and participatory decision making will be permitted. Again, organizations structured along these lines are familiar in both the developed and the underdeveloped world. In the second case of manipulated participation, the elite permits discussion, and possibly decision making, but retains for itself controls over the means of opinion formation and decision making in order to determine the outcomes that are suitable for their purposes. Such organizations are also familiar; one radical critique of capitalist democracy makes this its central argument, for example.

At the radical end of the spectrum lies what Peruzzo calls 'power participation'. By this, she means those forms of social organization in which there is some degree of popular control over their central direction. One variant she identifies is 'co-management', in which power over an organization or process is shared between different competing forces. One example might be a development project in which the funders and the representatives of local groups have established some forum whereby they mutually arrive at decisions about the shape of the project. Examples of these kinds of organization are much rarer than the earlier kind, wherever one looks. They are likely, in practice, to be unstable social forms since they seek to institutionalize different forces with different goals. Most of these forms of dual power are extremely short lived. The forces that are in play are not fixed and static but are constantly shifting in their relative strength. Sooner or later, and it is usually sooner, one or other will triumph. Even those relatively long enduring forms, like the control over the Vienna arsenal that lasted from 1918 to 1927, are eventually resolved with the victory of one force over the other (Duczynska, 1978: 56). The final form that Peruzzo identifies is 'self-management', where the participants in an organization or process collectively decide upon the aims, objectives and conduct of the matters in hand, and are in a position to reach informed decisions that they then have the power to execute. Such forms are extremely rare, whether in the developed or the developing world, and are more likely to be found in the area of voluntary associations rather than in productive or governmental spheres.

Clearly, it is to this latter form of self-management that the more radical proponents of the participatory paradigm adhere, but others are clearly satisfied with more limited variants. The explanation for the paradox that we observed earlier thus becomes clear. The wide theoretical appeal of the participatory paradigm is explained by the fact that its extremely attractive rhetoric actually conceals a variety of different meanings for the term 'participation'. Some ways of articulating the participatory paradigm bring it back very closely indeed to the dominant paradigm. Others represent a radical break with conceptions of modernity and development, but find it hard to establish any alternative vision to guide intervention. The stresses upon community and participation can lead to a variety of practices from the cynically manipulative and calculating through to the subversive and risky. In sharp contrast with the clarity of the old dominant paradigm, this paradigm is open to a multitude of interpretations. The dominant paradigm, by contrast, is difficult today to justify theoretically, but in practice it provides a 'tool-kit' that seems to be capable of generating solutions to urgent practical problems, many of which may well be theorized in terms of the participatory paradigm.

The extreme diversity of the theoretical substance present in the participatory paradigm makes it necessary to draw some very clear distinctions within it. We can identify two broad variants of the participatory paradigm. These both claim to base themselves upon the idea of the participation of the communities that will be developed, but have quite different interpretations of what they mean by this. As a consequence, they have quite different ambitions and strategies.

The negotiated variant

The first version of the paradigm is what we may term the 'negotiated variant'. In some of its formulation, this is very close to the continuity variant of the old dominant paradigm, but it usually accepts rather more of the argument for a diversity of kinds of knowledge and different possible measures of development. In contrast to the continuity variant, it recognizes both the centrality of structural constraints upon development projects and need for the population to be more involved in formulating the aims and methods of any development project. In this, of course, it simply reproduces some of the general problems we have seen are present in the overall participatory paradigm. It proposes, however, a clear resolution to these problems. What often terms itself 'communication for development', perhaps in recognition that it sets itself rather more modest goals than those of psychic transformation that underlay the classical paradigm of development communication, accepts the external constraints that issues of the distribution of social power place upon it. It argues that while these structural constraints may indeed lie at the root of the social problems it wishes to address, resolving them is extremely difficult to achieve. Nevertheless, it believes that it is possible to settle for rather less and still make a substantial change for the better: 'there are some approaches, however, that can be useful in narrowing the socio-economic hiatus in development through communication strategies, despite the absence of major structural changes at the macro level' (Melkote, 1991: 216–17).

In order to find the space to operate, the negotiated variant attempts to develop a series of strategies as to how those changes that a social system is able to accommodate may be facilitated. If it is forced to accept that the division between rich and poor, both materially and informationally, is the fundamental problem in a given country, it nevertheless attempts to find ways to use communicative techniques that can improve the lot of the poor. Such a programme necessarily focuses on smaller scale problems and solutions than did the dominant paradigm. Minor changes in practices in this or that area are more likely to be possible without any serious challenge to the existing social structure (Chin, 2000: 33). The piecemeal, unsystematic, and thus un-system-threatening, nature of such proposals would also be more likely to commend them to possible sources of support, for example local and national government or the international aid agencies.

One important consequence of attempting to negotiate a space for the kinds of small-scale development projects that are possible within a social structure whose power distribution is taken as beyond serious question is that there is a much stronger impulse to seek ways of involving people in communication through their own existing channels and media than in the more resolutely modernizing variants. The key communicative mechanism is no longer the 'big' mass media but the 'small' appropriate media (Melkote, 1991: 206–7). Following from this, there is a renewed interest in the social setting of media consumption and a rediscovery of the traditional means of communication. One important divergence of this approach from the classical formulations of the dominant paradigm is that it is prepared to

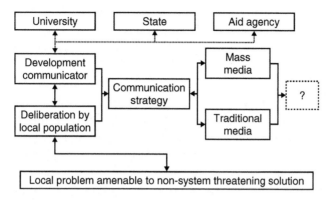

Figure 4.2   The negotiated variant

consider that traditional, non–modern, social structures and media might have a role at least as important as that of the modern mass media in the communication of change.

The basic structure of the negotiated, or communication for development variant, is outlined in Figure 4.2. As is apparent, this version of development communication differs somewhat from the dominant paradigm and its continuity variant. Although some of the players remain the same, their relationships are markedly different. In particular, the local population are no longer the pure passive objects of a process over the setting of whose goals they have no say whatsoever. On the contrary, in this variant they have an initiating role both in terms of their knowledge of the situation and the problems it contains and in the formulation of a communication strategy designed to overcome them. The official, 'modern' world of state, aid agency and expert are no longer accorded a superior status in defining the problems, identifying a solution, formulating communication strategies and managing change, although they remain outsiders intervening to promote change (Bessette, 2006). The mass media, those irreducibly modern elements in a society, are still present in the communication strategy, but they now have no privileged position over and against other, more traditional forms of communication. On the contrary, they co-exist with other forms of communication.

The problems with this model, however, are equally evident from the diagram. However much development communicators may now be required to share with the local population the task of identifying the problems and formulating their solutions, it is likely in practice that many of them will have some sort of relationship with another, outside agency, in this diagram represented as university, state and aid agency. Although modern and traditional are more evenly balanced in this model, it is the modern elements that have the predominant place, even if it is only in terms of deciding the boundaries of the 'resolvable problems' that are fundamental to this approach. What is more, it is not at all clear who amongst the local population defines the problems and their possible solutions. As we saw above, traditional communities can be as much the site of conflicting interests as are modern communities, and often those interests will come to different conclusions about the nature of the problems facing them and propose different solutions. Although there is no statement one way or another available, it is consistent with the logic of this model that it is the official representatives of the local community, whose activities are sanctioned by the state, who will define the problems and their possible solutions, since the adoption of any other strategy would be likely immediately to confront precisely those problems of power that this approach seeks to avoid.

In its overall structure, this variant represents an attempted depoliticization of the participatory model. Politics, however, are integral to any situation in which there is an unequal distribution of wealth and power. Remaining more or less silent on the relationships between the communication project and both the local and national structures of social power means, in effect, that it is the definitions of the real problems and of the kinds of desirable steps that can be taken to solve them that are favoured by the powerful and will be the ones that are accepted. The variant thus has deeply conservative implications, whatever the good intentions of its adherents. By refusing to confront what it honestly recognizes as the key determinants of any situation, it ensures that it will only ever be engaged with those kinds of change and development that are predicted to produce outcomes beneficial for the ruling order.

A very clear example of the way in which an attempted alliance between the existing structures of social power and popular participation ends up obscuring critical issues is the Mexican Instituto Nacional Indigenista (INI), which runs a chain of radio stations devoted to indigenous programming, and is much praised in the literature as an outstanding example of participatory communication (Dragon, 2001). As their main student remarks, 'the fundamental question about indigenous participation in the INI network is whether or not its sponsor, even occasionally, can act as catalytic agent and thus play a positive role in indigenous people's development efforts' (Vargas, 1995: 241). While she records that there is very much that is positive in the work of stations like Radio Margarita, which provide both an outlet for indigenous culture and a site in which some of its meanings can be interrogated and contested, there are very clear limits to what is permitted: 'the [non-indigenous] general manager and, to a lesser extent, the [non-indigenous] programme director, have the power to decide on the station's policies, goals, and the use of its resources' (Vargas, 1995: 245). This is a picture of an institution very close to Peruzzo's account of manipulated participation. It is therefore not surprising to learn that the station does not represent a forum for the discussion of political issues central to the life of the indigenous population. One has to recall that, shortly after this study was conducted, one part of the indigenous population of Mexico rose in armed revolt against the national government. In Radio Margarita, however, 'the staff has faced tremendous constraints in producing programmes that might be interpreted as 'political', especially local news' (Vargas, 1995: 242).

The radical variant

The second main variant of the participatory paradigm makes a much more radical break with the original assumptions. This 'radical variant' fully accepts that communities, even in developing countries, are marked by inequality. However, it takes these as a starting point for change and consciously seeks to find ways for groups that suffer severe developmental disadvantage, for example, women, poor peasants, agricultural labourers, and so on, to articulate their own views and interests. It wishes to find ways that such people can empower themselves, organize as a social force and achieve the kinds of developmental change that improve their conditions.

Here, the role of the 'development communication expert' is hardly recognizable compared with the previous accounts. It is to assist in the formulation of a programme of empowerment, to help articulate it in a form that can be readily disseminated and to provide expertise in the construction of media strategies. These can be designed to mobilise popular support for a particular project amongst the disadvantaged, or to influence public opinion in general in support of it, or both at once. Unlike the negotiated variant, this approach rests on no prior acceptance of the limits to desirable social change and no uncertainty about the nature of the local community it attempts to assist. On the contrary, it identifies the most disadvantaged within the population as the people most in need of assistance and most likely to benefit from change. In other words, it accepts that the task is not simply a technical one of communication but essentially a matter of politics. This model is illustrated in Figure 4.3.

For these reasons, the affiliation of the 'development communicators' is likely to be with a non-governmental organization rather than a state or official aid agency, and their tasks are likely to be defined much more in terms of the facilitation of social and political action rather than simply the design of messages. In this perspective, it is taken as likely that a particular general social problem will first be identified by a group that experiences it in a particularly acute manner, but it will be one that is either shared by the wider community of the underprivileged or at least resonates with their own experiences of deprivation. The intention is to design a political strategy, using whatever communication channels seem appropriate, first to make the wider community aware of the problem, and perhaps engage them in political action, and secondly to influence the mass media, and through them public opinion, to achieve change on the part of the state.

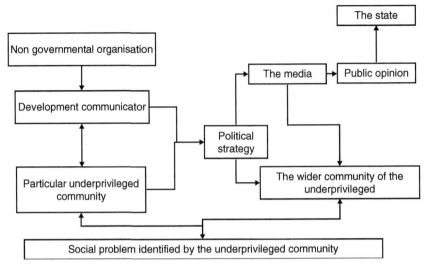

Figure 4.3   The radical variant

The distance between this model and the original dominant paradigm of development communication are obviously considerable. The radical variant, with its stress upon popular empowerment, addresses the critique of the dominant orthodoxy to a degree that is absent from both the continuity model and the negotiated variant. It begins with no predetermined view of modernity or development, but rather with the definition of social reality provided by the poor and dispossessed. It does not privilege the expert or the state and relegate the mass of the population to the role of the objects of history. On the contrary, it places popular action and activity at the centre of its programme. Mass communication is not abstracted from the real social relations in which it is embedded, nor prioritized over other forms of human communication, but on the contrary it is seen as only one form of human exchange, useful for some purposes but of limited value for others.

There is much in this version to attract the critical, or even radical, thinker. It does indeed address the central problems of 'underdevelopment' in ways that the former variants do not. It recognizes that the sources of poverty and its attendant woes are political and economic, and require action at the political and economic level to be rectified. It places the self-activity of the masses at the centre of its ideas about political mobilization. Unlike any of the other versions, it is concerned with the view from below, and it seeks to place no *a priori* limits on what may be thought, said or done, to improve social conditions.

On the other hand, however attractive it may be, the radical variant of political empowerment is not without problems. Naturally, setting itself these kinds of objectives, the relationship of direct dependency between the development communication experts and the state that marked earlier variants has now become, at the very least, rather strained. Neither at the local, the national nor the international level are ruling groups predisposed to give substantial support to people who state quite explicitly that their main aim is to discomfort those self-same ruling groups and remove from them some or all of their wealth and power. As Servaes put it: 'it is not in the interest of dominant classes, at national or international level, to implement policies and plans that would substantially improve the conditions of the lower classes or masses' (1996b: 39). Writers in this tradition therefore tend to look to other sources of support for their projects. In particular, non-governmental organizations (NGOs) are seen as an alternative source of funding and organizational capacity, although these also have their own political agendas.

The putative communicator needs not only to consider the political sensibilities of possible funding sources but also the character of the demands thrown up by popular voices. The radical variant is particularly challenged by the value relativity that we saw follow from the blanket rejection of modernity. If one starts, as this variant does, from agnosticism with regard to social values, then how is one to discriminate between demands and issues? To put the matter very bluntly: it is by no means clear that all popular expressions are valuable and desirable. The fact that people are poor and oppressed does not invest them with saintly qualities of political discrimination. This is certainly the case in developed western societies. One can immediately think of numerous examples in Europe and the USA where there have been expressions of popular racism. No doubt similar instances can be found in developing countries. If one is committed, as a matter of principle, to valuing and respecting 'popular voices', then what grounds would one have for not supporting these efforts at public communication? Taken seriously, the celebration of multiplicity can be used to justify anything at all, no matter how barbarous. In a less extreme sense, it is not at all clear that theories of development that are distinctly non-western, are by that token radical, or represent a challenge to the structures of oppression. Indeed, some of the examples cited as positive models of alternative structures seem, at crucial points, to have collaborated with the existing state powers rather than sided with the poor and the oppressed.

The radical variant also encounters problems with the relationship of local communities to the wider structures of power in a society. It is not simply that national structures of power do not generally fund and encourage radical local initiatives: quite often, they vigorously repress them. Unless one falls back on the discredited negotiated variant, and says that only those radical local initiatives will be considered that do not raise the possibility of state intervention, then one is forced to develop a strategy for meeting such eventualities.

The radical variant has no single answer to this conundrum. Some writers are silent and others effectively adopt the position of the negotiated variant, but one current within it does provide an answer that is extremely radical. Basing itself mainly on Latin American experiences, its analysis generally begins from the nature and experiences of social movements, rather than from development projects (Dervin and Huesca, 1995: 176). In the context of highly repressive and very corrupt regimes, any reliance on donor-based strategies necessarily extracted a very high price from participatory projects 'even in terms of the lives of not a few of their members' (Mato, 1999: 70). The alternative approach, in the words of one of its main theorists, recognizes that the '… democratization of communication is necessarily part of a broader process of redistribution of political power … The social mobilization necessary to attain this redistribution involves building alternative channels of communication, developing a different explanation of social reality, and adaptation of media'. (White, R., 1995b: 235). Very far from sharing with the negotiated variant worries about the dangers of alienating the powers that be, this variant claims that it is precisely to the degree that grass roots organizations display 'aggressiveness' that they have been able to achieve even local success. On some occasions, they have even 'been a major influence in national political change' (White, R., 1995a: 110).

The place of communication strategies is not, in this account, central to the overall conception of change. Rather, it is seen as part of a process of popular mobilization, and without that mobilization is likely to prove of 'only limited value as liberating medium' (Thomas, 1996: 218). This approach requires a rather different kind of 'change agent' from the traditional model of the social scientific communications graduate well-trained in quantitative methods in the best mid-Western universities: 'Successful popular theatre performances call for an organised build-up before the actual performance. Committed cadres prepare audiences beforehand; they organize cultural analysis sessions and provide perspectives on the larger struggle' (ibid.). At this point, however, as even the language attests, the radical variant has come much closer to explicit theories of social change in the socialist tradition.

Conclusions

In the last three chapters, we have traced the development of a set of ideas originally developed in order to aid the USA in the struggle against communism through to the very different situation of non-governmental organizations operating in the 1990s and early 2000s. Naturally, there have been major changes in almost all aspects during these forty or fifty years of history. As the result of our survey, a number of important points stand out.

The first of these is that, as Rogers argues, 'the dominant paradigm of development has not passed (as had been thought in 1975)' but on the contrary continues, in one form or another, to have a robust life both in theory and in practice (Rogers, 1989: 85). While this conclusion may not come as a surprise to those working professionally in this field, it certainly needs stressing from the point of view of more general reflections upon communication. Standard historical accounts more or less write off the influence of the original model after the 1970s (Sreberny, 1991). We have seen how this is quite wrong, and that in, for example, health communication, a more or less unmodified version of the original model is still robustly alive and influencing policy. That this is the case invites a more general comment that relates to one of the minor themes of this book. Simply because an idea or theory is no longer considered what we can only term 'fashionable' in universities does not mean that it is therefore incorrect, uninteresting, or uninfluential. The ideas of development communication certainly contained many errors, and perhaps they are no longer interesting to academics outside of specialized historical accounts, but they are certainly still influential in the world outside of the academy. That is a powerful reason for continuing to take them very seriously indeed.

Secondly, although the original model has proven surprisingly robust, the impact of both practical failures and academic critiques has meant that there have been several efforts at revision. These range from the minor modification of the introduction of a 'feedback loop' into the original model through to the complete re-thinking of the radical account. In this evolution, there are changes in the attitude towards state intervention and modernity. In the dominant paradigm and its successor, the state is seen as a major actor. It is one of the main repositories of an unquestionably desirable modernity. In the participatory paradigm, the state is at best neutral, and there is a much greater degree of scepticism towards the claims of modernity. Opposite to that, the role of the mass of the population, and the nature of their knowledge and beliefs, are re-evaluated in an increasingly positive sense. At the same time, the role of the experts, and the status of the knowledge they bring to bear on the problems under consideration, goes through a change. In the dominant paradigm, the expert is closely allied with the state and is a strong actor in communicating the values of modernity. Indeed, it could be suggested that in the classical model the expert is the prime actor, since it is modernity understood as scientific knowledge that is the central element in the process, and this can be argued to reside more fully with the scientist than with the politician or the bureaucrat. In the negotiated variant, the expert occupies an uneasy mediating role between the state and the community. In the radical variant, the expert is more closely identified with the population and, while still active, functions in a supportive rather than definitional role.

Thus, although the negotiated variant of the participatory paradigm is, in practice, quite close to the continuity variant of the dominant paradigm, they rest on different underlying assumptions. For the dominant paradigm, the state and the expert are the point of origin for developmental change. For the participatory paradigm, the community is the point of origin. In the case of the negotiated variant, the state is recognized as a factor limiting the extent to which the views of the community can be translated into developmental action. Its theoretical place, then, is within a different paradigm than that of the continuity variant, despite its practical similarities. It is with the radical variant that the implications of the shift are most clearly revealed. Here the state and the other agencies of social power are seen as benefiting from the social structures that maintain communities in a state of immiseration and, at least in the view of its most consistent adherents, the aim of communication is to assist in the transfer of power from its existing sites into the hands of the people so that they may improve their lot.

5

CULTURAL AND MEDIA IMPERIALISM

The dominant paradigm encountered two sorts of criticism. The first, which we examined in the last two chapters, were concerned with what we might term its 'internal' shortcomings. Critics examined the structure of the paradigm and identified this or that problem. They proposed changes, in the case of the participatory paradigm rather radical changes, that were designed to address the perceived shortcomings in its characterization of development and modernity and in its proposals as to how the media could be used in efforts to improve peoples' lives.

The other class of criticisms related to the omissions in the original intellectual framework and we may say that they were concerned with the 'external' shortcomings of the paradigm. In particular, the critics singled out the dominant paradigm's neglect of the structural factors that they identified as obstacles to the process of change. The dominant paradigm had begun from a belief that social change was the aggregate of individual change, and it had therefore been concerned with understanding individual beliefs and attitudes in order to find ways to alter individual behaviour. It tended to be blind to the macro-structures of economic and political power and, critics argued, so long as these were ignored, the real reasons for the misery of so many millions of people would be misidentified and the wrong remedies would be attempted.

The alternative was to confront these structural imbalances of power directly: 'If communication scholars are to exercise a healthy influence on society, it is indeed imperative that they pay more and more attention to research philosophies that can productively stimulate social change in a structural sense' (Dissanayake and Belton, 1983: 137). This search for structural constraints on development led on the one hand to concerns about the kinds of social relationships existing within a country that were very often quite close to those developed by the more radical proponents of the participatory paradigm, but they also led well beyond them into an analysis of the relationships between the developed world and the developing world. As one hostile account noted, 'No longer was development focused on Indian villagers or African farmers; now it had to do with global economic power and the purposes of the mass media' (Stevenson, 1993: 47).

The new approach involved a different analysis of the problems of development. This departed from the concerns of the dominant paradigm in focus, methods and idiom. In our terms, it represented a new paradigm, which we will term the 'imperialism paradigm'. At the same time, it was as much concerned to effect change as were the alternatives, and it advanced a political programme that proposed a set of practical steps that could be taken to alter the conditions that lead to continued underdevelopment for so many millions of the world's population.

Dependency theory and self-reliant development

The starting point for the new paradigm was that even though the colonial empires were rapidly passing into history, it was patently obvious that formal political independence did not end the relations of subordination and domination between developing and developed world. The mechanisms of control were now less overt than the colonial governor and his military garrison, but they seemed to be proving at least as effective in denying the population of developing countries access to decent standards of life. There evidently existed mechanisms that were less visible, but at least as powerful, as the direct coercion upon which the European colonial empires had been built.

The clearest general formulation of this view was to be found in the work of Andre Gunder Frank. He analysed the states of Latin America, which had been independent from the formal control of Spain and Portugal for many years but which were trapped in a cycle of poverty out of which they found it impossible to break. According to Frank, despite their political freedom, they remained subordinated to 'the metropolis' (i.e., primarily the USA) through the latter's control of economic life and consequent appropriation of the surplus that productive activity generated inside the country (1967: 5–9). Frank argued that the developed countries stood in an exploitative relationship to the less developed ones: surpluses that were generated in Latin America were diverted to North America. At the same time, the developed countries constantly interfered, both consciously and unconsciously, in the economic, political and social life of the developing world in ways that polarized the societies and set their citizens at odds with each other. The consequence was that the processes that led to the development of the advanced countries trapped the less advanced ones in a continuing cycle of poverty: 'One and the same historical process of the expansion and development of capitalism throughout the world has simultaneously generated – and continues to generate – both economic development and structural underdevelopment' (1972: 9).

The fundamental argument of writers like Frank was that 'the most important hindrances to development were not internal but external' (Servaes and Malikhao, 1994: 9). According to this theoretical position, there was a 'centre' consisting of the developed economies and a 'periphery' consisting of the underdeveloped world. The two were mutually interlinked: 'This view also implied that development in the centre determined and maintained underdevelopment in the periphery. In fact, the two poles were structurally connected to each other' (ibid.). The condition for the prosperity of the developed was the misery and exploitation of the underdeveloped world, and it was in the interests of the developed world to maintain its control over the international flow of capital, goods, and services in order to continue to reap extraordinary benefits that its population would not be able to generate by their own efforts.

The path to development for the people of the developing world lay through throwing off these multiple forms of domination and subordination and building their own economic lives independently: 'To remove such obstacles, it was argued, each peripheral country would have to dissociate itself from the world market and opt for a self-reliant development strategy' (ibid.). Frank himself specifically ruled out the export-oriented developmental strategy. Attempts to develop industries with an export potential, such as automobiles, diverted resources away from more urgent national tasks. They sustained the control of a narrow and corrupt elite in alliance with the businesses of the developed world. Such strategies 'result in underutilization of national resources, improper use of resources which might have been more adequately employed in promoting self-sustaining economic development, deepening inequalities in the distribution of national income, and the creation by these industries of vested economic, social and political interests which are committed to continuing policies of underdevelopment' (1972: 110–11).

One powerful model of the kinds of self-reliance was obviously that provided by the 'socialist countries'. While these were bitterly divided between themselves, even to the point of military conflicts, they were clearly united in their stress on 'self-reliant development'. Under the label of 'socialism in one country', they pursued autarchic paths of economic development, using state power to control foreign trade and plan national development. Given the subsequent outcome of the autarchic path, it is important to remember that during the period under review, they seemed to be in possession of a superior developmental model to that of the west. One major reason why they formed such a strong pole of attraction to nationalist elites in the developing world was because planning really did seem a vastly better method of economic development than did the market. Between 1953 and 1970, manufacturing volume in the oldest major capitalist economy, that of the UK, grew by roughly half; in the newer, and much more successful, USA, it almost doubled; in developing Japan, it grew by about three-and-a-half times. By contrast, in the USSR it grew by about five times. Taking a longer view, the record over the half century before 1970 was even more strikingly favourable to the communist path (Barratt Brown, 1974: 113).

The problem of the domination of the developing world by the power of the developed world and the possibility of an alternative pattern of social development were seen as closely linked, because these 'socialist' countries often found themselves in conflict with the developed capitalist countries. Writing about the problems facing the producers of culture in the contemporary world, Dallas Smythe argued: 'The first and historically unprecedented front is the emergence of socialism in, chronologically, the Soviet Union, Eastern Europe, China, North Korea, Cuba, and parts of Indo-China'. He immediately went on to link this economic challenge to the west with its increasing domination of the flows of culture and the possibility of reversing that process through the adoption of the 'socialist' model: 'The second [problem] is the accelerated penetration by the cultures of developed capitalist nations of the so-called less developed parts of the world ... in some less developed and presently non socialist nations there is the problem of making the cultural transition directly to socialism' (Smythe, 1981: 100). The failure of the dominant paradigm to offer a satisfactory alternative path to development meant that its historic opponent, Stalinist Marxism, found a new and wider audience both amongst the political elites of the developing world and amongst those who wrote about the flows of cultural products around the world.

Because this renewed emphasis upon national self-development under the control of the state machine was particularly attractive to the leaders of many newly independent nations its political consequences were increasingly argued between governments. It was in international forums like the United Nations that the push for a re-ordering of the economic and political relationships in the world, often called the 'New International Economic Order', found its clearest expressions. In the field of communication, there was a parallel development in the growing demands for a 'New International Information Order', which was predicated upon the collective strength of the developing countries and the socialist countries in UNESCO: '... the new international information order became an issue ... fundamentally because a sufficiently strong coalition of social forces had accumulated to enforce the new order – at least as a political programme, even if not as an immediate reality' (Nordenstreng, 1984: 5). The very success of the struggle against colonial empires meant that there were now many newly independent developing countries with votes in international organizations, and a programme that appealed to them could expect to win a sympathetic hearing in a forum like UNESCO.

The dominant paradigm had been closely linked to the political realities of the first years of the Cold War, and the imperialism paradigm was similarly linked to this new international situation. At the same time, the dominant paradigm rested upon a genuine intellectual foundation, which could not be reduced to the crude expression of political interests. The well-documented fact that various US government agencies funded much of the work in development communication does not disprove the results of that research. The same was true of the new paradigm. However much it was involved with political conflicts, the new paradigm also had a theoretical dimension, which we will explore in this chapter, before going on in the next chapter to consider how they were expressed in the political context of UNESCO.

Schiller and the foundation of the imperialism paradigm

Critics of the imperialism paradigm sometimes argue that it lacks clear definitions and precise meanings, and that things mean different things for different writers at different times. It should therefore be treated more as a 'discourse' than as a 'theory' (Tomlinson, 1991: 8–9). It is certainly true that there have been many different interpretations of imperialism, media imperialism and cultural imperialism, but we have seen that there have been many interpretations of the participatory paradigm, and we shall certainly encounter a wide range of ideas about globalization, often flatly contradictory. This diversity is certainly a problem, but it is not one unique to theories of imperialism. The danger with the strategy of constructing a 'discourse' is that there is a temptation not to stick closely to what the writers one is considering actually wrote. In this case, we can avoid that danger because, while we can accept that there have been many very loose uses of the terms at stake, it is possible to point to a relatively coherent body of theory, that developed by Herbert Schiller, which is unarguably central to the whole debate. There is a strong case for comparing Schiller's intellectual role in the development of the imperialist paradigm with that of Lerner's in developing the concepts of the modern personality, empathy and development. It is just as legitimate to take Schiller's theoretical formulations as definitive for the imperialist paradigm as it is to take Lerner's earlier work as definitive in respect of the dominant paradigm.

The starting point of Schiller's analysis of the mechanisms of domination in the field of the mass media was changes to the media industries in the developed world. He began to develop his scholarly reputation with a more general analysis of the links between the main centres of corporate power and the US military, and the theme of what was then known as the 'military-industrial complex' was one that was to remain with him in his better known studies of international communication (Schiller and Phillips, 1970). He extended his argument, in the best known of his books, to the claim that the US communications industries not only operated on a very large scale but were also integrated closely into the rest of the military-industrial complex. He traced the ways in which, from the very beginnings of broadcasting, there had been much greater governmental interference in regulation than the commonly read histories recorded. In particular, he identified the allocation of a sizeable portion of the spectrum to general governmental, and particularly military, usage, as a forgotten, or suppressed, dimension in that history. US foreign policy in the field of information had used the idea of the free flow of communication as part of the struggle to break the hold of the British and French colonial empires, and the news agencies that were based on them, over international information flows, to attack restrictions on the import of US films, and subsidies for local producers. When the US proposed that the slogan of the 'free flow of communication' be written into the founding charter of UNESCO, it had the additional advantage of being 'a highly effective ideological club against the Soviet Union' (Schiller, 1976: 30). From at least the start of the Korean War, he argued, military control over the allocation and usage of radio and television frequencies had been substantial. There was a close correspondence between the interests and needs of the military and of large-scale industry, which together were enough to determine the direction of US domestic and foreign policy. The then revolutionary developments in satellite communications were, he claimed, clear evidence of the ways in which this alliance of business and military were extending their control over international communication, and consolidating the power of the US as the dominant state. As he much later remarked: 'the satellite project had one unambiguous goal. It was intended, and succeeded, in capturing control of international communication circuits from British cable interests' (Schiller, 1996: 93).

This concentration upon the domestic realities of the US cultural industries was the main focus of Schiller's work on the mass media. Contrary to what is popularly supposed, he was not primarily concerned with the international effect of the US media, but with the ways in which they acted to destroy human potential inside the USA itself. The bulk of his most famous book, and particularly the extended discussion of the 'Democratic Reconstruction of Mass Communications' that closes it, is concerned with US conditions and US possibilities. It was primarily because of their strength in the home market that US culture industries were in the process of taking over the world. In Schiller's account, US control was expanding rapidly and rested on a close link between private enterprise and government, particularly in its military aspects: 'Each new electronic development widens the perimeter of American influence, and the indivisibility of military and commercial activity operates to promote even greater expansion' (Schiller, 1970: 80).

Schiller went on to list many of the government propaganda initiatives, military broadcasting facilities and foreign policy objectives, and the complex of international acquisitions, programme exports and advertising expenditure, that together constituted what he saw as 'the global American electronic invasion' (Schiller, 1970: 79–92). One of the major reasons for the very considerable impact of Schiller's book was that he attempted one of the first, and most thorough, 'inventories' of the international trade in television programmes and the spread of US ownership around the world.

The aim of Schiller's analysis was to show how the USA was developing what he saw as a genuinely imperialist control of the world. This new imperialism was different from the old colonial empires that were then in full retreat. Instead of direct colonial rule, the new US imperialism was much more indirect. Certainly, it rested upon military force, as the war in Vietnam made only too plain, but its mechanisms were also economic and ideological: 'what lends sophistication to the still-youthful American imperial structure is its dependence on a marriage of economics and electronics, which substitutes in part, although not entirely, for the earlier, "blood and iron" foundations of more primitive conquerors' (Schiller, 1970: 5).

Schiller was attempting to develop a much more subtle and complex account of the nature of contemporary US imperialist control of the world through the power of its mass media than was necessary for analysing the old colonial empires. In those earlier cases, commercial and technical factors were directly linked with military and political control. The decision to develop broadcasting was generally taken by the colonial administrators, who imported both the model of social organization and the technology directly from their home countries. They financed the broadcasters, appointed the staff, supervised the output and generally shaped the institution to fit the needs of imperial rule. When the colonial powers were forced out, control of broadcasting fell to the newly independent governments, and its future no longer depended directly upon decisions taken in the interests of London or Paris.

This formal independence, however, did not mean that broadcasting was now able to develop in the interests of the whole of the population of developing countries. There had been a 'transition from a state of formal total subordination, colonialism, to a condition of political independence and national sovereignty' (Schiller, 1970: 4). Both in former colonies and in those states that had always been independent, or had achieved independence long ago, like the countries of Latin America, there remained a range of mechanisms that acted together to subordinate the media to the demands of the imperial powers. Figure 5.1 outlines the nature of some of the possible control mechanisms. On the one hand, there were the familiar mechanisms of direct control. While political control was only strongly present in the case of actual colonies, the embassies of both the former colonizers and other powerful developed states, notably the USA, remained important players in the local political scene. In the case of former colonies and independent developing states, there was always the

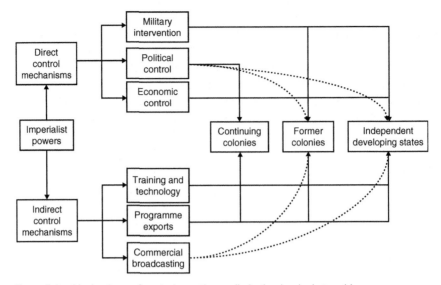

Figure 5.1   Mechanisms of control over the media in the developing world

possibility of direct military intervention if the threat to imperial interests was perceived as great enough. Although perhaps a remote possibility in a country such as India, there were plenty of examples of smaller countries, particularly in Latin America, where the local great power had always felt free to defend its interests through invasion and occupation. Such interventions, exemplary and educational though they might be to other countries, nevertheless remained the exception. Across the range of states, economic control, exercised through the ownership of shares in the press and private broadcasters, was a much more mundane and unexceptional way in which the local media could be subjected to foreign control.

The very existence of broadcasting outlets, particularly television stations, had a further major consequence: broadcasting requires programming. The standards of good programming were determined, in the first instance, by the views of the professionals who worked in the broadcasting organizations. They could acquire such programmes in two ways. The first, and obvious one, was to make them. Almost certainly, this is what the vast majority of them would have liked to do. The main obstacle to that was not technical expertise but finance. Most of the television stations in developing countries were simply too poor ever to dream of working on the range and quality of the programmes available in developed countries.

There was, however, a second possible way to get such programming. They could buy it on the international market, where the prices were much lower. One of the most striking pieces of evidence that Schiller introduced into the debate was that, in the late 1960s, the international price of a half-hour episode of US TV drama ranged from $4200 in the UK down to $22 in Kenya (Schiller, 1970: 88–9). Because the exporters could set prices so low, their products represented bargains for the purchasers. For around $40 an hour, they could buy a programme that had cost thousands, perhaps hundreds of thousands, of dollars to produce. They got high quality programming at a very low cost. The consequence, however was that the audience, too, came to base its standards of quality on those prevailing in the richest countries and came to have a ruthlessly critical attitude to the lower production values of local products.

Buying programmes on the international market, and primarily from the USA, thus had the short-term advantage that it allowed poor local broadcasters to transmit high quality material while remaining within their budgets. But it had the longer-term cost of making it extremely difficult for local producers to produce competitive material and thus effectively locked developing countries in to dependence upon a supply of programming from the developed world every bit as securely as would direct economic or political control of their broadcasting institutions.

In addition to these mechanisms, however, Schiller identified a further factor that he saw as, if anything, more important, even though it operated in an even more indirect manner than did training, technology and programme exports. This factor was 'the spread of the American system, the commercial model of communication, to the international arena' (Schiller, 1970: 93). In the USA, he argued, the interests of equipment manufacturers, broadcasters and advertisers had meant that the complex possibilities of the new medium for use in public debate, education and general social improvement had been marginalized in the construction of a wholly commercial communication network. This depended on the sale of advertising for its primary finances and thus subordinated public communication, more or less directly, to the needs of large corporations. In other countries, there had been different developments, and broadcasting was not always a purely commercial enterprise. Schiller argued that this model was now being exported internationally and that the success of this mission was essential to the future of capitalism: *'Nothing less than the viability of the American industrial economy itself is involved in the movement toward international commercialization of broadcasting'* (Schiller, 1970: 95). Without the internationalization of the commercial model of broadcasting, there would be no outlets for advertising material. Without advertising material, there would be no markets for US cars, soft drinks, soap powder, and other commodities. Without markets for their products, US industries would experience a crisis of overproduction and the consequent depression and unemployment. Without material expansion and rising living standards, US capitalism would re-enter the nightmare of the 1930s. Mass communication had thus become central to the survival of capitalism and the survival of American capitalism depended on the spread of the model of commercial communication around the world.

This economic theory of the importance of advertising to the survival of capitalism has been remarkably influential on many writers on critical media analysis other than Schiller and it merits some further explanation. In most accounts, it rests on a version of Marxist economics that is technically termed 'under-consumptionism'. Its status is hotly debated within Marxism itself, since it can be taken to imply that capitalism can avert crisis through stimulating demand, either through advertising or Keynsian measures of state expenditure. It was most rigorously developed in the US by Paul Sweezy, who elaborated it extensively in his work on theoretical economics (Sweezy, 1942). Its great currency in leftist circles during the period under review was due to the more concrete account of the workings of the world economy he co-authored in the 1960s with Paul Baran. In their view, it was endemic to contemporary, monopoly capitalism, that it produced more goods than could be profitably exchanged, and therefore faced the constant threat of another recession. What was needed was something that could stimulate consumption. Along with military expenditure and luxury consumption on the part of the capitalist class, they identified advertising, and thus the media, as crucial to the continued expansion of capitalism: '... the economic importance of advertising lies not primarily in its causing a reallocation of consumer expenditures among different commodities but in its effect on the magnitude of aggregate effective demand and thus on the level of income and employment' (Baran and Sweezy, 1966: 124). Schiller shared this framework with another major theorist of media imperialism, Dallas Smythe, who wrote that 'In order to manage demand, monopoly capitalism "invented" the mass media of communication' (1981: xiv).

Schiller argued that the problems of cultural production and consumption could not be seen solely in terms of the development needs of the poorer countries. The same system that prevented the utilization of the potential of communication technology for development in the Third World was also operative inside the USA and had disastrous effects: 'The fetters that bind American talent and limit its national engagement are essentially the same as those which are hobbling the social utilization of global communications' (Schiller, 1970: 163). To be sure, material conditions in the USA were far superior to those in developing countries, but there too what Schiller called 'the forces of enlightenment' faced a struggle against the power of capital to win an audience for policies that could avert 'social catastrophe' (Schiller, 1970: 157–8). With the outstanding exception of the recent work by Richard Maxwell, commentators on Schiller's ideas, both sympathetic and critical, tend to ignore this central reality of his work (Maxwell, 2003). They often neglect the fact that in his most famous book, as well as in most of his later works, the main emphasis of his analysis was upon the realities of corporate capitalism inside the USA, and their effects upon the life of the American media and American people, rather upon the imperialist depredations it was wreaking abroad (for example, Schiller, 1973, 1989, 1995, 1996, 1998, and many others).

Inside the USA, Schiller sought to find social movements that could be won to a struggle against the commercialization of public speech. For Schiller, there was no such thing as a unique US culture. There was a culture produced by the major mass media, but there were other sources of creativity in the oppositional movements, particularly the black movement, that embodied different cultural values, and he saw it as important to help and encourage such movements to contest the dominant commercial model. The failure to challenge commercial culture inside the USA meant that the outside world saw only a single 'American' culture. The international role of the US cultural industries was a result of their complete subordination to capital inside the USA itself. The US was the country that had: '... gone furthest along the road to corporate control' (Schiller, 1989: 5). This 'emergent imperial society' was exporting its own model of culture and promoting the control of international communication by US capitalists (Schiller, 1970: 147).

Internationally, and particularly in the developing world, he argued that it was essential to develop national communication policies that could lead to a disengagement with a world television environment dominated by the USA (Schiller, 1975). Despite his advocacy of such policies, however, he remained as critical of the internal structure of developing countries as he was about the USA itself. Just as he saw the US as a society in which there were different pressures and different cultures, and just as he saw US national communication policy reflecting the interests of the dominant class in the USA, so he saw the danger that the national communication policies he urged developing countries to adopt would simply reflect the interests of ruling groups in those societies, and do as little for the cultural and material well-being of the mass of the population as corporate control of US culture did for the population of America. Since both those who worked with Schiller's ideas and his bitter critics have tended to ignore this dimension of his work, it is worth quoting exactly what he said at some length:

In most of these [non-socialist developing] countries, the opposition to external dom-ination is ambiguous at best. For the ruling, propertied stratum, the anti-imperialist rhetoric that often characterizes the utterances of leaders of these states has at least two objectives. In the first instance, it may provide the local ruling class, or a segment of it, better bargains in the ongoing deals and disputes with the transnational corporations and the governments that represent the TNCs. Second, it offers the domestic population a (distant) target for its anger – partly, but only partly, obscuring the role of the local privileged class ... In practice, national information policy in most developing countries is really property class policy with a national flavor and rhetoric. (Schiller, 1982: 269–70)

In theory, at least, Schiller was just as clear that there was no such thing as a single homogenous national culture or policy that expressed the will of the entire population in developing countries as he was in the case of the USA.

This point is worth emphasising, given some of the later criticisms directed against the imperialism paradigm. It was not Schiller alone who identified this problem of national elites using the rhetoric of independence to justify their own interests. On the contrary, the theoretical recognition of the limitations of the governments of developing countries is a recurrent theme in analyses within the imperialism paradigm. For example, a very similar point was made by Beltrán, commenting in retrospect on the analyses of the sixties and seventies that explored the failure of development: 'The conclusion of those critics – scholars, politicians, media practitioners – was that the oligarchic elite subduing and exploiting the mass had also become dominant in the sphere of communication and culture, thus enhancing their power to favour the status quo' (1988: 2). Jan Servaes expressed very similar views nearly two decades later: 'While the modernization paradigm legitimates the interests of Western political and economic interests groups and their "bridgeheads" in the Third World, the dependency theory meets the economic and political needs of those Third World elites who want to play an autonomous role' (Servaes, 1996a: 39). The problem, as we shall see, is that this clarity about the class structure of developing countries, and the motivations of national elites that was present in theoretical writings, was often not so clearly articulated in political practice.

The effects of structural domination

The overall picture that Schiller, and the many other writers who worked to develop the paradigm, drew was one in which the technology of international communication was increasingly dominated by the USA, the trade in programmes was dominated by the USA, ownership of media outlets was increasingly dominated by the USA, and the commercial model of broadcasting was spreading from its original home in the USA. One central consideration was the effects of all this upon the population of the subordinated countries. The first consequence of commercialization was that the developmental potential of the media was being destroyed. While he was clearly among the critics of the dominant paradigm, Schiller did not reject the idea of the use of the mass media as a mechanism to aid development. In a striking passage, he wrote: 'The informational apparatus now available for national use is much more than glamorous instrumentation; if sufficiently and intelligently applied it is an engine for great forward drives in the developmental process' (Schiller, 1970: 109).

For Schiller, at least, the quarrel with the dominant paradigm was not that it was a flawed attempt to impose modernity upon societies for whom it was completely inappropriate. On the contrary, he agreed wholeheartedly with Schramm that there was an urgent need to use the mass media to assist in transforming developing countries for the better. The problem for him was that the desirable educational and developmental messages were confined to the margins of the media, whose central core was dominated by a flood of foreign entertainment material that bore no direct relation to the immediate problems facing the mass of the population, and which he believed was promoting the wrong kind of modernity and the wrong kind of development.

It was in this way that the subordination of the media of developing countries to those of the USA had its most serious effects. By ensuring the domination of the commercial model of communication, the inequalities of wealth and power that were structural features of imperialism were reinforced through the effortless daily consumption of media products. Schiller held the view that the content of the media was the crucial issue, but he noted that the main mass media were not at all concerned with development content in the majority of their output. The problems of development communication were insoluble so long as the central means of communication remained subordinated to commercial goals: 'The world's desperate communication needs, first for literacy and education, but also for meaningful information, are deeply dependent on and influenced by the communications structure and system that operate in the United States'(Schiller, 1970: 162).

This educational deficit was reinforced by the fact that the prime audiences for the products of western commercial culture, notably television, were at that time the elites of developing countries. They possessed the wealth to be amongst the first individual purchasers of television sets, and they were more likely to have the linguistic skills, not to mention literacy levels, that permitted them access to the print media. To them, the imperialist media made a seductive proposal, which is outlined in Figure 5.2. The media offered a set of psychological resources that were

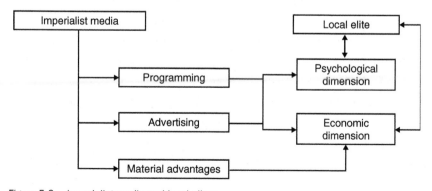

Figure 5.2   Imperialist media and local elites

embedded in both the advertising and programming that they presented. These both originated in the developed world and, naturally enough, their version of psychological normality was characteristic of that world. The elites of the developing world were invited to consider these representations of the physical and psychic features of the developed world in contrast to the realities of their own countries. To the extent that they found these representations attractive, they became distanced from the world and the people around them. Some of them might actually leave for the developed world. Their energy and skills, and the investment in their education, would forever be lost to the struggle for overall development. Others would try to use their wealth and privilege to import the commodities of the developed world and recreate as much of the landscape glimpsed on television in the midst of a radically different social setting. Western clothes, air conditioning, Mercedes Benzes, and swimming pools became the badges of a detachment from the common lot of the surrounding population. That population, far from being partners in the effort of national development, became the despised traditionalists whose only useful function, if they failed to make the transition to modern life, was as servants or sources of tax revenue.

Alongside these psychological effects, the imperialist media also had economic effects. At one level, they offered employment to an influential layer of the population – journalists, producers, copywriters, market researchers and so on – who also formed part of the elite. More substantially, the mass media acted to promote and circulate the idea of a world built upon the purchase and consumption of commodities, rather than on an older 'natural economy'. They therefore acted as intensifiers of the pressures towards capitalist modernization. As Figure 5.3 illustrates, the process was conceived of as a one-way, top-down process of transformation very similar in structure

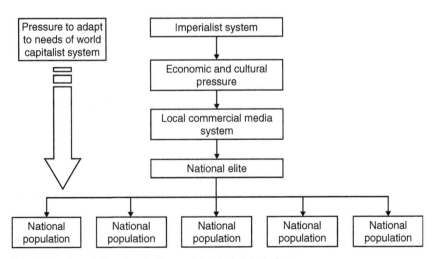

Figure 5.3   Imperialism, local elites and developing societies

to that proposed by the original dominant paradigm. Any developing country was under siege from a variety of forces, economic, military, political and ideological, that sought to bend the whole of that society to the needs of imperialism. One of the main entry points of these pressures was through the influence of the media upon local elites. The structures and content of these media played a central role in persuading the elite to use their influence, whether persuasive or coercive, to transform the societies over which they ruled into a form suitable for capitalist exploitation.

To the end of integration into the world capitalist system, local industries and agriculture had to be transformed. Old beliefs and value systems had to be discarded. In the place of handicraft and subsistence agriculture would come capitalist agriculture and its attendant support services. In the place of communal values and traditional beliefs the dominant ideas of developing societies would come to be possessive individualism and a desire to purchase and consume commodities. Schiller's objection to the dominant paradigm was not that it preached modernity, but that it was the wrong kind of modernity and that its remedies were marginal to the main activities of the media in developing countries. Schiller applauded the aim of the development communicators to improve the technical level of production in agriculture, to increase the level of awareness about basic reproductive and health matters, and generally to provide the element of a modern outlook on the world. What he argued, however, was that these were effectively only marginal to the overwhelming drive of the main mass media to transform the whole of society in the direction of capitalist modernity, which offered luxury to the elite while providing nothing for the masses.

Media imperialism and cultural imperialism

Schiller's original thesis had been primarily about relatively narrow issues, and he did not use the terms 'media imperialism' or 'cultural imperialism' in his path-breaking book. It would perhaps be most accurate to term the theoretical position elaborated there the 'structural subordination paradigm', but it was extended in a number of important directions by Schiller himself, as well as by the other researchers working in the same area, and the more developed position can certainly be termed the 'imperialism paradigm'. Schiller himself, along with other writers in the same tradition, later used both the categories of 'media imperialism' and 'cultural imperialism', although they did not always distinguish very clearly between them, and it was these terms rather than the more careful analysis of the original thesis, that came to shape the common understanding of this position. In fact, as we have seen, the central argument of this school of thought was that the structural domination of the media systems, which might be considered media imperialism proper, was central to the introduction of 'alien' patterns of thought, behaviour and culture, which might be considered cultural imperialism proper.

The main difference between the concepts of cultural imperialism and media imperialism lies in the fact that the former term is much broader in its scope than is the latter. Media imperialism was narrowly concerned with the structures and content of the media themselves. Boyd-Barrett, in a classic article, defined media imperialism as 'the process whereby the ownership, structure, distribution or content of the media in any one country are singly or together subject to substantial external pressures from the media interests of any other country or countries without proportionate reciprocation of influence by the country so affected' (Boyd-Barrett, 1977: 117). Both the agent and the object, in this definition, are identifiable 'media' and 'media interests', and no wider claim is made about any supposed effects upon the culture as a whole.

Cultural imperialism, on the other hand, involved very much more than simply the media alone and 'includes the results of international media, educational and cultural systems' (Golding, 1977: 291–2). While it is, to a substantial extent, dependent upon the media, cultural imperialism cannot be reduced to the actions of the mass media. The range of cultural practices that would undoubtedly have to be included in any account of cultural imperialism is very wide indeed. Obvious examples that come to mind are: aspects of sport, and notably the introduction and development of cricket in the Indian sub-continent and part of the Caribbean; food (notably the spread of US fast food chains internationally); religion (notably the spread of Christianity in Africa); and clothing (notably the spread of the business suit and the tie throughout the world).

From the point of view of the analysis in this volume, the problem with such an inclusive category is that it involves institutions whose history and practices are radically different from those of the mass media, and are therefore very difficult to deal with under the same heading. Natural language provides an excellent illustration. This is undoubtedly an important, many would say the most important, element in culture, and it is clearly central to the mass media, but obviously it has a much wider and more complex life than simply its presence there. It rests upon powerful institutions, both historical and contemporary, which are quite distinct from the mass media. In many former colonies, the official language remains that imposed by the erstwhile imperialist power, and serves as the main language of education, government, business and often also the mass media. It has been argued that this dominance has been at the expense of the development of the linguistic resources of indigenous languages and thus constitutes a form of linguistic imperialism (Skutnabb-Kangas and Phillipson, 1997: 51). A similar case has been argued concerning the rise of English as the dominant world language, even in countries that have never been colonized by the UK or the USA: 'A working definition of English linguistic imperialism is that the dominance of English is asserted and maintained by the establishment and continuous reconstitution of structural and cultural inequalities between English and other languages' (Phillipson, 1992: 47).

This linguistic imperialism might in part be borne by the mass media, but is also powerfully inscribed in quite distinct institutions such as the British Council, one of whose main functions is propaganda for the teaching of, and testing in, English language proficiency as a passport to international success. Another institution that leaps to mind is the circuit of international social science. This unquestionably reproduces the dominance of the languages of the old imperialist countries; the language in which the vast majority of the proceedings of the International Association for Media and Communication Research, for example, are conducted is English, and the official alternates are French and Spanish. Studying the mass media, however, is notoriously distant from the practices and institutions of the media, and the one cannot be reduced to the other.

Schiller himself came to prefer the broader category, writing that *the concept of cultural imperialism today best describes the sum of the processes by which a society is brought into the modern world system and how its dominating stratum is attracted, pressured, forced, and sometimes bribed into shaping social institutions to correspond to, or even promote, the values and structures of the dominating centre of the system'* (Schiller, 1976: 9). According to one hostile writer, this was because it gave 'neo-Marxists' like him a purchase on 'the totality of dependence and dominance relations' (Lee, 1980: 41).

However that may be, it is clear that this broader meaning was, at least, implicit in Schiller's earlier formulations, and it is difficult to see how one could theorize media imperialism without at least some concept of a wider cultural imperialism. It is certainly the case that the narrower definitions of media imperialism, like that advanced by Boyd-Barrett above, are much more susceptible to serious investigation than are broader concerns, but in concentrating upon the media it is important to recognize that the issues at stake need to be understood within that broader context. Media imperialism can be used as an exemplification of broader issues, and in doing so, nothing substantial will be lost from the case that was put forward by Schiller and his co-thinkers. Whatever substance there is to the term media imperialism is as a specific set of processes that would constitute part of a more general category, including other specific sets of processes, that might be termed cultural imperialism.

The mechanics of media imperialism

Schiller's work on the US domination of global communication immediately found an echo in a flood of books and articles from all points of the spectrum, politically and geographically (for example, Tunstall, 1977; Mattelart, 1979;

Smith, 1980; Guback and Varis, 1982). Even writers hostile to Schiller's theoretical and political orientations added greater or lesser amounts of empirical detail to an account that was already established and whose main contours were fairly well understood.

Boyd-Barrett divided these findings into the 'four modes of media imperialism', which form a convenient framework for organizing the mass of material. The first of these was the phenomenon of mass communication itself, as a technology of one way communication that has been developed and elaborated in the developed world. The second was the organization of this technology into particular kinds of state organizations (as in Europe with the BBC or the then ORTF) or along commercial lines pioneered in the USA. These institutional facts were supplemented by a third element, that of professional norms of media production, which again were first developed in advanced western countries and exported in their fully finished form to quite different environments. Finally, the actual content of programming, the nature of media narratives or the very concept of news itself were first modelled in the west, and either exported in finished form to the developing world or imitated so far as was practical by practitioners trained in the west (Boyd-Barrett, 1977: 119–29). These four factors were embedded in concrete mechanisms that together shaped the dependent nature of media systems. They acted to influence, if not determine, both the technical and personal characters of broadcasting in developing countries and the kinds of programmes they broadcast.

The equipment needed to both broadcast and receive radio and television programmes, or for that matter the presses needed to print a newspaper or magazine, were indeed designed and built in the developed world, and were adapted to the social and market conditions prevailing there. The same was true of the institutions that used these technologies to produce programmes. They had been implanted into developing countries with very little sensitivity to local needs. For example, the introduction of radio into those parts of Africa colonized by the British and French had been the direct result of the political decisions of the imperial powers, and had been very strongly influenced by their military needs in the struggle against Germany and Italy during the Second World War (Mattelart, 1980: 233–4). In the Caribbean, a similar colonial pattern was evident (Brown, 1997: 162–3). One of the common legacies of the departing rulers was a media structure heavily influenced by the models in their imperial homelands. This was most obvious in the case of broadcasting, but it was also true for the press in some important cases: the dominant section of the press in India, at least until very recently, was written in English, and many of the titles (*Times of India*, *Indian Express*) echo the newspapers of the UK. In the case of Latin America, where the colonial power had been defeated long before the development of broadcasting, the influence was rather more indirect, but here financial power ensured that the US 'succeeded in conveying an image and model of commercial broadcasting as the norm, an ultimate standard against which all other models were judged' (Fox, 1997: 27).

The issue was not solely one of technology and institutions but also of content: 'When we speak of transfer we are referring not to the transfer of technology alone but also the transfer of socio-cultural institutions with economic and political implications, institutions ready-packaged with organizational and program formats and even contents' (Katz and Wedell, 1978: v). The technologies themselves, the media institutions, and the programme structures that went with them, had evolved to satisfy parts of the cultural lives of rich, developed countries. There was no reason to believe that the cultural needs of developing countries would be identical. The accepted standards of production, not to mention the sheer quantity of production, imposed intolerable burdens on poor societies (Katz, 1973). The institutional arrangements for a broadcasting station might be ones that were entirely appropriate for relative political independence of the BBC in London, but the different political cultures prevailing in developing countries meant that in too many cases permanent government interference was more or less guaranteed. Alternatively, it might have a commercial model dependent upon advertising that was appropriate for the disposable incomes and consumption patterns of Middle America but which more or less guaranteed difficulty and discontent in a developing country.

Technological developments, particularly the emergence of broadcasting satellites, were threatening to exacerbate this subordination. Despite their potential for cultural and educational uses, satellites threatened to 'attack' the media systems of independent countries with a flood of entertainment programming (Schramm, 1968: 16). These developments posed a threat to the established UNESCO policy of encouraging the free flow of information around the world (Anon., 1970a). It seemed more and more to be in reality a 'one way flow' (Anon., 1970b: 27). Direct broadcasting satellites could be owned and run from outside the country that received their signal, and therefore they threatened to undermine the state's control of broadcasting and communication (Le Sueur Stewart, 1991). This was a real cause for concern amongst independent states, who shared 'the widespread conviction that the form and content of the television system in a country is an aspect of national sovereignty' (Mowlana, 1985: 41).

The problem was exacerbated by the fact that the telecommunications industries, and particularly their most technologically advanced sections, were not only open to foreign capitalist penetration at all levels but their infrastructures were designed to favour disproportionately the interests of large companies, both domestic and foreign, and the needs of the ruling elite (Sussman, 1981: 20–1; Hamelink, 1984: 80). The optimistic view that telecommunications would accelerate development was little more than a slightly revised version of the old dominant paradigm (Sussman and Lent, 1991: 16–17). Even those states that adopted the most sophisticated technologies, and who took steps to ensure that they were as far under their own control as possible, faced the fact that 'the end result will be reinforcement of the internal and external dependency status' (Mody and Borrego, 1991: 164).

The people who worked in media systems of developing countries were likely to have been educated along European or American lines. They received their professional training either in an advanced country or at the hands of experts flown in from there (Golding, 1977). Whatever their subjective intentions and their private commitments, it was argued, the professional personae of media workers in developing countries acted to make them effectively as alien in their own countries as their colonialist predecessors had been. Technology and training were instruments of continuing subordination to the developed world since 'the influence on standards and norms of training, professionalism, modes of organization and production ... draw the media away from the cultural base of a relatively poor country, identify various occupations with their metropolitan counterparts and ultimately influence the local forms of production' (Cruise O'Brien, 1976: 6).

The content of the media in developing countries was similarly heavily marked by dependence upon the developed world. Investigations of the origins of the television output carried by broadcasting stations in the developing world bore out the basic point made by Schiller. The most significant development on the original position was that the later studies, contrary to what is often claimed, displayed a more nuanced view of the relationship between the TV companies of the developed world and those in developing countries. Tapio Varis, an author prominent in developing studies of international flows, wrote that 'foreign stations have usually adjusted themselves to the local culture' (Varis, 1975: 30).

When, a decade later, the same author repeated the study, he concluded that 'When studying the international flow of television programmes and news in 1972–73, we concluded that there were two indisputable trends: (1) a one way traffic from the big exporting countries to the rest of the world, and (2) a predominance of entertainment materials in the flow ... The 1983 study confirms that no major changes in the international flow of television programmes and news have taken place since 1973' although, again contrary to many later criticisms, he went on to note the increase in regional programme exchanges (Varis, 1985: 53). A very large, if methodologically somewhat controversial, study of Western Europe came to similar conclusions, although a more general survey by the same authors suggested that the USA was joined by other advanced countries in the export of programmes (Chapman et al., 1986: 70–80; Gould et al., 1984). Looking at the source of programme exports, Nordenstreng and Varis concluded that 'in international television programme production the United States has led markets in the mid-sixties by exporting more than twice as many programmes as all other countries combined', although they noted that this dominance appeared to be declining and, again contrary to later criticisms, pointed to Mexico as an emerging programme exporter (Nordenstreng and Varis, 1974: 39–40).

Within these general findings about the flow of programmes, particular attention was paid to the international circulation of news, which was taken as a clear example of the ways in which the media of the developed world determined the content of what was available in the developing world. Because of the costs of producing original international news (indeed, any news), discussions of the nature and origins of this material tended to focus on the big news agencies. Studies of news flows predated any concern with media imperialism; Schramm himself had conducted a major study in the field. One early writer reached the conclusion that the news supplied by the major agencies gave a distorted picture of the world and argued for the need to sustain alternative information exchanges to attempt to redress the balance (Robinson, 1969/1981 and 1974/1981). From a different ideological perspective, Hachten concluded from an analysis of news flows that the existing pattern of news flows was 'essentially a legacy of colonialism' (Hachten, 1971: 51).

The studies fitted directly into the evolving imperialism paradigm, which concentrated on the then dominant providers of international news. Studies identified four large western agencies, Associated Press (AP), United Press International (UPI), Reuters, Agence France Press (AFP), and one large Soviet agency (TASS), which between them effectively controlled the international flows of news (Boyd-Barrett, 1980: 15–19). In the definitive study of the 'Big Four' international news agencies, Oliver Boyd-Barrett showed that they were, in fact, dominated by primarily national logics. This was true in two ways. In the first place, all of the agencies had some relationship with the governments of the country in which their headquarters were situated. The closeness of these links ranged from the open and obvious, in the case of TASS, through official subsidies (AFP) and secret subsidy (Reuters), to the occasional tendency of US agencies to withhold stories for a time, since 'When the President of the United States calls you in and says this is a matter of vital security, you accept the injunction' (AP's General Manager cited in Boyd-Barrett, 1980: 149). The second, and perhaps more generally important, way in which the agencies operated according to a national logic was that AFP, UPI and AP all operated as national news agencies and found their largest single markets for general news in their home markets. Although Reuters did not operate as a national news agency, and had proportionately more international clients than its competitors, the UK was still its largest single market.

As well as being tied to a small number of developed states, all of the Big Four agencies found the bulk of their clients and their revenues in the rest of the developed world. The structure of their reporting efforts reflected the interests of these clients; the agencies produced more news about more subjects from the developed world than from elsewhere. Their international strengths, particularly in the developing world, also reflected the national interests of their home countries. This factor had been particularly strong in the nineteenth century, when 'the early pattern of agency expansion reflected a mixture of the imperial, political, investment and trade interests of their respective home countries' (Boyd-Barrett 1980: 155). While that close relationship had become weaker with the collapse of the colonial empires and the rise to global dominance of the USA, it nevertheless remained the case that this heritage strongly influenced the location of bureaux and the flows of information.

The consequence of these factors was that the news available to developing countries was subject to a number of pressures. First, they were much more likely to receive news about developed countries than about their neighbours or other countries in a similar situation. Secondly, the news about other developing countries was filtered through the priorities of news agencies of the developed countries. Very often, news from a neighbouring country was gathered by a local agency report, sent back to the home office in the developed world and then re-transmitted to the developing country. Sometimes, news from a developing country in which there was no bureau was collected in a neighbouring country before being fed back to a head office, and then relayed in the general news output of the agency. Figure 5.4 illustrates the structure of these relations. The news agencies, despite their global reach, are centred in the developed world. They gather and transmit the majority of their material within and between these countries. The flow

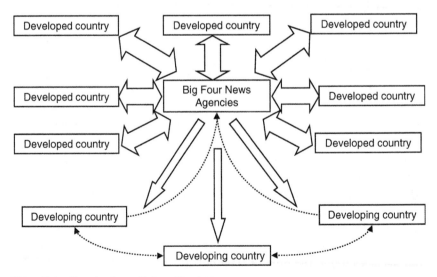

Figure 5.4   The structure of international news

of material to the agencies from the developing world is meagre compared with that which links the developed countries. At the same time, the agencies transmit their output to the developing world, but because of their poverty, far fewer media outlets there can purchase and use this material.

Developing countries thus faced a flood of inappropriate news and a dearth of the right kinds of material. While they might learn all about the hatches, matches and despatches of the royals, or sport and entertainment stars of the developed world, they were much less likely to learn about a significant political, let along technical, development in a country that faced similar circumstances to themselves. The elite of developing countries, let alone the ordinary people, were starved of the kinds of information that they needed to help them plan policies for national development. What people got in Nigeria, for example was 'news *of* Africa but *for* non-African audiences' (Golding and Eliot, 1979: 162). The population of the richer countries, who might be persuaded to back political and economic action to alleviate the suffering of the poor of the developing world, likewise heard of the wars, famines, and disasters of the developing world, but little of the successes, or the daily life, of people in the developing world. As the Chair of the Non-Aligned News Agencies Pool (NANA) set up to counter this western dominance put it, the Third World made three charges against the western news agencies: they did not carry enough news of developing countries; the material they did carry was neither adequate nor relevant; and they projected a 'wrong, biased and prejudiced image of the developing countries to the world' (Mankekar, 1978: 48). Writing in the mid 1980s, Mowlana reviewed 447 studies of news flows between 1973 and 1985, and concluded that the overall findings were that structure of international newsgathering and news flows acted to reproduce the inequalities and prejudices of the imperialist system (Mowlana, 1985). The prospects for development depended on breaking this control over what the population of the developing world knew about itself and the world in which it was obliged to operate.

The overall conclusion from these studies was that, very far from the media constituting a key mechanism for the spread of empathy and modernity, and thus acting as a key agency in development, it increasingly appeared as though they were acting to distort developing societies in such a way as to perpetuate their subordinate status in the world and increase the difficulty of their ever being able to achieve a decent standard of life for all of their citizens. As one writer from the developing world put it: '...the transfer of modern media technology may, in fact, increase the dependency on foreign capital, and on foreign sources of information and culture, and consequently may exert a definite control over the tastes and wishes of the inhabitants of developing countries.' (El-Oteifi, n.d.: 5).

This onslaught on the cultural lives of people newly liberated from colonial rule of course stimulated resistance, and many of the leading theorists of cultural imperialism, whether they were located in the core or on the periphery, saw their scholarly work as assisting in those struggles. The theory of cultural imperialism was every bit as closely tied to the project of social and political action as was the dominant paradigm. But while the link between theory and practice was very close, it also raised a range of very difficult problems, and the theory itself became embroiled in many diverse political struggles. It is to that political project and its theoretical consequences that we turn in the next chapter.

6

THE FAILURE OF THE IMPERIALISM PARADIGM

The imperialism paradigm was not developed as a purely academic exercise. On the contrary, it was from very early on closely tied to a programme of action. The close link to action followed the precedents set by both the dominant paradigm and its participatory alternative. There was, however, an important difference. Because it focused on the structural constraints to development, the imperialism paradigm was concerned with politics in the direct and narrow sense of being concerned with governments and states. To the extent that it was concerned with the communication policies of states, it was confronting the making of policy within states. To the extent that it was concerned with core-periphery relations, it was confronting the relations between states. The intense debates that it provoked were thus political as much as academic, and involved a much wider range of participants than simply the scholarly community.

A close relationship between a scholarly account of reality and proposals for political action is in many respects a positive one, particularly when the subject under consideration touches on the impoverished lives of millions of people. The move from theory to politics, however, is also the move from reason and evidence into the realm of power, and that is not necessarily a positive step. In the course of its development, the imperialism paradigm found itself closely identified with a range of political forces and, in order to accommodate their needs and interests, there were changes within the paradigm. At the very least, these amounted to a shift in emphasis that blunted some of the insights of the original formulations. While the paradigm prompted a range of political actions, in practice only some of these were taken up, and then by forces and in context that rendered them significantly different from the original formulations.

As a consequence, the proponents of the paradigm very quickly found themselves under attack from two distinct directions. On the one hand, there were challenges to the theoretical framework itself and, on the other, attacks on the political positions with which it had allowed itself to become identified. To the extent that these latter were not entailed by the theory itself, the paradigm should not have been threatened by political criticisms. The decisive issue for any paradigm is the extent to which it offers a coherent and convincing explanation for the nature of the world. The fact that in practice it has become associated with some discredited political force is not a decisive refutation of the power of the paradigm itself. In this case, however, the theoretical paradigm became so closely identified with its political implications, and indeed was so significantly altered to fit the needs of political struggles, that when the latter were discredited it was more or less impossible to rescue the paradigm from the general intellectual wreckage.

The road to UNESCO

The theoretical basis of the imperialism paradigm identified two obstacles to the use of the media to achieve positive social change. The local ruling classes of developing states and the global structures of domination were both hostile to the kinds of policies that would be needed to realize national development. Very often, the two were seen as mutually dependent. As Cees Hamelink expressed it, after the end of colonialism: 'The former political–military coercion by the external colonialists shifted to the internal colonialism of the national ruling class. And in many cases these ruling classes were the mere figure-heads for the former colonial power' (Hamelink, 1977: 132). Lack of development meant that those who ruled a particular peripheral country were dependent upon their continued subordinate relationship with the rulers of the core countries for their powers and privileges. In return, they ensured that the core countries had unrestricted access to the resources of the peripheral countries over which they ruled.

There was a classical political response to this kind of analysis. At least as long ago as the struggles in China in the late 1920s, Stalinist Marxism had developed a strategy that sought to identify those sections of the elite who were genuinely in favour of national independence, and ally with them against those who were mere puppets of imperialism (Isaacs, 1951). In this account, the 'national bourgeoisie' who were in opposition to the imperialist domination that was preventing their independent capitalist development needed to be won to an alliance with the progressive elements amongst the masses and supported by the socialist camp. The resulting bloc would engage in struggle against the 'comprador' bourgeoisies and the imperialists who backed them and whose interests they served. The main lines of this analysis were taken over more or less wholesale in the development of the imperialism paradigm (Salinas and Paldan, 1979). In one very clear version, the nature of the anti-imperialist bloc was spelt out in detail: 'The workers and small capitalists (independent distributors) joined forces to push for national control of Canadian cinema, whereas Canada's prominent capitalists (national theatre chains) and the international capitalists sought the cooperation of various sectors of the state machinery to keep their control intact' (Pendakaur, 1990: 167). Dallas Smythe shared the same views, noting a division between 'national capital' and 'that sector of capital within the colony that prefers policies within the colony that favor foreign capital over the interests of the population and resources within the colony' (1990: 17).

The inevitable result of this analysis was to downgrade the importance of the internal conflicts within a developing society while stressing the conflict between the periphery and the core. At best, the theorists of the imperialist paradigm effectively assumed that the work done by the adherents of the participatory paradigm constituted the 'national' practice of the imperialist paradigm. They themselves devoted their energies to developing national communication policies for use in the international arena (Rodrigues Dias et al., 1979).

The main efforts of the proponents of the imperialist paradigm were directed at changing the relations between states, not those within states. As one writer bluntly put it: 'An alternative to this new subtle way of domination is the urgent need for a global struggle in defense of national sovereignty, cultural identity, legitimate traditional values and an autonomous, two way flow of objective information' (Gonzales Manet, 1986: 57). This focus on states and their rights meant that the international organizations of the United Nations system were the main site where political work could be done. Most notably, the United Nations Educational, Social and Cultural Organisation (UNESCO), which was the main body concerned with inter-state cultural relations, became the centre of attention and activity (Nordenstreng 1984: 13).

This shift towards working within international governmental organizations meant that the imperialism paradigm and its advocates were exposed to a radically different set of forces from those that operated within countries. Within countries, conflicts of interest are the accepted currency of politics in all but the most extreme totalitarian states. Both the dominant paradigm and its participatory alternative operated within national frameworks in which internal differences and disputes were taken as starting points. The world of inter-state relations, on the other hand, is one in which states appear as formal, singular, entities confronting their peers through the representatives of their governments. Dissenting internal voices have no official status, and their representation depends entirely upon the goodwill of a recognized state. However much an analysis might recognize differences and conflicts inside a country, as far as UNESCO is concerned states are manifested solely in the shape of their governments and only those governments have rights and votes in the decision making process. These realities meant that, however careful and nuanced were the analyses of the internal structures of states made by the imperialism paradigm, the practical concentration upon inter-state relations meant that all that really mattered was the way that countries voted in the key international forums, and notably UNESCO.

It was in UNESCO that the theoretical formulations about media and cultural imperialism were operationalized into a political programme. This came to be known as the New World Information and Communication Order (NWICO) and was designed to complement, at least terminologically, the New World Economic Order, adopted by the United Nations General Assembly on May 1 1974. The proposed new arrangement of the media was given several different names: New International Information Order (NIIO); New International Information and Communication Order (NIICO); New World Information Order (NWIO). If there were once political subtleties in these terminological differences, they are of limited contemporary relevance, and the terms are today effectively interchangeable. The policies developed for the NWICO were intended to challenge the distortions of communication that had been analysed by the theorists of the imperialism paradigm.

These new policies were rooted in the needs and interests of states, as is clear from a brief examination of the wording of some of the main sections of the 1974 'Declaration on the Mass Media' which was the first official attempt at embodying the NWICO: 'Art I.1. The mass media in disseminating information and opinion have a responsibility to do so in a manner which is compatible with the mutual respect of the rights and dignity of States and peoples ... Art III. Since the two-way flow of news is fundamental to the strengthening of peace and international understanding, States and information media in each country have the right to diffuse reports of national events to others beyond their borders ... Art X. The responsibility of States in the international sphere for the activities of mass media under their jurisdiction is governed by customary international law and international agreements.' (Bielenstein, 1980: 'Flow Chart'). The language was not an aberration. All of the debates around NWICO were saturated with the assumptions of the political primacy and internal unity of existing states.

The detailed history of the 'struggle' inside UNESCO has been recorded frequently elsewhere, and we do not need to review its progress in any detail here since we will not add anything of substance to the works that are readily available to the interested scholar (Nordenstreng, 1984; McPhail, 1981; Wells, 1987; Gerbner et al., 1993). The historical studies agree that the main proponents of the NWICO were the recently independent countries that made up the non-aligned movement, but they were quickly supported by the USSR and the 'socialist camp'. This alliance had the almost automatic implication that the NWICO would be opposed by the 'free world' under the leadership of the USA. It also ensured that the debate would be caught up in the conflicts of the Cold War.

The MacBride Commission

Partly perhaps to avoid provoking a serious crisis, and partly because the available base of knowledge was genuinely limited, decisions on the 1974 Draft Declaration, as well as subsequent drafts, were postponed and 'further research' was commissioned and undertaken. Much of the internal history of the NWICO is in reality a story of UNESCO-sponsored conferences and meetings, crossed with meetings of an ever broader group of interested bodies from the OAU (predictably anti-imperialist) to the US Senate Foreign Relations Committee (predictably paranoid about the USSR). Some interesting quotations that give a direct sense of the tenor of at least the earlier phases of the debate are provided by Berwanger (1980).

The value of some of the results of this research effort was questionable. The fact that the proposals for a NWICO were caught up in the ideological struggles of the time meant that they often resulted in rhetoric that was entirely barren from the point of view of scholarly investigation. There were, however, genuine investigations carried out under the auspices of the UNESCO debate. Many of the detailed studies cited in the preceding chapters were made possible by funding from UNESCO, which was also the publisher of the resulting monographs. Neither were all of the actors and researchers governments or intergovernmental organizations. There were many non-governmental organizations (NGOs) heavily involved in the debate from the start.

So politicized was the debate, however, that the status of non-governmental organization was not a guarantor of independence. This was particularly true of prominent actors like the World Press Freedom Committee and the International Organization of Journalists, who were major and interested parties in the conflict, and whose actions were particularly closely tied to influencing governments and UNESCO (Kleinwächter, 1993: 16–17). Kaarle Nordenstreng later went so far as to claim that: 'The commercial publishers, mainly based in the Western capitalist countries, proved to form a coherent entity ... Their line coincided – and was coordinated with – the political position of leading western governments, particularly the USA ... as a matter of fact, some NGOs have largely turned into government organizations' (Nordenstreng, 1993: 106–7).

However that might be, some of the NGOs involved in this debate could in no way be seen as stooges of government. Prominent examples that do not fit easily into the Cold War demonologies of either side were what was then the International Association for Mass Communication Research (IAMCR – now the International Association for Media and Communication Research), and the World Association for Christian Communication (WACC). While these organizations were, and still are, clearly independent of governments, the fact remains that the logic of the struggle for a NWICO tended to drag even those into a discourse dominated by states and their struggles to realize their interests.

The final, climatic, attempt to resolve the political issues through further research was the establishment in December 1977 of an 'International Commission for the Study of Communication Problems', which came to be known as the 'MacBride Commission' after the name of its Chair, the

Irish politician Sean MacBride. The main concrete result of the battle over the NWICO was the Report of the MacBride Commission, which despite the many compromises in its composition and deliberations did provide a very comprehensive review of the state of international communication (MacBride, 1980). The Commission made a series of 82 recommendations for action on the part of UNESCO and its member countries when it presented its final report to the General Conference in Belgrade in 1980. Despite the bitter hostility that the Commission experienced, very few of the concrete proposals that were produced seem exceptional in retrospect. The US representative on the Commission, Professor Elie Abel, wrote a number of qualifying notes to the text, as did others including Sean MacBride himself, but the only members who made general comments on the text as a whole were Losev (USSR), Masmoudi (Tunisia), Marquez (Peru) and Somovia (Chile, then living in Mexico).

Most of the suggestions were never implemented, but one, which said that UNESCO should give 'consideration … to organizing a distinct communication sector' (269–70) did lead to the creation of an International Program for the Development of Communication (IPDC). Nordenstreng wrote much later that 'It was obvious that there would have been no IPDC unless the movement towards NWICO … would have first stirred up the Western interest to react' (Nordenstreng 1999: 261). It should also be noted that the Commission accepted more or less wholesale the dominant paradigm's account of the role of communication in developing countries: 'Development strategies should incorporate communication policies as an integral part in the diagnosis of needs and in the design and implementation of selected priorities. In this respect communication should be considered a major development resource, a vehicle to ensure real political participation in decision-making, a central information base for defining policy options, and an instrument for creating awareness of national priorities (MacBride, 1980: 258).

The prospects for the IPDC having a vigorous life, or for UNESCO acting on any of the other proposals, were much curtailed when in December 1984 the USA, followed by the UK and Singapore, withdrew from UNESCO activities, taking with them their contributions, which together amounted to around 30 per cent of the annual budget (Galtung and Vincent, 1992: 88–95). While it established itself as the source of funds for some worthwhile capacity development projects, the IPDC was neither designed nor resourced to address the central issues of world-scale imbalances that NWICO identified as crucial to the establishment of a more equitable communication order.

The other major outcome of the debate was the establishment of the Non-Aligned News Agencies Pool (NANA) and a number of regional pools, for example in Africa and the Caribbean. This, again, was an initiative between governments, although it was formally independent of the problems in

UNESCO. The aim of these projects was, and is, to provide an alternative to the domination of the international news flow by the big news agencies, identified in the imperialism paradigm as providing a service tailored to the needs of news organizations and audiences in the developed world. Despite very considerable efforts, lack of adequate financial resources has tended to mean that the services provided by these organizations have been marginal to the main flows of world news (Boyd-Barrett and Thussu, 1992).

Overall, the results of the intense political activity by scholars around the NWICO were extremely limited. Entering the world of state politics, and identifying some states as the source of problems, and others as the agents of the likely solution, meant that the project was bound to become embroiled in more general issues of international relations. In particular, any proposals touching on issues of communication and government were bound to become involved in the long struggle between the USA and the USSR, in which both sides were only too ready to use to their own political advantage any issue that touched a chord of genuine international concern.

The end of the paradigm

The imperialism paradigm was formulated in the late 1960s and early 1970s and quickly commanded substantial intellectual and political support around the world, but by the mid 1980s it was in full retreat. The very rapid rise to prominence of the paradigm can partly be explained by the wave of anti-imperialism that dominated world politics at that time. The reasons for its equally rapid demise also have partly to do with changes in the political situation. The December 1984 withdrawal of the USA from UNESCO, and the subsequent effective abandonment of the project for a New World Information and Communication Order by the latter organization, was undoubtedly a major setback for the imperialism paradigm. By the end of the 1980s, another important international political development undermined the surviving support for the paradigm. As we have seen, the debate over international communication had always been related more or less directly to the Cold War, and the imperialism paradigm, not to mention its political expression in NWICO, was no exception. The Cold War came to an abrupt end with the collapse of the communist states of Central and Eastern Europe in the years 1989–91. The end of communism dramatically weakened the position of the protagonists of the paradigm. The communist state apparatus and their client organizations had provided both political and material assistance to the supporters of NWICO. After 1989, the states that formerly backed NWICO were under different management. They were much more receptive to the views of the US, not to mention to US media. What was more, at least some of the NGOs involved in the debates had been more or less official proxies for those states. The International Organization of

Journalists, one of the main supporters of the project, lost much of its official support after 1989, and by the mid 1990s it had been kicked out of its Prague headquarters, to linger on as a much-weakened force on the margins of international debates. In the new world of post-communism, there were no longer the sources of official support that were essential for the sort of campaign aimed at influencing states and international organizations that had been waged a decade before.

These reversals in the world of international politics no doubt demoralized many of the writers who had devoted their careers to the imperialism paradigm, but they were not in themselves fatal to their theoretical ideas. Although the paradigm and the political project were closely linked, political reversals do not automatically lead to intellectual collapse. A set of ideas can be aided or hindered by political developments, but its explanatory power can only be undermined by a confrontation with other, more cogent, ideas that demonstrate its inadequacies and provide a superior explanation of reality.

There were four sorts of intellectual reasons that contributed at least as much as changed circumstances to the marginalization of the imperialism paradigm. The first class of reasons had to do with internal weaknesses of the paradigm itself. The second class of reasons concerns changes in the field of communication and media studies that raised serious questions about the validity of some of the conclusions of the paradigm. The third class of reasons was changes in the nature of communication media during the last quarter of the twentieth century. The fourth class of reasons has to do with changes in the nature of the audiences for the mass media themselves, considered in the aggregate.

Internal contradictions of the imperialism paradigm

The most important internal problem facing the imperialist paradigm was the self-defeating consequences of the strategy of concentrating attention on the international level. While the political setback on its own, demoralizing though it was, would not necessarily destroy the intellectual project, the way in which the paradigm had been developed in order to facilitate the political project had meant changes that caused very serious problems.

In its original formulations the paradigm had, as we have seen, clearly recognized the internal differentiations, indeed the existence of class struggle, within states. The local elites, who controlled the newly independent states, were seen as often constituting a part of the problem since they were in league with the imperialist states. The price of the UNESCO-based strategy that purported to offer a remedy to this was that this important insight was abandoned, or at the very least de-emphasized. Alliances between states involved keeping silent about what was going on inside some of the countries with which one wished to ally. From being part of an oppressive class structure that depended upon the continued misery of the domestic populations, the ruling elites of countries were offered an alternative role. Those elites prepared to oppose the US and its friends in the workshops and conferences of UNESCO became important allies of the scholarly proponents of the new order. While all of the real crimes and shortcomings of the US and its allies were catalogued, often in tedious detail, there was, at the very least, a tendency to neglect some of the more egregious repressive actions of those states that were allies of the movement. So, for instance, the 'Action Programme of the Fourth General Conference of the Non-Aligned News Agencies Pool', thoughtfully reprinted by the IOJ, detailed the very real threats posed by the USA to Cuba and Nicaragua, the racism and aggression of the apartheid regime in South Africa, the oppression of the Palestinians and Israeli aggression in the Lebanon, and so on. The war in Afghanistan, military rule in Poland, and the role of dictatorships throughout the developing world, not to mention the human rights record of the Cuban government hosts themselves, all passed without mention (IOJ, 1988: 103–11).

The struggle between the USA and the USSR was the dominant reality in international politics during that period, and it was more or less inevitable that any proposal to effect serious change would become caught up in that struggle and its horrible consequences. Looking back many years later, three of the major actors drew the conclusion that 'What started as a clear North–South issue soon turned into a quagmire of Cold War politics. In some respects the NWICO was hijacked by the two Cold War superpowers and used to settle their scores, old and new' (Vincent et al., 1999: viii).

Ambivalence about the role of the Stalinist states was a long-standing feature of the work of many theorists of the imperialism paradigm, not to mention the wider left. As Nordenstreng, who was undoubtedly one of the key architects of the strategy, wrote with the benefit of hindsight, the famous Symposium in Tampere that really launched the project of a new world order in information and communication: 'did not have anything critical to say about the socialist countries or the Third World' (Nordenstreng, 1993: 266).

There is no way of knowing the real motivations of the proponents of the imperialism paradigm. Some, like the late Dallas Smythe, were true believers in the virtues of the 'socialist camp' Others may have been opportunists who saw the patronage of states as stepping stones in their careers. Still others may have been reluctant allies of what they privately recognized as monstrous dictatorships but saw as the lesser evil in a global struggle for social justice. Whatever the motive, in practice, the strategy of winning UNESCO meant at the very least silence on the suppression of journalists and free speech in country after country.

Sometimes, it meant going just a little further. Nordenstreng and Varis wrote that 'the crucial boundaries in the world do not occur between nations but within them', but more or less immediately concentrated upon the struggle between the US and its socialist foes (Nordenstreng and Varis, 1973: 393ff). On the basis of that opposition, they went on to provide a theoretical justification for the suppression of free speech in the German Democratic Republic: 'When a capitalist society is transformed into a socialist one, the freedoms of the old press are usually restricted or abolished in order to break the bourgeois hegemony ... [an] interesting example in the modern world is the German Democratic Republic' (Nordenstreng and Varis, 1973: 401–2).

Most of the people who held views like this would these days regret them; the point is not to remind them of their past indiscretions: the current author has also made political mistakes that he would rather forget. The point is to understand what theoretical compromises were involved in the strategy, and ultimately to give one major reason why it was such a complete failure. As Hamelink later admitted, 'the debate on this issue was not helped by the fact that quite a few political elites in the South were rather actively committed to censuring their own citizens and foreign journalists and had little qualms about the occasional killing of those who exercised free speech claims' (Hamelink, 1997: 417; see also Kleinwächter, 1999, and Nordenstreng, 1999). What an alliance with the indefensible did was to hand those who wanted to retain the status quo the most powerful weapon imaginable, both politically and intellectually.

Anti-communism was a pervasive theme in opposition to demands for change, notably in the USA (Roach, 1992). Thus Dante Fascell, who had been a Democratic Representative from Florida since 1955 and a foreign affairs activist in Congress, wrote in opposition to the demands for change that there was a 'philosophical struggle between those nations that do not generally wish to restrict information flows and those that view restrictions, such as prior consent, as fundamental' (Fascell, 1986: 6). What had emerged in 'international forums' was a threat to what Americans took 'for granted as self-evident truths'. This threat came about as a result of the combination of 'communist ideologues [and] many Third World leaders in a concerted effort to frame what has been termed a "New World Information Order"' (Fascell, 1979: 12). One could multiply this sort of rhetoric ceaselessly, particularly from the writings of Leonard Sussman, for whom 'some [unnamed] proponents of the new order were blatantly, harshly totalitarian' (Sussman, 1983: ix). However, it is also undoubtedly the case that the charge of collusion with tyranny that they levelled at the proponents of the new order had more than a little truth in it. When Sussman pointed out that the founding conference of NANA was held in India and addressed by Mrs Gandhi in the middle of the State of Emergency, he had identified a central weakness in the project (Sussman, 1977: 29–31).

Versions of the incapacitating consequences of this central weakness turn up again and again in discussions of the reasons for the failure of the practical proposals of the imperialism paradigm. The focus on winning the support of national elites, for example, meant that the structural imbalance upon which they rested, most universally upon gender imbalances, was never addressed, and the claim to be attempting to redress imbalances was thus at best half-hearted (Roach, 1993: 290–3). Similarly, the need to align oneself with the existing institutions of the state disabled those attempting to change and improve the media systems of developing countries. Thus Kumar identified Doordashan's news as being as indifferent to the ideas of the new order as those of organizations in the developed world, and Vilanilam, examining the role of the Hindu religious epic on Indian television argued that 'cultural invasion … need not always be from without; it can occur from within' (Kumar, 1996: 282ff; Vilanilam, 1996: 83).

The only overall conclusion that it is possible to draw from a brief review such as this is that the theoretical inconsistencies of the imperialism paradigm were ruthlessly exposed by the UNESCO-oriented strategy. The original analysis had placed at least as much weight upon the effect of internal social structures in constraining development as it had upon the international dimension, but the practical strategy it inspired only took up the latter issues. In identifying the struggle between states as the central motor of change, the practical project consigned the theoretical insight into the structures of states to irrelevance. The practical defeat of the strategy may have been the result of some unpleasant *Realpolitik* by the USA (assisted of course by the UK and Singapore), but the intellectual problems were internal to the project itself. When in the course of the 1980s and 1990s a number of critics from different intellectual traditions came to write about the shortcomings of the imperialism paradigm they had a relatively easy time of it largely because of the ways in which its original theoretical insights had been distorted to fit the demands of tactical alliances with social forces whose intentions were anything but the welfare of the poor.

Developments in communication and media theory

Inside communication and media theory, there were a number of theoretical developments that changed the intellectual climate within which debate took place, and which have been labelled 'new revisionism' (Curran, 2002). These affected the general field of scholarship, but had a particularly powerful effect upon the study of international communication. There was, as is very well known, a general shift away from seeing the mass media and its products as the instruments of power and the site of domination, and a new emphasis upon the active role of the audience in determining the meanings derived from media consumption. A number of key propositions that underlay the media imperialism thesis were subjected to critical review in the light of the new orthodoxy, and found to be manifestly inadequate.

The first of these revisions was the new stress upon the multiple social contexts of media consumption. The theory of media and cultural imperialism had, at least in the version advanced by writers like Schiller and Smythe, claimed to demonstrate first that the international trade in television programming was dominated by US products and that these saturated the schedules of broadcasters in the developing world. The consequence, in Schiller's words, was that 'the public media are the foremost example of operating systems that are used in the penetrative process' (1976: 9–10). The result of these actions by the media and other agencies of socialization was a 'cultural takeover of the penetrated society' (1976: 8). The programmes shown on television changed the ways in which people, or at the very least influential people, in developing countries viewed the world and aligned their values and aspirations more closely with those of the corporate USA. In other words, the media (alongside education, business culture, and so on) had a direct and predictable effect upon the minds of the audience that consumed them.

The first objection to this position was that investigations showed that there is no single social activity that constitutes 'media consumption'. On the contrary, it differs dramatically around the world. Particularly in the case of television, the nature and context differ radically from culture to culture and even within any one culture over time.

One very good example of this was the studies collected by James Lull (Lull, 1988, 1990). They demonstrated that there was a broad spectrum of different social settings in which television consumption took place. At one end of the spectrum was the case of the USA, where the individual 'nuclear' family had its own distinct and separate living quarters, within which there were commonly several television sets. While it might have been the case a generation ago that the mode of consumption was in the family group, now viewing was increasingly fragmented along generational lines. In the middle of the spectrum were those societies in which television viewing retained strong class inflections, for example in Latin America. Not only were families likely to be larger, and children likely to remain in the family home longer, but there were also servants who lived in the same house and who watched television together with their employers. Towards the other end of the spectrum were those societies, notably India, in which the family unit was much more 'extended', and included many more pairs of adults and their offspring, and in which the viewing experience was strongly marked by patterns of gender relations. At the far end of the spectrum lay those societies in which the limited availability of television sets meant that viewing was a collective experience involving various families, often in the house of a powerful and wealthy local individual.

Given this wide range of settings, and the range of different forms of social organization and power relations that were embedded in them, it seemed obvious that there was no single activity such as 'viewing', and that any socially informed theory of reception would necessarily find that there were different interpretations of television texts both available and realized in different contexts. The simple uniformity of effect that was attributed to theories of media imperialism was therefore unlikely to be true. If watching television meant such different things in Illinois and Dacca, then it was unlikely to be the case that the meanings of what was being watched would be the same, even if the actual programmes were very often identical.

Powerful support for this view came from the new emphasis placed upon the activity of the audiences for media products. The origins of this approach lay in the studies of the 'dominant ideology' undertaken within the tradition of cultural studies, notably by David Morley, but they quickly proved much more generally applicable and came to form something of an orthodoxy that remains dominant even today. What Morley, and a host of succeeding writers, showed was that differently constituted groups, and indeed individuals, bring to one and the same media artefact a wide range of beliefs, knowledge, understanding, and so on, and thus are likely to construct the meaning of media texts differently. Since the audiences for imported programming in different countries around the world naturally brought to the experience of viewing a vast range of different cultural resources, and since the repertoire of comparisons and references they possessed differed equally widely, the results of their discrete constructions of meaning were likely to be radically distinct.

The US drama series *Dallas*, which was widely popular around the world during the 1980s, provided the exemplary case. Since it embedded a great deal of what can be taken to be 'American values', it was often identified as the exemplar of the problem against which the imperialism thesis was constructed. Ien Ang noted that 'the *Dallas* phenomenon functions as an alarming bogey' symbolizing the danger of US cultural imperialism in the discourses of critical intellectuals around the world, and notably in Western Europe (Ang 1985: 2–3, 92–95). In response to this sort of critique, she demonstrated that the interpretations of Dallas actually made by women in its Dutch audience differed very widely from one another, even within an extremely small and unrepresentative sample. What these interpretations had in common was not that they demonstrated the workings of an ideology of domination but that they articulated the multiple pleasures that such a work could produce.

Ang's work, which can be located fairly firmly within the 'cultural studies' tradition of analysis, was complemented by a study from the much more positivist 'uses and gratifications' tradition, which showed that Israelis of different ethnic backgrounds and US citizens had quite different 'readings' of one and the same episode of the soap opera (Liebes and Katz, 1990).

Some of the studies that concentrated upon examining the kinds of interpretations audiences made of US television programmes showed that there were what appeared to be liberating effects from watching foreign programming. Contrary to the claims of the imperialism paradigm, which saw US programming as acting to erode the positive features of local cultures, it was possible to see the international flow of programming as permitting for the first time the articulation of what was present but un-say-able in a culture, allowing internal critiques of the limitations of cultures, and providing the basis for fresh thinking and creativity.

A very interesting case was that reported by Miller in a brilliant article on the reasons for the enormous popularity of the US soap *The Young and the Restless* in Trinidad. According to Miller, Trinidadian culture has two contradictory aspects, the respectable culture that stressed morality and sobriety and the culture of 'bacchanal' that celebrated excess and indulgence. Both of these aspects are strongly present in the everyday life of all Trinidadians. Broadcasting, like much of official culture, is dominated by the respectable dimension of culture, and finds it almost impossible to produce programmes that embody the dimension of 'bacchanal'. Trinidadian television thus embodied two aspects of the national culture, but while the respectable and official dimension could find expression in the locally produced news, the highly disrespectable and unofficial dimension of bacchanal could only be articulated by an imported drama programme, that was interpreted by the audiences through the lens of their own background and experiences. As Miller wrote: 'There is a sense, then, in which the imported program has the potential to articulate that aspect of the "local" which the locally-produced cannot incorporate given its continuous eye on the external judgemental gaze' (Miller, 1995: 220).

Taken together, these results posed a major challenge for the cultural imperialism paradigm, which had argued that the fact that US programmes could be shown to dominate the broadcast environment of many countries meant that the population was being subjected to a process of mental indoctrination into American ways. The evidence seemed flatly to contradict this. US programming might, or might not, dominate the international flows of television, and the same show might be broadcast in fifty or one hundred countries, but all that this meant was that there would be fifty or one hundred different cultural responses and interpretations. Far from producing a standard tendency towards the acceptance of US values and beliefs, watching US television programmes led to the most diverse forms of cultural consciousness.

Changes in media structures

At the same time as developments in audience research were calling into question the assumptions about the dominating power of the US media, studies of production were starting to question whether this domination of the global media market existed any longer. In the place of a single, US-based production centre dominating the whole of the world trade in television programmes, it was increasingly argued that technical and economic changes were rendering the world a more complex place, in which there were multiple centres of production and exchanges flowing through many different channels. As one influential writer put it: 'We must allow for flows within flows, patterns of distribution that do not fit into the familiar and simplistic model that show total domination of international television by the United States' (Tracey, 1985: 23). While it may have been the case that in the early years of television broadcasting, local stations were dependent upon international sources for technical advice, professional models, and indeed programming itself, this all changed as they matured and developed.

The most obvious of challenges to the idea of a single dominant centre was the development of satellite television. The old communication technologies were bounded by distance and political geography. Communication satellites, on the other hand, have footprints that naturally take no account of political geography. The consequence is that the problem of 'spillover' is no longer a marginal question that affects only border areas. In all but the very largest countries, someone else's satellite signal is always available.

Satellite, and associated cable distribution systems, provided the basis for a new, non-national television (Negrine and Papathanassopoulos 1990). Around the world, commercial broadcasters found that they could utilize this new technological potential to find their way into markets that had previously been closed to them. So, for example, advertising funded commercial broadcasting found its way in to Sweden and Norway despite the opposition of national governments, as the result of satellite signals that were up-linked from London. Commercial competition was introduced into Indian television as the result of the News International 'Star TV' service, originating in Hong Kong (Page and Crawley, 2001).

The development of video recorders, while technically unrelated to satellite broadcasting, had a similar effect of opening up previously closed broadcasting markets. The international movement of people in response to the development of a global economy means that there are large populations in the developed countries who originate, or come from families that recently originated, outside of their borders, and retain strong cultural ties with the lands of their family origin. The national broadcasters of developed countries served the cultural needs of these groups very badly, and the spread of the video recorder permitted them to view programmes originating in other countries, notably those from which they originated or which have cultures more similar to theirs than that of the country in which they were living. So, for example, people whose families originated in South India, but who live in Britain, found that they could now have access to video recordings of popular Indian films and television programmes (Gillespie, 1995: 78ff). As these markets developed, so the preferred technology shifted, and video has been supplemented by dedicated satellite TV channels re-broadcasting, for example Indian and Chinese programming, to audiences in Europe.

A third set of technical developments, this time in telecommunications, made it possible to transmit large quantities of data over long distances much more cheaply. This meant that, for the first time, it became a realistic prospect to edit a newspaper in one location and to publish it more or less anywhere in the world. One of the effects of this use of remote printing was to make the development of a newspaper press distributed throughout large countries a technical possibility for the first time. So, in the US, a new title, *USA Today*, evolved to exploit this new technology, and other established newspapers, notably the *Wall Street Journal*, developed multiple outlets and effectively became national newspapers.

But the potential of this development was not exhausted by the possibility of constructing a newspaper market within one country. On the contrary, it could be used to construct a truly global media artefact. The *Wall Street Journal* led the way in developing editions in Europe and Asia, and has been joined by a number of other titles, most notably the *Financial Times*, which has added European, US and, most recently, Asian editions to its London home paper. Although so far only a relatively narrow range of titles have developed such a global perspective, it seems clear that technical developments have meant that even the least portable of communication technologies has found a way of transcending the limits of time and space.

Overall then, it no longer makes any sense to conceive of the world as made up of closed, self-contained communication spaces that are commensurate with the boundaries of the state system. The flows of communication in the contemporary world are much messier than that: media no longer respect political geography and audiences have access to information originating from a range of sources. As a consequence, it no longer makes any sense to think of the media system of one state dominating or influencing those of another state. Media imperialism may or may not have been an accurate description of the past, but technological developments have made it increasingly inappropriate for the contemporary epoch.

Changes to the audience structure

The development of capitalism has rendered the borders of the national state permeable not only to material and to symbolic goods, but also to people. The last half of the twentieth century has seen vast movements of populations around the globe. There has been, particularly, a movement from Asia, Latin America and Africa into the developed world. The large cities of Western Europe and North America are today the home to millions of peoples who trace their family histories very directly back to other continents. This human diversity, of course, is also an ethnic, linguistic and cultural diversity.

This diversity represents a major challenge to the project of the modern state. One of the primary aims of such bodies was the establishment of uniformity. Within the national territory, there was to be one faith, one legal system, one educational system, one language, one culture, and so on. In order to establish this uniformity, a battery of measures – coercive and persuasive, physical and symbolic – was deployed. Media systems were built around this ambition for national uniformity. The very names of broadcasting organizations embody this aspiration: British Broadcasting Corporation, Radio Telefís Éireann, Arbeitsgemeinschaft der öffentlich-rechtlichen Rundfunkanstalten Der Bundesrepublik Deutschland and Zweites Deutsches Fernsehen, Radiotelevisione Italiana, and so on almost without exception. Sometimes the state was more or less success-ful: the culture, language, religion and methods of one group came to be the effective norm. Sometimes, the state failed, and popular usages remained obstinately differentiated. The failures were reinforced by the new migrations. In some cases, they presented the state and its dominant culture with a wholly new and radical challenge.

The imperialism paradigm accepted the official definition of there being homogeneous national cultures that were in some sense or another 'authen-tic' and which could be identified and defended by the appropriate cultural institutions. This belief that populations could be considered homogeneous in their ethnic, linguistic, cultural and spiritual life was obviously incorrect, at the very least in the vast majority of cases. This was true of the USA, the source of so much of the programming that the imperialism paradigm had denounced, and it was evidently the case in countries whose borders and populations were artefacts of colonial history that were the supposed victims of the homogenizing tendencies resulting from the dominance of US programmes.

Studies in the developed world demonstrated that the movement of pop-ulations, creating what were increasingly called new diasporas, combined with the global trade in cultural goods to produce wholly new cultural formations. No longer was the choice between, on the one hand, remaining a 'migrant', attached culturally and spiritually to some (mis)remembered youthful experiences or idealized but unvisited homeland, to which one would, at some point, return in triumph to fully possess, and on the other hand complete and full assimilation into the culture of the new homeland, at the price of dropping the language, culture and beliefs of one's personal origins. Instead, there was now the third option of constructing a new, syncretic or hybrid culture. Calling this a process of 'translation', Hall argued that these groups 'are not and will never be *unified* in the old sense, because they are irrevocably the product of several interlocking histories and cultures, belong at one and the same time to several "homes"' (Hall, 1992: 310). These shifting patterns of population produce effects both in the developed world and in the less developed. The *'sapeurs'* of Congo-Brazzaville studied by Freidman and the 'Bhangra beat' youths of Southall in London studied by Gillespie are equally products of these 'interlocking histories and cultures' (Freidman, 1990; Gillespie, 1995).

In both cases, a new sense of identity is negotiated out of the available materials both of the 'home' culture and the 'new' culture, but it is one that is distinct from both of its sources. In the case of the *sapeurs*, the commodities of life in the French capital, particularly those associated with the social elite, are appropriated and transported to a completely different setting. They are deployed in a public display whose meaning is neither an affirmation of an essential 'French-ness' nor a denial of its Congo African other, but a negotiated stance whose aim is simply to display a particular social position (Freidman, 1990: 316). In the case of young people in Southall, Gillespie says of the music that '... it allows for an assimilation of the values of urban British youth culture in combination with a continued attachment to the values shared with parents and rooted in the sub-continent' (Gillespie, 1995: 46).

These considerations point to a much more general question. The extent of the shift in the dominant way of thinking about the mass media, and about the more general questions of social theory within which it is situated, is indicated by the discussion of diasporas, post-colonialism and hybrid identities. This general movement is the subject of the next chapter, which inaugurated the dominance of a wholly new and distinctive paradigm but before turning to that we need to consider what we may term the 'afterlife' of the imperialism paradigm.

The persistence of the imperialism paradigm

Support for the NWICO dwindled rapidly in UNESCO in the mid 1980s, and by the 1990s it had more or less disappeared from the official discourse (Nordenstreng, 1999: 262). The Windhoek Declaration of 1991, sponsored and later adopted by UNESCO, operated within a quite different intellectual framework. Its paradigm was much more influenced by the free market and the free flow of information than even writers like Schramm had been. The Declaration contained much that was representative of a serious response to the problems of emerging democratic media in the African continent, even if it did seem equivocal on some key points of contention like monopoly and independence, but it had nothing at all to say about the continuing domination of the flow of international news by a small number of organizations centred in the developed countries. So, item 2 read in part 'By an independent press, we mean a press independent from governmental, political or economic control' (UNESCO, 1996: 18). The meaning of this sentence depends entirely upon a fine point of English punctuation. Without the comma, the sentence means that it is government alone that is a problem. With the comma, it means that there are three kinds of objectionable control, none of which is prioritized. On the other hand, later formulations in the declaration, like item 6, represent political and economic pressures as simply different modes of one and the same governmental control. No doubt diplomats are paid handsomely to produce these kinds of fine nuances that are capable of being subject to different ideological interpretation.

In reality, the UNESCO texts of the 1990s were transparently written with an eye to persuading the US administrations, notably those of Clinton, to rejoin the organization. Nothing that would offend their sensibilities appears in the texts. Having said that, the evils that are identified and denounced were, and are, real evils, just as were the ones identified and denounced by the NANA, detailed above. The new leadership of UNESCO made every effort to bury the NWICO project and its associated research in an effort to entice its major paymaster back into membership. These efforts were long unsuccessful and it was the administration of George W. Bush who finally rejoined UNESCO on October 1 2003. The UK had rejoined in 1997, following the election of the Blair government. At the time of writing, only Singapore of the original trio of resisters remains outside the organization.

That did not, however, mean that the issues that had been raised in the debate disappeared. On the contrary, they persisted, albeit in new places and in new forms. The central idea that US media were contributing to the destruction of national cultures resurfaced and played a major role in international debates over EU cultural policy and around the General Agreement on Tariffs and Trade (GATT) and its successor, the World Trade Organisation (WTO). Elsewhere, there was more or less direct continuity of ideas, issues, and even personnel over the decades. There were also cases where new writers introduced some significant changes of perspective, but continued to address the same core issues.

The continuation of sharp international debate over the alleged threat from US media exports had little to do either with the worries of developing countries or with Cold War politics. On the contrary, the countries now expressing concern about the inflow of US cultural commodities were economically advanced and unequivocally capitalist. The most notable spokesman of this new 'anti-imperialism' was the French politician Jack Lang, who was Minster of Culture and Communication between 1981 and 1986, and again from 1988 to 1993. As such, he was a spokesman for a series of initiatives in both the EU and wider bodies like the GATT that addressed the protection of national film and television industries (Grantham, 2000). Most notably, he was able to lead the struggle to secure an exemption for film and television from the Uruguay round of GATT. The cultural exemption had originally been placed in the 1947 founding treaty of

GATT to allow the protection through exhibition quotas of national cinema film industries. It had become, by extension, used to cover protection for other cultural products, most notably television broadcasting. The USA was strongly opposed to the continuation of these exceptional arrangements, and indeed continues to be opposed to them in the (currently stalled) Doha Round. (For a very detailed account of Article IV see Neuwirth, 2002.)

In the case of the European Union, the concern to protect national and European television industries from foreign (that is, US) competition resulted in a major policy instrument, the much studied Directive on *Television Without Frontiers* (technically, "Council Directive 89/552/EEC of 3 October 1989 on the coordination of certain provisions laid down by Law, Regulation or Administrative Action in Member States concerning the pursuit of television broadcasting activities") and in modified form, still in force although at the time of writing undergoing revision (Collins, 1993; Venturelli, 1998; Ward, 2002. They have differing views of the issues at stake).

The radical ambition to alter global communication flows, and the theoretical basis upon which the policy had been built, did not, however, entirely disappear. As Schiller put it in a famous article, there was a strong case to be made that the world had not yet entered the post-imperialist era (Schiller, 1993). The efforts to continue with the paradigm were much reduced in scope, but there remained a number of intellectual and political activists who tried to develop the ideas. Some of the original actors in the NWICO debate, like Schiller himself, continued to operate within more or less the same intellectual framework. Others made some very important adjustments to the way the paradigm was articulated while continuing with its original impetus. Most prominent amongst these were the intellectuals and activists gathered around the World Association for Christian Communication (WACC) and its journal *Media Development*. WACC became by far the most important NGO continuing activity on these issues, and it has published a continuing flow of material addressing issues of international information inequality. WACC, as we have seen above, was also the home to many of the ideas and practices of the more radical forms of the participatory paradigm. The work that they facilitated in the continuation of the imperialism paradigm was deeply influenced by that stress upon participation. While they provided financial and organizational backing for MacBride Round Tables that attempted to extend the analyses undertaken by the UNESCO Commission, there was a new emphasis on the poor and oppressed. The theme of the 'right to communicate', which had been sidelined in the power politics of UNESCO, came to the centre of the work done around WACC. The state system was no longer the sole preoccupation of activity, although naturally all policy-oriented research seeks to relate in one way or another to the state machine.

The emphasis now, however, was much more upon human rights and freedom (Hamelink, 1994).

A further arena in which the ideas and the personnel involved in the struggles over the imperialism paradigm became involved was the debate around the World Summit on the Information Society (WSIS) organized by the International Telecommunications Union (ITU) and starting in Geneva in December 2003. Once again, the arena of debate was one provided by official, mostly inter-governmental organizations, and once again the terrain favoured the state based agenda. Although the spectre of communism is today very far from haunting Europe, or anywhere else for that matter, there were those who saw the danger of 'the efforts of some governments and radical nongovernmental organizations nostalgic for NWICO to regulate the content of domestic and international news and information flows over the Internet' (Koven, 2003: 38).

The passage of time, however, meant that new issues and new personnel became involved and the language and focus began to shift. The term 'imperialism' more or less disappeared from polite conversation in the academic world for about a decade. It was, presumably, judged too redolent of Marxism, which had been assumed to be dead and buried along with the regimes of Eastern Europe, to be worth taking at all seriously. What in fact happened is that some writers in this tradition now used the more fashionable term 'globalization' to cover what was more or less the same set of phenomena. One outstanding instance of this re-labelling is the work of the US scholar Robert McChesney (Herman and McChesney, 1997; McChesney, 1999: 78–118). In this account, the US media system is seen as having much the same overall role and general effects that were attributed to it by Schiller. The development of a global media market, notably in television, and its domination by ten large companies, the bulk of them from the USA, is leading to a transformation of the media systems in most countries around the world. According to this school of thought 'the most important effect of media globalization has been the spread and increasing and cumulating domination of a commercialized media' which leads to the destruction of alternative models of broadcasting (notably the European public service tradition), the weakening of alternative cultures, and the erosion of the public sphere (Herman and McChesney, 1997: 136ff). In line with the 'active audience' critique sketched above, the authors take a much more nuanced view of the cultural effects of these developments, and in particular are more sensitive to the contested nature of national cultures than were their predecessors of a generation before. What we cannot find in these writers, however, are any of the characteristic theoretical formulations that are present in what we may term 'strong' theories of globalization. These latter were the dominant ways of thinking about the world, and about the place of the media in the world, during at least the 1990s, and it is to these that we now turn.

7

GLOBALIZATION AND THE MEDIA

The decline of theories of media and cultural imperialism was precipitate. By the early 1990s, they had become marginal to debates about international communication. This decline was the result of both political and intellectual defeat, and was part of a much broader retreat of leftist ideas and movements during the 1980s. There is no question that the concept of globalization has replaced the imperialism paradigm as the main way of thinking about the international media. New ideas reflected new times as much as new thinking.

Theories of globalization are of much wider application than simply in the media. It is not possible to isolate only those parts of these more general theories that have to do with the mass media without doing some violence to their internal coherence, but we can at least attempt with globalization what we did with the earlier theories and try to consider their utility in understanding the ways in which the contemporary media operate and their impact on social change. In this chapter, we will examine some of the main theories of globalization in order to show that they can be said to constitute a different paradigm for understanding international communication.

This task confronts some difficulties. For one thing, there is no single theory of globalization that commands common assent. On the contrary, there are numerous competing theories of globalization. As Held and his collaborators put it after an exhaustive investigation: 'no single coherent theory of globalization exists' (Held et al., 1999: 436). There is a certain banal agreement that globalization means greater interconnectedness and action at a distance, but beyond such generalities theories differ in fundamental ways. To take one egregious example, the leading theorists are divided over the relation between globalization and that other central contemporary concept in social theory, namely modernity. Probably the majority of writers would agree with the proposition that 'if globalization means anything, it means the incorporation of societies into a capitalist modernity, with all the implications of the latter – economic, social, political and cultural' (Dirlik, 2003: 275). They differ, however, as to what that entails. For Giddens and Appadurai, globalization is constituted in and through the spread of modernity (Giddens, 1990; Appadurai, 1996). For Robertson, modernity is clearly a distinct process from that of globalization (Robertson, 1992). According to Volkmer 'modernization refers to nations and states, globalization to communities of an extra-societal kind' (Volkmer, 1999: 55). For other writers, Albrow for example, and at least implicitly Bauman, the global age is the period that comes after modernity (Albrow, 1996; Bauman, 1998). Finally, there are writers such as Herman and McChesney in the field of media, who seem to have no time for the concept of modernity. For them, capitalism is the master category of the age, and they use the term 'globalization' to mean something barely distinguishable from imperialism (Herman and McChesney, 1997). Not all of these writers can be grouped together as part of the same current, but we will show that there is enough common ground, even between theorists who differ radically on secondary issues, to constitute a sufficiently distinct body of thought as to be labelled a globalization paradigm.

The second problem is that much of the discussion of globalization takes place amongst scholars who would describe themselves as social theorists. They tend to operate at a very abstract level, and are not much concerned with evidence about the world they are discussing, or even with formulating their ideas in ways that might be subject to evidential review. As one critic put it: 'there is an almost spectacular lack of evidence in the work of commentators ... associated with the globalization theory' (Hesmondhalgh, 2002: 177). In the place of evidence, we find 'opinions, views and prophecies about the direction of the world, and critiques of concepts assumed to be parochial, essentialist and racist' (Freidman 2002, 15). It is very hard to tell whether theories with these characteristics are valid or not.

Taking due account of these two problems, we will, to a much greater extent than in the preceding chapters, be obliged to synthesize the globalization paradigm out of the work of a variety of writers. There is no author whose work we can say commands the same status as did that of Lerner or Schiller in earlier paradigms. Synthesis is problematic as it inevitably runs the risk of distorting the character of the original theories from which the paradigm is constructed. The only way to avoid the charge of wilful misrepresentation is through careful documentation of the claims made about the original theories.

It is possible to identify ten distinct characteristics that underlie the most prominent theories of globalization. Not all of them are present in all theories, but together they form the conceptual framework within which the globalization paradigm operates. They define the kinds of questions that are asked, how research should be conducted, and even what counts as evidence. In this chapter, we will outline what they say before moving, in Chapter 8, to consider how far they correspond to the contemporary world.

Strong and weak theories of globalization

The first task is to make a general distinction between two kinds of theories of globalization. In the last chapter we noted that the work of some writers employs the vocabulary of globalization but in fact operates within a different intellectual framework. Works in this tradition we identify as 'weak' theories of globalization. In weak theories, it may well be the case that there have been modifications to the concepts used and the conclusions drawn, but the system of thought, the underlying paradigm, remains the same as in the preceding period.

The alternative is what we may term 'strong' theories of globalization, which recognize the radical novelty of the current epoch. In these theories, both the object of social thought and the theories and methods appropriate to its study differ from those of earlier times. It is this difference that renders globalization a new paradigm and it is with theories that stand within that framework that we are concerned in this chapter.

A radically different kind of theory

Strong theories of globalization represent themselves as being radically distinct from preceding theories. They may discuss the same issues, and even conceivably reach the same conclusions as earlier theories, but they operate with a quite different set of underlying assumptions. Strong theories of globalization argue that the world in which we exist today has radically different parameters from that of preceding epochs. It displays features, most notably the degree of interconnectedness, that are 'strikingly new' (Appadurai, 1996: 27). These new social forms demand new ways of thinking that are quite different from the concerns of previous theories. As one enthusiast put it: 'the iconoclasm of globalization lies simply in the implicit demand to re-envisage the world that arises once the nature of the complex global interconnectedness and the process of time-space compression and action at a distance are recognised' (Tomlinson, 1997: 173).

The characteristic feature of the global age is the generalization of features that were fragmentarily present in earlier epochs (Robertson, 1992). The epoch of globalization is different to the extent that the development of existing tendencies has reached a point where the resultant of their interaction is a new social order. A clear example of the way in which this is understood in relation to the media is Chris Barker's account of global television, whose defined distinctive global character resides in the fact that: 'Globalization is constituted by a set of processes which are intrinsic to the dynamism of modernity and as a concept refers both to the compression of the world and the intensification of consciousness of the world as whole' (1997: 25). Tomlinson follows Giddens to make a very similar case for the general field of global culture (Tomlinson, 1999: 47ff). It is the pervasiveness of the new order, the lack of any space outside of it, and the intensification of certain social relations arising from the constant processes of interaction that is radically new and that necessitates a new theory.

We may say that globalization constitutes a new epoch in human history. By this is meant that the constitutive social laws of the period of globalization are fundamentally different from those of earlier periods. These may be variously described as the epoch of capitalism, or high modernity, or industrial society, depending upon the ideological position of the commentator. Perhaps some of their characteristics are carried over into the period of globalization, but the way in which they interact, the presence of new elements, and the overall resultant of the conflicting forces is such as to render the social system one that operates according to different laws from those prevailing in the past.

Methodological innovation

This new and radically different social order demands a new and different kind of theory. Just as the emergent industrial capitalism brought forth political economy, so globalization brings forth a different theory with a distinct methodology. In sharp contrast to the 'reductivism' said to characterize Marxist-inspired theories of imperialism, strong theories of globalization reject this attempt at monocausal explanation and to stress the complexity and indeterminacy of relationships in the globalized world: 'The new global cultural economy has to be understood as a complex, overlapping, disjunctive order, which cannot any longer be understood in terms of existing center-periphery models … The complexity of the current global economy has to do with certain disjunctures between economy, culture and politics which we have barely begun to theorize' (Appadurai, 1990: 296). For him, the explanation of culture in terms of economic determination may well have worked in the past, but it is incapable of helping us understand a world in which there are necessary non-correspondences between different kinds of social practice.

This desire to disaggregate the different levels of social and cultural life, and the belief that they can only be understood in terms of their own autonomous dynamics is not a view peculiar to Appadurai, although he expresses it extremely directly and spells out its implications very clearly. It is a recurrent theme in much writing about globalization. For example, Giddens writes that globalization is 'a complex set of processes, not a single one' (2002: 12–13); Beck states that 'the various autonomous logics of globalization – the logics of ecology, culture, economics, politics and civil society – exist side by side and cannot be reduced or collapsed one into another' (2000: 11); Held and his co-authors say that 'to explain contemporary globalization as simply a product of the expansionary logic of capitalism, or of the global diffusion of popular culture, or of military expansion, is necessarily one-sided and reductionist' (1999: 437). Accordingly, it is not surprising to read that 'the composition, the global flow and the uses of media products are far more complex than [Schiller's naïve account] would suggest' (Thompson, 1995: 169).

Theories of globalization are therefore generally very critical of attempts to offer a single explanatory factor for the dynamics of the media, or any other part of the social system for that matter. In their view, one of the key characteristics of the contemporary world that marks it out from earlier periods is this necessary complexity.

A new relationship between theory and practice

Theories of globalization are differentiated from the preceding paradigms we have examined in that they are disarticulated from any clear practical consequences. The development paradigm and the imperialism paradigm were mapped onto the main ideological division of their age, so it is hardly surprising that we can find divergences between them at many points. There were, however, important ways in which they shared an understanding of the nature of knowledge, and they were united in a concern to provide guides to social action. Schiller and Schramm may have had a great deal to argue about in most areas, but they both began from a horror at the conditions under which vast numbers of people attempted to eke out a living. Both believed that it was possible to understand the reasons why this state of affairs persisted and make plans for conscious human intervention that would change the situation for the better. Both believed that it was possible to reach a degree of certainty in one's understanding of the world through special techniques of enquiry that warranted knowledge as scientific. Both agreed on the desirability of moving towards a state of modernity, although of course they differed as to the contours and content of modernity. Both believed that this movement constituted development and could be described in unequivocal terms as progress. Both, in practice, relied on the state to hasten the generalization of modernity. While they quarrelled bitterly about many things, it was a family quarrel.

The family in which this quarrel took place was, of course, the Enlightenment family, of which both theories were clearly children. This Enlightenment heritage is as strong for Schiller's underlying framework, derived more or less directly from Marxism, as it was for the advocates of 'policy science'. Both schools shared the classical Enlightenment project of rationally understanding the world and using that understanding to guide actions designed to improve it.

So far as can be determined, there is no explicit concept of social practice that flows from theories of globalization. The idea of development as a process resulting from conscious expert intervention is now problematic. A number of countries have achieved what is unmistakably 'development' following a quite different path, in which the undirected workings of the world market rather than state policy appeared to be decisive, and this suggested that the old interventionist theories were mistaken (Kiely, 1998a: 9). The successes of the 'Asian Tigers' and China threw strategies based on theories of dependent development into crisis. These real examples of countries transforming themselves into powerful capitalist states with many of the attributes of modernity, were cited as support for the neo-liberal theories of development that were from the 1980s embodied in the so-called Washington Consensus (Kiely, 1998b: 30ff). In this account, capitalism itself has found a way of overcoming what for an earlier generation appeared to be its major shortcoming: that it condemned the vast bulk of the world's population to lives of ceaseless toil and near starvation. The route to development was by constructing an export oriented economy that functioned according to capitalist principles. Through these measures one could achieve rates of growth that in a few years would transform a country from backwardness to developed status.

On the face of it, these changes left little room for the kinds of policies advanced by earlier paradigms. The process of development now appeared to be an autonomous one that required no special policies on the parts of any social agents. The domination of capitalism did not condemn the bulk of the world's population to stagnant misery from which they could only be rescued by the determined action of state power.

The fact that these advances almost everywhere depended upon the persecution of internal dissenters, sucking surplus out of the countryside by manipulating savings and prices, and holding down domestic consumption through repression in order to generate a greater surplus, did not appear to represent a specific developmental policy. After all, other states that stagnated adopted equally repressive policies. Development was now seen as something that happened, rather than as something that policy scientists or progressive intellectuals made happen.

More narrowly, recognition of the global nature of the contemporary media appears to make it impossible to propose concrete action to change things. If the media landscape was limited by the boundaries of the state, and if the state was the force that had the power to control the nature and content of the media, then it was clear what the site of political action should be: to influence the media one needed to influence the state. If, however, the media now operated on a scale vastly exceeding the state, and if their activities were no longer subject to control by the state, then it becomes increasingly difficult to see not only what policies might be developed to improve the situation but also who might have the kind of power that could implement them.: '... the increasing perception of the global integration of the media and their centrality to the futures of all national economies has encouraged a mood of fatalism in which all positive action, like that proposed in NWICO, seems like blowing against a hurricane' (French and Richards, 1996: 32–3). In a world in which the media are independent of national governments, it makes little sense to ask those states to regulate the media in pursuit of pro-social objectives.

To the extent that theories of globalization recognize conscious action as a necessary element in social change, the preferred actor tends to be the entrepreneur. It is the figure of Bill Gates, of Larry Ellison, or even Rupert Murdoch, who is central to driving forward the interconnectedness of the world, of abolishing local isolation, of developing global integration and facilitating the mobility that is central to the contemporary epoch. Whatever the personal views of their proponents, theories of globalization recognize that the nature of the business activities that such entrepreneurs personify tend to drive globalization and thus to increase the sum of human happiness.

The fact that the theories of globalization are relatively distanced from social action compared with their predecessors has important consequences for both the coherence and the status of evidence in this paradigm. Paradigms that become embedded in practice quickly build up a body of practitioners who are trained in their implementation, gather the kinds of evidence preferred by the paradigm, write documents discussing the strengths and weaknesses (usually the strengths) of the paradigm within which they function, and so on. Sooner or later, the demands of practice also become tests: one of the reasons why development theory became discredited was precisely because it was perceived not to work. Theories linked closely to social practices thus have a marked tendency, if they are successful, to attract institutional support that reinforces and extends the paradigm: this is what Kuhn called 'normal science'. But they also, just because they are implicated in practice, subject themselves to a constant interrogation by those who examine the concrete results of interventions based upon the theories. The globalization paradigm, very weakly linked to practice and often displaying an abstraction from concrete evidence, has not experienced this ossification into orthodoxy. One can still write almost anything that one wishes and claim that it is an instance of globalization. Who, after all, is in a position to argue that what you say is not an instance of globalization? And if there is no practical consequence of your theoretical position, it becomes relatively difficult to test its claims.

The centrality of the media and communication

Strong theories argue that globalization has a distinctive and new social dynamic in that it places considerable emphasis upon media and communication as central to contemporary social reality. This is hardly surprising given the more general concern of different intellectual currents with the information society, with weightless economics, and with simulacra. After long being on the margins of social theory, the media are today everywhere accepted as constitutive of social reality in contemporary society.

Communication media are central to any theory that sees 'action at a distance' as a central feature of globalization. To the extent that globalization is constituted in and through networks and the resulting circulation of symbols rather than things, then the immateriality of media products are emblematic of the process of globalization. Barker, for example, identifies the technological advances made possible by digital networks and writes that they 'enable media organizations to operate on a global scale by assisting in the process of internal organizational communication and in allowing media products to be distributed across the globe. Both functions of new technology are intimately bound up with the globalization of media in general and television in particular which, it can be argued, are laying the foundations of a global electronic culture' (1999: 51).

These characteristic features of contemporary media have effects far beyond simply the field of cultural production and consumption. The media, and in particular the electronic media, are much less bounded by physical distance than are the bulkier products of material production or the territorial imperatives of political organizations. As Waters put it: 'Symbolic exchanges liberate relationships from spatial referents.' As a consequence the greater the relative weight of symbolic content in human exchanges the more globalized social relations are: 'it follows that the globalization of human society is contingent on the extent to which cultural arrangements are effective relative to economic and political arrangements ... [and] ... the degree of globalization is greater in the cultural arena than either of the other two' (Waters, 1995: 9–10).

Alongside this claim about economic shifts from physical production to symbolic production, and very often overlapping with it, is the claim that the enabling powers of technological advances, notably in the fields of computing and telecommunications, which have been particularly influential in media and communication, are what makes the global epoch possible: 'it is in large part due to these media and transport technologies that the world, or at least much of the world, is now self-consciously one single field of persistent interaction and exchange' (Hannerz, 1996: 19).

Formulations such as these refer to a complex of distinct social processes, which do not possess the same character or dynamic: banking is different from broadcasting, even in the global epoch. Although writers like Waters tend to run the different sorts of exchange together (1995: 145–50) this is not essential to the claim that the media are a particularly important site of globalizing tendencies. It is certainly the case that the financial markets that exercise such immense sway over the destinies of whole economies and the lives of millions of people are pre-eminently symbolic exchanges. Discussions over the extent to which such transactions are definitive of contemporary economic life are important for theories of globalization, but for our narrower purposes it is important to distinguish between those kinds of symbolic exchange and other kinds, notably those embodied in media artefacts. The transmission and reception of a programme on Star TV or CNN is a symbolic transaction, but one of a different order from currency transactions. It is true that both depend upon a range of technological developments in computing and telecommunications that have significant overlaps, but they are distinct social processes and they must be considered separately.

The growth of supranational organizations

Strong theories of globalization claim that the powers of the contemporary state are much reduced. It follows from this that states are no longer a privileged site for social analysis, particularly with regard to the mass media. While once it may have been the case that the boundaries of states were the effective boundaries of social life, including its cultural dimensions, the erosion of the power of the state has meant that it can no longer be considered the sole arbiter in such matters. Cultural phenomena in general are best understood as the resultant of practices operating at the two linked levels of the global and local.

This general crisis of the state in the global epoch was identified in the 1980s by Raymond Williams, who wrote that 'the nation state, in its classic European forms, is at once too large and too small for the range of real social purposes' (1983: 197–8). As a consequence, it is being undermined 'from below' by new localisms like distinctive ethnic and national identities, as well as 'from above' by new forms of transnational organization, like the European Union. The state is today a weaker determinant of social organization than it was in the immediate past (Peiterse, 2000). This inability of the state to manage the social relations within its borders is not the special shortcoming of 'failed states'. On the contrary, it is a characteristic of all states, even the strongest: 'the military, economic and cultural self-sufficiency, indeed self-sustainability, of the state – any state – ceased to be a viable prospect' (Bauman, 1998: 64).

The general argument is that there is emerging a world society in which the state is less and less a significant actor at all levels, the economic, the political, the cultural and so on (Beck, 2000: 4). A major site of this erosion of the state from above has been the development of media delivery systems that are not bounded by political geography. The developments of satellites, and the internet, as we have seen, provided powerful arguments against the state-oriented policies that followed from theories of media and cultural imperialism. The negative argument logically follows through to a positive assertion of the role of new media technologies in constructing a global order. As Appadurai put it 'electronic mediation transforms pre-existing worlds of communication and conduct .... [and] ... neither images nor viewers fit into circuits or audiences that are easily bound with local, national or regional spaces' (1996: 3–4). In contrast to the press and broadcasting, which were 'children of the modern nation state ... directed towards a national community', the reach of satellite television is much broader than the nation state and the internet is boundless by design (Hjarvard, 2002: 71–2). They are thus related to broader groupings of people, perhaps global and perhaps regional in their constitution, but certainly not closely identified with a single national space. In effect: 'we are witnessing the 'deterritorialization' of audiovisual production and the elaboration of transnational systems of delivery' (Morley and Robbins, 1995: 1–2).

One consequence of this is quite close to the arguments put forward by Herman and McChesney: broadcasting is more and more dominated by 'co-financed and co-produced products ... made on a global assembly line and ... aimed at the world markets' and 'these mega-corporations are shaping a global space of image flows' (Morley and Robbins, 1995: 32). The main difference, however, is that while Herman and McChesney identify these global media corporations as centred in a small number of developed countries, and predominantly in the USA, the globalization paradigm tends to give them a degree of autonomy from national states: 'Global television refers to television which in its technology, ownership, programme distribution and audiences operates across the boundaries of nation-states and language communities. Global television in this sense is transnational television' (Barker, 1999: 45).

The extent to which these global cultural products have completely eroded national cultures and replaced them with a global culture is much contested. The idea that there is an actually-existing single global culture is sufficiently improbable as to command few or no supporters (Smith, 1990). At most, claims are made for some elements of cultural life, notably news, being properly global in content, but in most versions of strong globalization there is recognition of the persistence of differences, at least for most people most of the time. World culture is, according to Hannerz: 'marked by an organization of diversity rather than by a replication of uniformity' (Hannerz, 1990: 237). At best, the 'cosmopolitans' who inhabit global culture are a relatively small number of people, at least at present, but they are relatively influential, since they tend to be occupationally involved in intellectual and cultural niches. They, and the products that they produce, dominate the international circulation of cultural commodities, notably feature films, and make a purely national audio-visual policy increasingly problematic (Askoy and Robins, 1992: 20).

In this account, the state has lost its ability to control the kinds of messages that circulate in the media, and has been forced to cede control to supranational organizations. A characteristic statement of the contemporary situation is that 'Regulatory control of international communication is transferred from national sovereignties to international regulatory organizations, such as the European Council, the WARC and the ITU. The dilution and eroding of state authority with regard to communication policy indicates the shift of authority for broadcasting on to the world community which regulates communication flows' (Volkmer, 1999: 65).

As a consequence, the key instruments of cultural policy that were essential to the construction of the nation state are no longer under 'national' control. They are thus no longer bound to produce and reproduce the rituals of national identity, neither at the grand level of national occasions nor at the much more mundane level of the daily selection and presentation of news and entertainment that fits well in to the official version of the nation. On the contrary, they can now pursue all sorts of different, even subversive, cultural logics that threaten to undermine the national state. It is impossible to avoid quoting two commentators on this topic at some length:

> The nation-state, in effect, having been shaped into an 'imagined community' of coherent modern identity through warfare, religion, blood, patriotic symbology, and language, is being undone by this fast imploding herteroglossic interface of the global with the local: what we would here diversely theorize as the *global/local* nexus. This dissolution and disinvention of *e pluribus unum* narratives can be seen happening in the United States from various angles and within multiple genres of discourse. (Wilson and Dissanayake, 1996: 3)

The national state was the central social institution at least since the middle of the seventeenth century. Theorists of international relations talk of the old order as the 'Westphalian system' of integral states that form the atomic particles of international relations. As one writer critical of this orthodoxy put it: 'Independent of theoretical premises, there is a broad consensus in the [International Relations] community that specifically modern principles or constitutive rules of international relations – state sovereignty, exclusive territoriality, legal equality, non-intervention, standing diplomacy, international law – were codified at the Westphalian Peace Congress against the background of the demise of pre-modern institutions of political authority' (Teschke, 2002: 6). In the new order, these political relations are undermined by the development of political and economic forces that have quite different boundaries. The 'Westphalian' state is no longer able to exert the same total control over its own destiny and that of its denizens. Transnational political organizations like the UN and the EU have eroded its power to act independently. Multinational corporations are so large and powerful, and the capital they command so mobile, that the state can no longer subordinate them to its regulatory regime. Global media are no longer tied to national boundaries but span the world and pursue audiences whose consumption patterns converge ever more closely. The state is simply no longer strong enough to put a boundary around a territory and a people and regulate all that they can do or watch.

The nature of the local

As Wilson and Dissanayake emphasize, the other way in which the state has been undermined is from 'below'. There has been a renewed emphasis on the local, which is invariably paired with the global, and sometimes elided into a process of 'glocalization' (Robertson, 1994; Kraidy, 2003). One of the main tasks of the modern state was to attempt to eradicate local differences at every level: law, custom, language, culture and so on. The local was identified as deviant from the standard practices of modern life within a state. Powerful cultural institutions, notably the educational system but also increasingly the mass media, were dedicated to propagating national standards in language, culture and behaviour. In the place of a myriad of local dialects, for example, there would be the Queen's English and, later, BBC English.

This process is seen by theorists of globalization manifestly to have failed. The recent political history of Europe demonstrates that the claim to have established nation states with a uniform citizenry has been unsuccessful. In Spain, and to a lesser extent in the UK, the centralising state has been obliged to make concessions to local interests, in political life, in language and in culture. Large groups of people (Basques, Catalans, Scots, Welsh, and so on) have obstinately refused standardization as either 'Spanish' or 'British' and insisted on their membership of distinct nations that are different in significant ways from the prevailing assumptions of the central state. To a greater or lesser extent, similar processes can be identified in many of the classical nation states created as part of the modern project. In the formerly communist countries, several states have actually broken up.

Although there is general agreement upon the importance of the local, theories of globalization are not always precise about what they mean by the category; one writer, indeed, proudly proclaimed that he had 'refrained from burdening [the local] with a definition that might have constricted analysis' (Drilik, 1996: 42). What is clear, however, is that in all of its uses in strong theories of globalization there is a pairing of global and local that intends to bracket out the state (Robins, 1991: 33–36). So far as I know, no one using the globalization paradigm ever writes something like 'global/national/local'. The national state is a category whose time has passed. Appadurai writes: 'Nation-states, as units in a complex interactive system, are not very likely to be the long-term arbiters of the relationship between globality and modernity' (1996: 19).

If the global is broader in scope than the state, then the local is narrower, and not necessarily aligned, or perhaps necessarily not aligned, with the boundaries of the state. Ohmae puts the issue very clearly in his opposition between the old order of the national state system and what he calls 'region states': 'What defines them is not the location of political borders but the fact that they are the right size and scale to be the true natural business units in today's global economy'. It is the system of region states (Emilia Romagna, Silicon Valley, the Paris Basin, Tokyo-Osaka, Hong Kong-Shenzen, the Thames Corridor) that take the decisive decisions in the modern world: 'theirs are the borders – and the connections – that matter in a borderless world' (Ohmae, 1995: 5). He goes on to argue that all that is left for the nation state is to cede power to these new formations: 'Thus, in today's borderless economy ... there is only one degree of strategic freedom that central governments have ... And that is to cede meaningful operational autonomy to the wealth-generating region states that lie within or across their borders' (Ohmae, 1995: 142). To the extent that there are still bodies that perform some of the functions of states, they are increasingly different from Westphalian states. The dynamic political forms in the contemporary world are more likely to be city states than national states (Hepworth, 1994).

If the local, however ill-defined, is clearly a form of social organization that is different from the Westphalian state, there is a division of opinion, or at least of emphasis, over the shape of significant local formations, particularly at the level of culture. In a very obvious sense, the English language use of the term 'local' is a spatial one. It is directly linked with the concept of locality and can be taken as signifying 'a relatively small place in which everyone can know everyone else' (Featherstone, 1996: 52). This sense is certainly present, particularly in the work of writers influenced by anthropological traditions (Friedman, 1994). It directs attention towards small-scale human organizations, where there is a relative uniformity of employment patterns and life courses, endogenous kinship systems, shared cultural experiences and so on. It denotes exactly the kind of social organization that is idealized as 'community' in some version of the participatory paradigm examined in an earlier chapter.

The contemporary world, however, is marked by new kinds of social relations that can be observed in the daily life of the great 'global' cities. The populations of the contemporary metropolis cannot be assimilated into the spatially based notion of the local. In cities like New York or London or Berlin or Amsterdam, for example, the human diversity of the population is evidently immense. One journalist (writing in the *Guardian*, of course) caught the reality of the population of a contemporary world city rather well: '[Lambeth College Students] ... faces were a snapshot of modern Britain, no two seeming to share the same pigment or physiognomy. This is today's reality, a London where three of your next four transactions are likely to

be conducted with people for whom English is not their first language'
(Williams, 2003: 3).

In such cities, and more generally in the contemporary world, there
are other kinds of association that do not depend entirely upon physical
proximity, but which have many of the other features that are associated
with the anthropological notion of locality. Hall described these kinds of
human organization thus: 'The emergence of new subjects, new genders,
new ethnicities, new regions, new communities, hitherto excluded from the
major forms of cultural representation' (1991: 34). These forms of social
organization, articulating, indeed often constructing, their own cultural
identities for the first time, form a second important dimension to the
global/local pairing. Their location is a social rather than a geographical
one. Appadurai writes: 'I view locality as primarily relational and contextual
rather than scaler or spatial' (1996: 178). In the old sense of the local, the
uniformity of experience arose from physical proximities that imposed a
common destiny on the population. In a world of constant geographical
displacement, it is a position in the social structure, rather than in geography,
that gives rise to common experience.

Both of these uses of the term 'local' are to be found in strong theories
of globalization, but the latter are more characteristic of the paradigm.
Hall's insistence upon the novelty of the forms of 'locality' he discusses
clearly identifies this usage with the idea of the radical difference between
the contemporary, globalized, world and any preceding epoch of human
history. The older version of the local is a common reality in preceding
societies. The newer version is unique to the contemporary world. Given
the emphasis in many versions of the paradigm on the compression of space
and time, and thus the destruction of the tyranny of physical place, this
broad definition of the local as an experience of power relationships rather
than spatial proximity is more in tune with the underlying paradigm than
one that privileges a particular geographical site as the defining mark of social
experience.

The absence of a controlling power

The assertion that the contemporary state system is in severe crisis leads
the strong globalization paradigm to deny the existence of any dominating
or controlling centre to the contemporary world. As Bauman put it:
'the deepest meaning conveyed by the idea of globalization is that of the
indeterminate, unruly and self-propelled character of world affairs; the
absence of a centre, of a controlling desk, of a board of directors, of a
managerial office' (1998: 59). Power in this world, whether it is physical
or symbolic in nature, is not concentrated in a single place. No state
is strong enough to dominate world politics and no company is strong

enough to dominate the world market. This general claim that there is no single dominant country or company in a globalized world is particularly pertinent in discussions of media and communication. Just like business and politics, cultural life cannot be seen as the result of the domination of one way of life over others: 'Globalization … is more than the spread of one historically existing culture at the expense of all others' (Beyer, 1994: 9).

This rejection of a notion of any single controlling centre stands in contrast to the central claim of the media and cultural imperialism paradigm. As articulated by Schiller, and not significantly challenged by any writer working within that school, the imperialism paradigm claimed that broadcasting around the world was dominated by US companies and programmes. The strong globalization paradigm argues that this is not the case: '… the United States is no longer the puppeteer of a world system of images but is one only one node of complex transnational construction of imaginary landscapes' (Appadurai, 1996: 31). Alongside the large US studios and networks, globalization theory claims, there are other companies, located elsewhere, that are producers and exporters of films and TV programmes in just the same way as is the USA.

The globalization paradigm argues that the trade in television programmes is far more complex than the imperialist paradigm allowed for, and that there are 'flows within flows' that do not fit the idea of US dominance (Tracey, 1985: 23). In the global epoch, the presence of a large number of confident and established broadcasters in a variety of different geographical locations means that the patterns of television are complex. There is no longer any one-way street.

This general proposition is developed in three different, and perhaps slightly conflicting, ways by different writers. The first of these is the continuing audience preference for national production, and the 'secondary' nature of US programming, in the main developed television markets. The second is the development of independent production centres in developing countries that are not historically part of the developed world and their entry into global patterns of programming exchange. The third is the emergence of regional markets organized around production centres that are independent of the US industry.

Multiple production centres and complex programme flows

The first element is best developed with regard to European experiences. Despite the popularity of US series in many countries, studies of audience appreciation have demonstrated that there is generally a preference for local production (Silj, 1988: 199). The reason for this is that US TV programmes are, quite naturally, produced with the taste of the US audience in mind.

That is their primary market and to succeed anywhere, they generally need to succeed in the USA first, and 'the evidence suggests that US viewers are unusually insular and intolerant of foreign programming' (Hoskins et al., 1997: 45). But if a programme meets the tastes and concerns of one audience extremely well, it is unusual for it to have the same properties in a different context (Bielby and Harrington, 2002). The programmes produced within a country thus tended to be better attuned than any import could be: 'Domestic programmes always receive the highest ratings in all European countries' (Silj, 1992: 38).

The preference for domestic programming is, however limited by the resources available to the broadcasters in a particular context. Because the US market is much larger, US shows in general tend to have higher budgets than do domestic programmes, and thus tend to be disproportionately attractive to viewers (Hoskins et al., 1997: 42). Consequently, when broadcasters are unable to fill their schedules with expensive domestic programming, which is a problem that has become particularly common since more and more channels have become available while the revenues to purchase programmes have been spread thinner and thinner, they tend to purchase imported programming (Litman and Sochay, 1994: 233–4). The 'best quality' imported programming, particularly in drama, available is that from the USA, which leads to the paradox observed by Silj immediately after his statement about the preference for domestic programming: '... the viewers' second choice always falls on American programmes and not programmes produced in other European countries' (Silj, 1992: 38). Contrary to the claims of the imperialism paradigm, the European evidence appears to show a robust preference for domestic programming and that the taste for US programmes is one that is acquired by default, as second best option. It is therefore unlikely that this second preference could have the kinds of effects claimed for it in the imperialism paradigm. Very far from US programmes destroying other cultures, they appear to complement them. Even the French were eventually seduced into loving US culture (Kuisel, 1993).

The second way in which the globalization paradigm recognized poly-centric broadcasting is in its identification of the existence and vigour of production centres outside of the USA. Quite apart from the production centres in the developed world, for example, in the UK, Germany, Japan, that the imperialism paradigm tended to ignore, the globalization paradigm has concentrated attention on broadcasters from developing countries, notably TV Globo in Brazil and Televisa in Mexico. These are two large and powerful broadcasters, both of which are located outside of the developed world and which offer global competition to the established players from the north. Globo, which by some reports is the second largest broadcast network in the world, was founded in alliance with Time–Life and subsequently developed in close association with the military government in Brazil but has since come not only to dominate TV production in that country but to become a major exporter of programmes around the world (Straubhaar, 1991: 48–9; Fox, 1997: 58–9). Televisa had a more problematic relationship with the PRI in Mexico, but also managed to establish itself as a major national producer and exporter. It even managed in the late 1980s to gain control of a small network of Spanish language stations in the USA, prompting claims of 'reverse cultural imperialism' from some writers (Fox, 1997: 57). Another, less well-known exporter is Radio Caracas Television in Venezuela (Fox, 1988: 31). In addition to these Latin American examples, it is possible to identify other national industries around the world that have a similar function, for example in Egypt.

The distinctive feature of these broadcasters is that they not only produce programming that is very popular in their own countries but that they have managed to develop forms, notably the Telenovella in Latin America, that are both distinct from US models and are exportable on a world market. Indeed, in many cases, studies show that it is these exports that are more successful than their American rivals. The most famous instance is that of the great success of the Mexican soap opera *Los Ricos También Lloran* ('The rich also cry') in post communist Russia (Baldwin, 1995). The popularity of these exports, despite the geographical distances involved, the different historical trajectories of the producing and consuming societies, and their very distinct cultural experiences, suggests that there are 'universals' other than those embodied in the Hollywood vision of the world that the imperialism paradigm had failed to recognize.

The third new element introduced by the globalization paradigm is the critique of the idea of a single global television market dominated by the USA. In the case of Western Europe, we have seen that while national programming dominates national markets wherever possible, and US programmes are the clear second preference for television drama, there are other exchanges that are independent of this dynamic. According to one detailed study, the share of US programming in the European market is a relatively small part of the total supply of material, and there are other significant players. The UK, for example, provided a substantial amount of material to some of the smaller European TV markets (Sepstrup, 1990: 86).

Regional markets

The single world television market can be broken down according to geographical markets or along the lines of different kinds of programming. It is the former dimension that has attracted most attention. In a number of areas, notably Latin America and East Asia, studies have noted the emergence of regional markets. Straubhaar, one of the first proponents of this concept, argued that while there was observable in Latin America a process of what he called 'asymmetrical interdependence' between the US and the rest of the continent, concentrating upon a single world marketplace obscured the fact that 'it seems to bear a strong regional flavour' (Straubhaar, 1991: 55). The reason for the development of these strong regional markets is because the programmes produced within them are more 'culturally proximate' than those produced in the USA and thus are more likely to be recognized and accepted as second choice programmes (Straubhaar, 1991: 55).

Subsequent writers have taken this idea even further and joined it with the thesis about the erosion of the power of the national state to argue that a shared 'Latinity', irrespective of geographical place in the Americas or particular citizenship, has emerged through the hemispherical flow of Spanish-language television programmes. In this account, the differences between Cuban émigrés in Miami, Mexican illegal immigrants in California, and the urban populations of Latin American states are secondary to a sense of a 'Latin-American community' that finds itself in international Spanish-language television programming, frequently produced in 'the new entertainment capital of Latin America, Miami, Florida' (Lull, 2001: 147). The consequence is that 'The Latin-American community can now connect via television programming internationally, and is therefore starting to overcome its history of cultural dependency' (de Santis, 2003: 73).

While this line of argument is most developed with regard to the Latin American region, similar regions have been identified as real or emerging markets elsewhere (Sinclair et al., 1996). In the case of 'Greater China', consisting of the PRC, Taiwan, and the Hong Kong SAR (plus, potentially at least, Singapore and the Chinese diasporas), all of which have strong elements of cultural proximity, it is only political obstinacy that is preventing the emergence of an integrated regional market (Chan, 1996: 146).

Some writers have detected a wider sense of cultural proximity than those present in the case of Greater China, which are based on historical and linguistic factors held in common by at least part of the populations in question. Discussing the export of Japanese musical culture, which admittedly has a somewhat different dynamic to that of broadcast television, Otake and Hosokawa note that East Asia as a whole is different from the West. In the latter case, the overwhelming weight of Japanese influence is in capital and technology. In East Asia, on the other hand, Japanese cultural products, and notably musical forms, also have a substantial impact: 'Karaoke is an indispensable tool for Asianising popular music in East Asia because it is basically targeted at the urban middle class'. This process of 'Asianization' cannot simply be assimilated into an undifferentiated modernization because it follows the example set by Japan of a country that has successfully modernized independently of western models and which now competes on at least equal terms with the historical homes of modernity in Europe and the USA. For the middle class in East Asia, this is an example, and by extension a culture, that is extremely attractive and provides a perspective within which to see their own hopes of social development. Japan is a society that has mastered the material culture of the west but retained its cultural differences. The appeal of Japanese popular music is that it embodies this alternative possibility: 'Karaoke in East Asia empowers the triple process of modernization, Japanization and Asianization of East Asia' (Otake and Hosokawa, 1998: 199–200).

The resulting picture of the international flow of television is thus much more complex and multi-layered than that proposed by the theory of media imperialism. Instead of a single market dominated by a single central production centre that ships programmes, and meanings, out to the periphery, there is now a series of different and overlapping markets. As two Australian writers put it: 'What emerges from this sketch of world television is the sense of a multilayered set of structures and a complex set of programme flows, none of which can be explained under the traditional media imperialism model. That model sees the US at the centre of a system of one-way audiovisual flows, with recipient nations at the periphery as passive consumers. The picture that emerges from a contemporary analysis is a veritable post-imperialist or post-colonial one, with no single centre and no automatic peripheries' (Cunningham and Jacka, 1996: 33).

There remains a global market in television programmes, but it is not dominated by the products of any one country. Beneath this global market, there are distinct and different regional markets (and indeed specialist niche markets), as well as continuing local markets, all of which have different dynamics. None of this can be said to provide the basis for the kinds of domination that characterized the centre-periphery relations that were central to the imperialism paradigm.

The emergence of global media products

Just as the erosion of the Westphalian state is seen as the result of the interaction of the forces of the local and global, which are simultaneously contradictory and complementary, so the final distinctive feature of the globalization paradigm stands at least partly in contradiction to the concept of market differentiation that we have just examined. The continuing viability of established production centres and the emergence of new players imply that the world trade in television programming is no longer dominated by the products of one country. At the same time, however, there is a growth of media artefacts that do not embody the cultural preferences of any one nation or state, and which are genuinely global in their appeal. These, too, are traded on the global media market and render claims of US domination even more absurd.

In this perspective, production is no longer exclusively determined, either in location or in content, by the needs of national markets. In the place of distinctively national products, the markets are now increasingly dominated by global products. In place of production firmly located in one particular place, capital is now globally mobile, and thus production can be shifted around the world more or less at will, in order to take advantage of favourable conditions. This argument is well developed for many of the traditional manufacturing industries, but it also has considerable relevance for the cultural industries as well. The erosion of the state as the central regulator of cultural life, the global movement of populations, and the development of global mechanisms of transmission, as well as complex patterns of international trade in television, implies that the circuits of meaning production are detached from the specific tastes of given and homogenous national audiences: 'hybrid cultures and transnational media corporations have made significant inroads into national cultures and national identities' (Held and McGrew, 2002: 36).

Neither are they in any sense 'western' in content and nor are they part of an apparatus of domination. While there do exist cultural artefacts that are widely diffused and of which it can be said that they have distinctive national identity tags, and which might be thought to contribute to the homogenization of culture along western lines, there are 'many other types of symbolic representation circulate widely too ... Instead of simply reproducing conditions of domination and repression, the market has created a rich source of material and symbolic resources which ultimately challenge the hegemony of state institutions' (Lull, 2001: 144–5).

Most of these new cultural forms display some degree of hybridity and they are the most important and significant markers of contemporary culture: 'the superculture is based on the premise that the hybrid is the essence of contemporary cultural activity' (Lull 2001, 157). 'Superculture' is Lull's own term for what others would tend to call the new global culture that is not locked in to the formation of any particular national culture: 'The concept of the superculture is based on the central idea that culture is the symbolic and synthetic, and that contemporary syntheses can be constructed from symbolic and material resources that originate almost anywhere on Earth' (Lull, 2001: 137). The term 'hybridity' is a much more widely used concept, which means something like the synthesis of two or more distinct cultural traditions in order to produce a different and new resultant cultural artefact or process. Up to a point, at least, such products can have a liberating and democratizing effect on the audiences that consume them (Pendakur and Kapur, 1997: 214–5).

The argument for the emergence of Lull's 'superculture' has two different forms, one relating to fictional and entertainment programmes, the other to news and current affairs. The argument with regard to entertainment material begins from the claim that the rewards to be gained from the global market are greater than those to be had from any given national market, even that of the USA. It therefore follows that it is economically rational behaviour on behalf of TV producers to make products whose prime audience is global rather than national.

This argument has been developed most persuasively by Joseph Chan, in his discussion of the transformation of the Chinese legendary tale 'Mulan' by the Disney Corporation into the animated feature of the same name. Chan argues that there is something of a tension between the original material and the need to produce a product with a global market: 'Given the equal importance of the domestic market and the global market to Disney, there is a tendency for Disney to give a foreign culture an American and universal spin ... For Disney, its challenge is to sell its animated features to the Americans and people in other parts of the world' (Chan, 2002: 232). Chan is a little uncertain as to whether he wishes to argue that Mulan has been entirely uprooted from its Chinese context or whether it retains some degree of 'authenticity'. He is very concerned, here and elsewhere, to distance himself from the imperialism paradigm, but as an honest scholar he worries as to whether his preferred analysis is really supported by the evidence. He argues that 'there is no question that the Chinese legend has been Americanised and Disneyfied' but he claims that there is a 'difficulty in differentiating the authentic from the hybridised' because there are many versions of the original (Chan, 2002: 240). Other writers are less hesitant, arguing that, at least in East Asia, 'the age of Americanization ... is over' (Iwabuchi, 2002: 269). In its place, there are the more regionally acceptable and less distinctively national products of the Japanese cultural industry. Japanese animation, for example, consciously chooses to represent non-Japanese physical types (Iwabuchi, 2002: 258–9). It is no longer the case that the products that circulate on a global scale need to be formed according to the cultural preferences of one dominant country, or even of the dominant countries as a whole.

The case that is made out for television news is even more definite. It tends to focus upon CNN, and particularly its international operations. Ted Turner claimed he was heavily influenced by the UNESCO-based critique of western dominance of news broadcasting, and consciously designed *World Report* to provide an alternative to that undesirable state of affairs (Flournoy, 1992: 9). The influence of this one programme echoed on throughout CNN, particularly in shifting its staff base, to render the whole operation genuinely a global one (Flournoy and Stewart, 1997: 71–82). Other writers have made stronger claims both for the non-national nature of CNN and for the influence it exerts upon global news. For Volkmer, although CNN may have had something of an American flavour in its early days, it is today the embodiment of a genuinely global operation that is radically different from transnational corporations. The latter begin on a national scale and expand to other countries, but CNN (and MTV) begin from the global and only subsequently, and to a limited extent, develop more limited markets (Volkmer, 1999: 113). As a result 'this global political communication ... results in the constitution of a *global public sphere*' (Volkmer, 1999: 4).

Conclusion: A new paradigm

These ten elements form the basis for concluding that globalization constitutes a new paradigm that is a comparable intellectual structure with earlier paradigms like those developed in the work of Lerner or Schiller. It is true that this paradigm is much less coherent, and it is difficult to identify one central theoretician as having outlined its main features, although Appadurai might be a strong candidate. Nevertheless, it constitutes a way of looking at the world that is sufficiently distinct from others as to merit this appellation.

The strong versions of the globalization paradigm claim that they are radically new theories developed to understand a radically new world situation. In order to do this, it is necessary to develop a new and non-reductive methodology. This new paradigm makes no claims to direct any form of practical activity that can lead to social change. One central feature of the new epoch is that the state system that dominated world affairs for the last four centuries has now collapsed, or is at least under severe strain. It is undermined by the development of supranational political forms like the United Nations and the European Union and by the growing power of transnational corporations. At the same time, there is a resurgence of localism, in both its classical spatial and its new relational form, although the latter is by far the most important. The reduction in state power means that it is no longer possible to point to any controlling centre or centres in world affairs, which now appears as a directionless and motiveless chaos, albeit a creative chaos. In the field of mass media, the production of programmes and other artefacts takes place in far more places than is recognized by the imperialism paradigm, and the resulting exchanges of programmes take place in differentiated markets where no one player dominates. In this new epoch, the mass media are particularly important since they are among the agents that embody the transcendence of the limitations of space that is a characteristic feature of globalization. These media that are so central to the constitution of globalization are also the bearers of a new form of cultural production that is truly global in scope and which transcends the limitations of particular national states. In both entertainment and in news and current affairs, there is an emergent and genuinely global broadcasting environment.

Because this paradigm rests on an attempted synthesis of a number of writers whose overall theoretical positions are often quite different, it is open to some objections. One is that we have here misrepresented this or that writer. Selectivity, however is endemic to all critical accounts of writers: a meta-discourse is necessarily different form the discourse itself. Ultimately, all that we can do is to provide ample citations of the writers discussed, and exercise care in interpreting what they say.

Other problems are specific to the method employed here. Not every writer we have cited can be said to hold to all of the propositions we have put forward, but it is fair to say that all of them operate within the conceptual space that is thus created. Perhaps these propositions are best thought of as negative limits. For example, we cannot find anyone who writes about global media and links it to some direct programme of social action. Similarly, none of the writers hold that there is a single centre of media production that dominates the world trade in television programmes. It is one of the claims of this chapter that writers using the term globalization can usefully be placed within this conceptual space.

The final set of problems concerns operationalizing what are presented as quite abstract ideas. Because we are concerned with one relatively small part of the globalization paradigm, we have often been able to cite rather more concrete propositions than are common in this area of study. Having outlined the paradigm, we can therefore move on to the next chapter and ask a different question: are these propositions borne out by the evidence? On the answer to that question hangs the validity and the utility of the paradigm itself.

8

THE LIMITS OF GLOBALIZATION

In one version or another, the globalization paradigm that was outlined in the last chapter is overwhelmingly dominant in discussions of media and communication, not to speak of other domains of the social and human sciences. The globalization paradigm is much more dominant than the 'dominant paradigm' of the 1950s could ever have claimed to be. It is in daily use amongst politicians, businessmen and journalists every bit as much as amongst social scientists. There is a very good reason for this; quite apart from the intellectual appeal of whichever version one happens to decide upon, theories of globalization all rest on some very solid foundations. It is idle to deny that the last quarter for the twentieth century, which we may take as the epoch in which theories of globalization came to command wide currency, experienced an explosion of human activity that transcended national borders.

In the case of the media, there are uncertainties about the evidence and what it means, which form the substance of this chapter, and we will discuss them at length below, but other areas of human activity are much more obviously accommodated in the paradigm. Telecommunications, for example, provides evidence that is completely unequivocal. Between 1975 and 2000, the time spent on international telephone calls over the Public Switched Telephone Network – mostly used by people talking to other people about business and life – rose by about 25 times. Their duration rose every year, even during recessions, from 4 billion minutes in 1975 to around 100 billion minutes in 2000 (ITU, 2000: 1). At the same time, there was a massive increase in the number of machines talking to other machines in different countries, notably through the new technology of the internet, which was specifically designed to allow machines anywhere in the world to exchange information with each other. The number of International Private Lines, mostly used for internet traffic, rose about tenfold between 1995 and 1998, from less than 25,000 to more than 250,000. In 1997, the number of these lines passed that of the Public Switched Networks (ITU, 2000: 3). The number of countries connected participating in the Internet went from seven connected to the US NSF internet backbone to

200 countries a decade later. By 2001, less than half a dozen countries remained unconnected (ITU, 2001: 1).

A similar picture can be drawn of the movement of people around the world. Passenger numbers on scheduled international flights, excluding special holiday charters, rose from just over 100 million in 1975 to more than 600 million in 2000 (IATA, 2003: 6). In 1975, 12,406,000 persons arrived by air in the USA and 12,053,000 departed. Roughly half of each total were US citizens. In 2000, the total for air passengers was 62,217,000 arrivals and 57,498,000 departures, with slightly more foreigners than natives moving in both directions (BTS, 2002: Tables 1–40; 1–41). The numbers of international tourists also show spectacular growth. In 1975, there were around 200 million international tourist arrivals in the whole world, but by 2000 the number was about 750 million (World Tourist Organisation, 2000). Much less happily, the number of international refugees rose between 1980 and 2000 from 8.4 million to 12 million, although the end of the war in Afghanistan meant that it fell back to 'only' 10.5 million in 2002 (UNHCR, 2003: 3). By any measure, this is a world in which international movement, if not an everyday commonplace for the entire population, is an increasingly familiar experience for relatively large numbers of people.

Above all, the thesis of the increasing importance of global trade and global capital flows to the world economy looks unassailable. Total world exports of goods and services were worth US$390.5 billion in 1970. By 2000, the figure was US$7786 billion (IMF, 2003). Movements of capital similarly grew at an enormous rate over the same period. In the period 1992 to 2000, capital inflows into the USA increased from US$170 billion to US$1,026 billion (IMF, 2003).

In the face of such persuasive facts, it seems otiose to question the explanatory power of the globalization paradigm. After all, if so many people, machines and money, are busy talking and moving around the world, then it must be the case that the global dimension is the appropriate frame for contemporary social analysis. Only a small minority of writers on contemporary social and human issues are prepared to resist this conclusion. In general social and political theory Hirst and Thompson are the best known writers (Hirst and Thompson, 1996). In studies of media and communication, Jean Seaton and Marjorie Ferguson are amongst the clearest critics (Curran and Seaton, 2003; Ferguson, 1992).

There is, however, a distinction to be made between the facts that demonstrate the global scope of contemporary social life and the way in which that material is theorized. The evidence cited above establishes that there is a great deal of global interconnectedness. The mass of supplementary evidence which can easily be cited only confirms that. What it does not do is establish the necessity of thinking about the world in any particular way. The facts of global interconnectedness are not enough to establish the validity of the globalization paradigm. There are a number of other possible ways in which lists of facts about global interconnectedness can be explained. In order to demonstrate that the globalization paradigm is the one with the best explanatory fit, we would need to demonstrate that the available evidence supported, or at least did not contradict, the main theoretical propositions of the paradigm, and that the paradigm adequately accounted for the most significant aspects of contemporary reality. In the last chapter, we identified the ten main propositions that underlie the profusion of strong theories of globalization, which we argued constituted the basis of the paradigm as a whole, and it is possible to examine each of these in turn to see how far the evidence of contemporary reality bears them out.

A new epoch in human history

The first of the elements in the paradigm is that the current age is, in Appadurai's words 'strikingly new' (1996: 27). This is the most difficult proposition to reach a firm conclusion about, since its validity depends in the end upon a judgement as to whether or not a combination of factors, each of which can be traced back to the past, are sufficient to constitute a new epoch. So, for example, Rantanen recognizes, correctly, that international news agencies date back to the nineteenth century, but still argues that the current epoch is a new and different one that is properly called globalization (Rantanen, 2003).

In part, the answer as to the validity of this proposition can only be established after we have reviewed the other aspects of the problem. Certainly, the present period will be marked by important features that are new and different from those prevailing fifty or one hundred years ago. Whatever we call the society we inhabit, it is clearly one in which rapid social change is a central characteristic. The globalization paradigm, however, is claiming not simply that there have been social changes, but that they are of such a nature, and are combined in such a way, as to render the contemporary world radically different from earlier periods. Whether this is the case depends upon two conditions: first, if all, or most, of the constitutive elements of the globalization paradigm are valid, then the proposition that we are living in a new epoch has at least the possibility of being true; secondly, whether or not these elements are combined in a new and radically different way. The applicability of the first of these conditions we can only determine after we have examined the discrete validity of each of the elements of the globalization paradigm. If we find that all, or most, of the elements in the paradigm are supported by the available evidence, then it is possible that the second condition might be valid, and we would need to reach a judgement about that. If the available evidence contradicts all, or most, of the elements of the paradigm, then of course the second condition would not apply.

On the other hand, we can certainly note at this stage in our investigation that many of claims made about the novelty and uniqueness of the global epoch have been made about the nature of social relations in earlier times. After all, writers not normally associated with contemporary cultural theory were writing about how contemporary industrial production operated on a global scale, taking raw material from the most inaccessible and distant sources, as well as selling its products right around the world, and how intellectual life was tending towards detachment from particular national states, more than 150 years ago: 'Modern industry has established the world market ... All old-established national industries have been destroyed or are daily being destroyed ... In the place of the old local and national seclusion and self-sufficiency, we have intercourse in every direction, universal interdependence of nations. And as in material, so also in intellectual production. The intellectual creations of individual nations become common property'. (Marx and Engels, 1848/1976: 476–88). We can say with some confidence that the evidence of global interconnectedness is not necessarily only to be explained by the globalization paradigm. It might fit better into another theoretical framework which does not depend upon the claim that we are living in a new epoch with different social laws to those that prevailed over most of the last two centuries.

The rejection of reductivism

The second of the propositions common to all strong theories of globalization is the methodological rejection of reductivism, and in particular economic reductivism. There are two slightly different ways in which this argument is advanced. The first, put forward by writers like Beck, is the unqualified claim that globalization demonstrates 'various autonomous logics [that] cannot be reduced or collapsed into one another' (2000: 11). The second, put forward by writers like Appadurai, states that 'the complexity of the current global economy has to do with certain disjunctures between economy, culture and politics which we have barely begun to theorize' (Appadurai, 1990: 296). The first approach leaves open the issue of whether reductivist explanations of social phenomena, while inadequate for the present might be appropriate for earlier phases of human history. In the second approach, the key word is 'current'. Its use suggests that in earlier epochs there was indeed some degree of conjuncture 'between economy, culture and politics' that was adequately theorized by older traditions of thought. The tradition towards which Appadurai points is that of Marxist-inspired theories of imperialism, which did indeed try to relate economy, society and politics very closely together, and there can be no doubt that in the field of media it is precisely this school that is being criticized by the theorists of globalization.

The approach adopted by Beck and others raises general issues about explanation in the human and social sciences that we cannot expect to resolve here. There is a long-standing and bitter debate about determination in social life, and economic determination in particular, that has been completely inconclusive for well over a century: in an earlier chapter, we briefly noted Weber's contribution, for example. The second approach, advanced by Appadurai, is making a more modest claim that it is the distinctive feature of global society that these linkages are non-existent, and we can approach an answer to that claim using much more modest intellectual resources. The claim of a disjuncture between the media, and general cultural activity, and economic and political life can certainly be tested.

In the 1970s and 1980s, the primary site for the discussion of global communication issues was, as we have seen, the United Nations Educational, Social and Cultural Organisation (UNESCO). As its title suggested, this was a body that considered the media primarily from educational, social and cultural aspects. True, its analyses did pay attention to the economic underpinnings of cultural production, and some of its prescriptions had definite financial implications, but the main focus of its activity was around specifically cultural questions. It was concerned with cultural imperialism, not economic imperialism, with national cultures not national economies. Those issues were recognized as important, but they were argued out in other arenas.

Since the collapse of the movement for a New World Information and Communication Order in the mid 1980s, the debate has shifted away from UNESCO. It has found a new site in the World Trade Organisation. As its title in turn suggests, this is a body that is first and foremost concerned with economic matters. There is indeed a struggle inside the WTO (and its forerunner organization the GATT) over cultural production, but it is over how far this can be incorporated into the general rules governing the trade in material and intellectual property. There is a continuing battle inside the WTO over the 'cultural exception', which rests upon a concession in the 1947 treaty that established the GATT (WTO, 1998). The evidence suggests that it is a battle which it seems is being won by those who wish to see trade in television programmes, films, music and so on treated as an economic matter, just like cars and petrochemicals and aircraft (Hollifield, 2004: 89–90). The evidence from the world of the international regulation of trade is thus very far from supporting the notion of a disjuncture between culture and economics. Quite the reverse; cultural activities are being ever more subordinated to the logic of economics.

If we take the case of the USA, even the briefest account of the activities of the Motion Picture Association of America would demonstrate that there is a very clear relationship between politics, economics and culture. For example, in February 2004 the US and Australian governments signed a

Free Trade Agreement, and the MPAA issued a press statement that said in part: 'Ambassador Zoellick is to be commended for securing a first-rate Agreement that provides full protection for the American films and TV programs' (MPAA, February 9 2004). Such examples are, of course, far from rare: in the course of 2003 the MPAA applauded Free Trade Agreements with Singapore, Honduras, El Salvador, Guatemala and Nicaragua (the last four acting together as the Central American Free Trade Association), and Chile (MPAA, 2000–2003). A mass of evidence points to the fact that the self-proclaimed 'little State Department' of the US motion picture and television industry remains as much the embodiment of the very close inter-relationship between economics, politics and culture as ever it was (Wasko, 2003: 211–12). There is no sign whatsoever a qualitative break that would render the current epoch, as Appadurai has it, 'strikingly new' (1996: 27).

The other way of responding to the claim that the world is now too complicated for us to attempt to explain it through a single lens, is to ask whether it is possible to say that one dimension of 'globalization' is the condition for the others. This view commands strong support. It is quite reasonable to say that the development of a global economic order, and in particular the spectacular growth of global financial markets, is the prime factor underlying the other dimensions of the contemporary world (Soros, 2002). If this is the case, then it hardly seems that these phenomena constitute the mark of some radically new social order, since one can make out a strong case for the economic order of preceding epochs as the condition for their other characteristics.

It therefore seems that the claim that the interrelationship between the levels of social life is different and much more disaggregated in the present epoch, is very far from self-evident. It is quite possible to cite evidence, particularly in the field of cultural life, that strongly suggests that economic and political factors are at least as important as ever they were, and that the condition for the global circulation of images and other cultural artefacts is the existence of a strong global market. Indeed, we might argue that, a priori, this dependence of cultural upon economic factors has accelerated in the present epoch because of the increasing incorporation of areas of human life directly into the world market. So, for example, one could argue that television broadcasting in India, which 20 years ago was more or less the monopoly of government controlled organizations, notably Doordarshan, and reflected political and cultural priorities rather than simply economic ones, has become much more directly related to the market as a result of the development of satellite television (Page and Crawley, 2001). A similar case can be made out for the broadcasting organizations of the former communist countries of central and Eastern Europe, not to mention China. These were, for a long period, relatively isolated from directly economic factors but have over the last twenty years been increasingly integrated in to the world market and responsive to many of the same pressures as operate on broadcasters in the west (Sparks, 1998a; Zhao, 1998). This process is not unique to the developing world. The BBC has, unquestionably and self-consciously, become much more concerned with revenue generating activities (programme sales, advertising supported services outside the UK, sales of products, etc.) than it was 25 years ago. In the case of television, the overwhelming weight of evidence is that broadcasters, once driven by a complex of political, cultural and economic factors, are increasingly subordinated to the economic logic of the market.

In the case of the press, the evidence is necessarily more problematic, since there is little international record of publishers with the same position and resources as the state and public broadcasters cited above. There is, however, certainly a belief amongst journalists, particularly in the USA, that the decline of family ownership and the rise of large scale chains means the subordination of the news agenda to the needs of commerce. Whatever the truth of that opinion, there is certainly no body of opinion expressing the view that newspapers today are less driven by market considerations than in the past.

It remains a question for general social enquiry as to the extent to which there is some degree of interaction between different kinds of human activity, but it is clear that the claim of the lack of relationship between the political, the economic and the cultural is every bit as unsustainable, and perhaps more so, as it was in earlier epochs. The evidence from the media is simple, clear and conclusive: economics is more and more the driver of media organizations.

Theory and practice

The sharp disjuncture between theories of globalization and the earlier paradigms with respect to the kinds of social action that might flow is much less problematic. There is indeed nothing in the theories we have examined that suggests particular forms of social and political action in the same way that the developmental and the imperialism paradigms led to forms of action. That is not to say that key theorists of globalization have not played a role in social and political life. On the contrary, some of them have been very active as advisors to governments, as ideologists for political parties, and as radical opponents of the process of globalization in the World Social Forum and similar movements.

The predominant form of this activism has varied from the gloomy acceptance of the market to outright enthusiasm, and while the degree of normative commitment does not follow directly from theories of globalization, the prevalence of this view certainly does. The recognition of the transformative power of the market, and the fact of its global reach, hardly constitute novel theoretical insights for globalization. The reason why these are now seen as unstoppable and uncontrollable forces for most of the people who think about globalization is that the collapse of the autarchic model of national development and the concomitant strengthening of the forces of the global market made very problematic all state-based theories of social amelioration. While this is obviously true of the Stalinist model of 'socialism in one country', it is also true of the Keynesian remedies adopted by many moderate socialists. Since both of the major state-based strategies for controlling the market appear to be in crisis, there seems to be no option but to, at the very least, accept it as an inevitable aspect of human life. Whether one welcomes this or merely tolerates it is not really relevant since there is no viable alternative.

There have been three ways that this conclusion has been resisted. The first, most notably represented by Paul Hirst, was to demonstrate that the process of globalization was and is much overstated by its theorists, and that therefore there remains at least some room for the traditional reformist programme of managing capitalism. The second, strongly present in some anti-globalization theorists around the World Social Forum, is to accept the existence and growth of the global market, but to condemn it and to seek to return to an earlier state of human development, in which there was more scope for the conscious, local, control of the economy. The third alternative, again strongly present in the World Social Forum, and often giving itself the relatively clumsy title of 'alter-globalization', accepts the existence of the global market, shares the condemnation of its effects, but argues that it provides the basis for a different, more humane form of globalization in which the driving force would be human needs.

All of these viewpoints can be derived from within the globalization paradigm, but none of them seem really to follow from it in the same direct sense as does, for example, the stress upon local ownership of development projects in some of the later versions of the development paradigm. There is a much greater disjuncture between the conclusions drawn from analysis and the normative stance which the theory enjoins. From the narrowly academic point of view, this may seem a strength of the globalization paradigm, but however that may be it is certainly a distinctive element of the approach.

How central are the media to contemporary life?

The problem of stress upon the central nature of the mass media to globalization is much more difficult to resolve. If we take this to mean that the media industry or media products are much more economically important in the current epoch than the production of physical commodities, then the case cannot really be sustained. While the global media corporations are very

Company	Turnover or Gross Income (USD millions)	Total Assets (USD millions)	Number of Employees
News Corporation	23,079	52,270	33,800
Viacom	24,606	89,754	122,770
Time Warner Inc	40,961	115,450	89,300
Sony Corporation	62,298	76,611	168,000
Boeing Company	54,069	52,342	166,000
General Motors	186,763	370,782	350,000
Royal Dutch Shell	179,431	152,691	110,000

Source: FT.com 2004

Figure 8.1   Comparative Scale of Companies in Different Sectors in 2002

large indeed, with turnovers of millions of dollars and thousands, sometimes hundreds of thousands, of employees, they are not exceptionally large by the standards of contemporary capitalism. Figure 8.1 compares three large media corporations with three large non-media corporations, and one corporation that spans both media and non-media. The three non-media companies were taken as representative of autos, aviation and petrochemicals, which are frequently cited as the key industrial sectors of the 'Fordist' phase of capitalism that dominated the first three quarters of the last century. As can clearly be seen, the media companies have revenues, assets and staff that are in the same order of magnitude as the 'old economy', but they are in fact rather smaller by most of these measures. In the case of Sony, its electronics manufacturing activities accounted for 61 per cent of revenues in the year to March 2003. Games (12 per cent), Music (7 per cent) and Pictures (11 per cent) were the other major sectors.

A second sense might be that media corporations are more global in their production and distribution than are those companies concerned with manufacturing material products, but this proposition is self-evidently not true. We may illustrate this by considering the same comparison between the media industries and the old industries we looked at above. The automobile designed by a company headquartered in Nagoya or Stuttgart is likely to travel around the world with only minor alterations, and perhaps be produced in more or less the same version in several different countries.

The airliner produced in Seattle or Toulouse will be more or less identical whatever the flag of the carrier that is painted on its hull. Petrochemical companies, notoriously, operate around the world extracting, refining and selling products everywhere, with only fairly minor alterations. The scale of operations of these classically Fordist corporations is highly globalized, and their products display a very high degree of uniformity in all markets.

In the case of cultural products, some (major Hollywood movies and TV dramas) can be sold in many countries with few modifications, while others (many magazines) can be produced in different versions to the same template in many different countries. Some, like the vast majority of newspapers, however, find it difficult to find a market outside of their locality, let alone in another country. There seems little warrant, then for claiming that symbolic goods are in some essential way characteristically global in form and can be contrasted sharply with the products of industrial production. To put it crudely, if one looks out of the window of a hotel in London, New York, Tokyo, Beijing, or almost any other major city, one will see the same vehicles, manufactured by Toyota or Mercedes-Benz. If one goes to the news stand, apart from a few magazines and a couple of financial newspapers, the products on sale will be different, and they will be in different languages. If one turns on the television set, then one can usually find CNN and sometimes the BBC, and on the domestic channels one will often find dubbed foreign series, but the top-rated programmes in most countries will be different and nationally-produced. In the case of the UK: 'most Britons … are obsessed by *Big Brother*, *Pop Idol*, *Eastenders*, Posh and Becks and Premiership football – all reassuringly (or depressingly) parochial' (Legrain, 2002: 8).

The withering away of the state

The fourth major hypothesis about globalization is that there is an erosion of the national state. The truth or otherwise of this proposition depends very much upon the way in which one thinks about 'the state'. If one means by it a body that directs national economic life, then obviously there has been a very significant weakening in the last couple of decades in many countries, both developed and developing. The most dramatic examples are the collapse of the communist regimes in Eastern and Central Europe after 1989, but the phenomenon is very much more widespread than that. Clearly, in some major western countries, most notably the UK, there has been a retreat from state ownership and from many types of state economic intervention. These policies are extremely well known and hardly need describing in detail. The first point to note about what we may term the 'end of the autarchic economic development model' is that it has worked itself out extremely unevenly across the world, both in the developed and the developing world. There is a considerable difference in processes and outcomes between the Britain of Thatcher and Blair and the Russia of Yeltsin and Putin. The differences are even wider if we consider China, Brazil, or the many developing countries in Africa and Latin America that have experienced IMF sponsored structural adjustment programmes. The second point is that they have not been adopted without contestation from within. Thatcher's Britain, for example, was marked by a series of conflicts over steel, coal and the motor industry in which the logic of closer integration into the world market was forced through against bitter opposition from workers who feared (usually rightly) for their future employment. Resistance to the policies that have achieved these ends has not been uniform around the world and probably its successes (for example European and US farmers who have managed to preserve very substantial subsidies and other forms of protection more or less intact) have been fewer than the defeats. The point to note, however, is that this economic retreat by the state has not been a directionless process accepted by everyone but a policy pursued by governments and international organizations. More or less everywhere, the state has been a voluntary participant in the shedding of its powers.

Given that this process has indeed taken place, the question is: does it obligate, in Bauman's words, a recognition that 'the military, economic and cultural self-sufficiency of the state – any state – ceased to be a viable prospect'? (1998: 64). This statement implies not only a loss of the power to determine economic policy but the collapse of a much wider range of powers as well. In this form, it is hard to see how it is not contradicted by the most obvious evidence. It is difficult to see how one might argue that 'the military … self-sufficiency' of the USA has 'ceased to be a viable prospect'. The very least we can say is that while there may have been a 'retreat of the state', the US state has retained considerable independent power across a wide spectrum of policies (Strange, 1996). After September 11 2001, this view has commanded increasing support. Price, for example, writes that he rejects the 'denial of national power and the depreciation of the state's capacity to make and enforce laws' (Price, 2002: 227). More generally, an understanding of the nature and meaning of the process leads us to a clearer understanding of the nature of the state of its role in the current epoch.

In the first place, the global market, no matter how free and how powerful, is not a self-regulating entity. On the contrary, the global market requires a set of laws and regulations that ensure its smooth functioning every bit as much as do other markets. The international organizations that might provide this regulation remain relatively weak and depend upon the continued existence of the system of nation states (Shaw, 1994: 178). There is no 'global' state that has the powers that the nation state has long enjoyed (Amin, 1997: 33). In practice, it is the concerted action of powerful states that is essential to the daily functioning even of the harmonious aspects of the market (Gilpin, 2000: 346–7). The enforcement of intellectual property rights is one obvious, and extremely important, contemporary example of how the global market depends for its functioning on the preparedness of states to enforce a common set of laws and regulations. The laws governing intellectual property are guaranteed by international treaties between states. The World Intellectual Property Organisation (WIPO), for example, makes it clear that 'only States can be members of WIPO' (WIPO, 2004). It is the failure of some states strictly to enforce these treaties that threatens the continued viability of corporations (pharmaceuticals, software, Hollywood, etc.) that depend for their profitability on control of such intangible and easily transported property. Within the mass media generally, the preponderant role in the international governance of media lies in the hands of nation states and their dependant inter-governmental organisations (Ó Siochrú and Girard, 2002).

When the world economy does not function quite so harmoniously, then the state as armed power remains an essential guarantor of 'its own' capitalists. As Ajiz Ahmed puts it, 'The first thing to be said about the relation between "globalization" and the nation-state is that the stronger the nation state the more easily the capital of its citizens can travel'. He argues that one major reason that the US has become one of the main international exporters of capital, and that it has come to have a dominant role in the global economy, is that 'the bearers of its capital could rely on the support, including the crucial military support, their nation state could provide them, anywhere in the world' (Ahmad, 1995: 46).

This right to use military force against its external enemies is, and has been at least since Westphalia, one of the main attributes of states. Indeed, in some of the classical texts of political theory, for example Hegel's *Philosophy of Right*, it is the defining characteristic. We do not need to rehearse the frequent wars between states and interventions of powerful states into much weaker ones in any detail: it is transparently obvious that at least some states are very willing to use this attribute of state power on a rather regular basis. It is true that armament expenditure fell during the period after the end of the Cold War, but in recent years it has risen again sharply, most notably in the USA, which today accounts for more than 40 per cent of military spending. The top five military spenders, the USA, Japan, the UK, France and China, account for more than 60 per cent of world military spending. With respect to the classic state function of the ability and preparedness to wage war, there is no evidence that the epoch of globalization has witnessed any decline of the state's powers (SIPRI, 2003).

Generalized to cover both the international and the internal attributes of a state, this stress upon the state as the site of force was famously present in classical social theory: 'Ultimately, one can define the modern state sociologically only in terms of the specific *means* peculiar to it ... namely the use of physical force ... the state is a relation of men dominating men, a relation supported by means of legitimate (i.e. considered to be legitimate) violence' (Weber, 1918/46: 77–8) . If we take this definition seriously, then there is little evidence that the state is declining in its internal functions. One of the clearest indicators of the extent to which a state can claim to exercise sovereign rights over its population is its ability to punish them for breaches of its laws. In this sphere, the state is not on the retreat. In the case of the USA, for example, there were, according to Amnesty International, some 1.7 million people held in jail in 2002 and this number has increased four-fold since 1980 (Amnesty International, 2004). Another, more detailed, estimate, stated that in 2002: 'the total number of prisoners under the jurisdiction of Federal or State adult correctional authorities was 1,440,655 at year end 2002. During the year the States added 30,088 prisoners, and the Federal prison system added 6,535 prisoners. Overall, the Nation's prison population grew 2.6%, which was less than the average annual growth of 3.6% since year end 1995 … Overall, the United States incarcerated 2,166,260 persons at year end 2002' (Harrison and Beck, 2003). The death penalty, that ultimate expression of the state's monopoly of physical force and its power over its denizens, was re-legalized by the Supreme Court in 1976 and has been exercised rather frequently since then.

At the other end of the political spectrum, Amnesty says of the People's Republic of China that 'Hundreds of thousands of people continue to be detained in violation of their fundamental human rights across the country, death sentences and executions continue to be imposed after unfair trials, torture and ill-treatment remain widespread and systemic, and freedom of expression and information continue to be severely curtailed' (Amnesty International, 2003). They state that, according to official figures in the public domain, more than 1,000 people were executed in 2002, and that this number is rising. They cite an unverified source giving the figure as an astonishing and utterly horrifying 15,000 per year.

Quite apart from jailing and slaughtering their denizens, there is little evidence that states are relaxing their surveillance over people and their movements. The aftermath of 9/11 has made it much more difficult to move between countries. Everywhere, immigration controls have been tightened, and new forms of identification, using the most recent technological developments, are being deployed both at the borders and for those already inside.

The rising tide of criminalization that Bauman rightly identified as one of the key factors of the current epoch is evidence of the continuing power and strength of the state, not of its destruction or attenuation (Bauman, 1998). What replaced the social-democratic state was not anarchy but harsh repression.

The withdrawal from attempts at autarchic economic management and the continuation of a strong emphasis on the international and domestic political functions of the state come together in the case of some of the more successful developing economies. If we look at the recent histories of Taiwan, Thailand and South Korea, not to mention the present realities of Malaysia, Singapore and, above all, China, we can see that a continuation of some key economic functions, notably the maintenance of a fixed exchange rate and controls over capital allocation and movement, and a high level of internal repression, directed particularly against attempts at independent labour organization, are common factors in these examples of rapid economic development. The point that Ahmad makes with regard to India surely applies much more widely to contemporary states: '... the new national bourgeoisies, like global capital itself, want a weak nation state in relation to capital and strong one in relation to labour' (Ahmad, 1995: 47).

If we examine the evidence from the narrower field of mass communication, we find that many of the claims for the attenuation of the state machine are based on a mistaken premise. As we saw with the critique of the media imperialism paradigm, the most common argument about the weakening of the powers of the state is advanced with regard to satellite broadcasting. This begins from the correct premise that the laws of physics and the realities of political geography do not coincide and that it is therefore possible to receive signals uplinked from one state within the boundaries of another. The state, it is therefore argued, has lost the ability to control the media environment within its borders.

The first thing to note about this argument is that cross-border flows of media artefacts have long been a feature of the mass media, from the smuggling of books promoting the wrong flavour of Christianity in the early modern period, through Radio Luxembourg and Radio Normandy in the days of radio, not to mention the BBC World Service, Voice of America and so on. In Europe in the age of terrestrial television, signals were frequently available in neighbouring countries: the Netherlands and Belgium relayed British TV programmes on cable systems long before the first satellite services were available, and East German television was constructed in conscious opposition to the freely-available programming of its western terrestrial rivals.

There is no doubt that the development of satellite television made it simpler to launch services that had the intention of reaching extra-territorial audiences. There are some extremely well-known examples of how this was done: the introduction of commercial television in Norway and Sweden, for example, was driven by satellite broadcasters uplinking from the more liberal commercial environment of the UK. Hong Kong is the base for the Murdoch-owned Star satellite signals that are directed at India and China (Page and Crawley, 2001). There is no doubt that these services have had a major effect upon broadcasting in the countries towards which they were directed.

It is quite another thing, however, to say that these notable successes represented evidence of any fundamental weakening of the state's powers with regard to broadcasting. They were cases in which the state did not utilize the full resources open to it, but the powers are still there. The best-known example of the state system using its powers to control what signals are available within its boundaries is provided by the story of *Med-TV*. This was in origin part of a political project for the construction of an independent Kurdish state, and was inspired by Turkish Kurds who, in the 1980s and 1990s, were engaged in a very bitter military struggle for national independence against the state within whose borders they live. This state, by constitutional edict, prevented broadcasting in any language other than Turkish. *Med-TV* programmes were produced in a number of European countries, notably Belgium, and the service was uplinked out of the UK under a licence issued by the British commercial broadcasting regulator, the Independent Television Commission (ITC). The content of *Med-TV* angered the Turkish state, which saw it as aiding and comforting those who wanted an independent Kurdish state, notably the Kurdish Workers' Party (PKK) that was the backbone of the armed struggle. The Turkish government accordingly put pressure on the ITC and the British Government, and eventually the ITC withdrew *Med-TV's* licence to broadcast and forced it to close down. The main historian of the station wrote: 'Although the Kurds of Turkey made extensive use of both the diaspora and the cracks or openings in the interstate world order ... the knots that bind the state to territory cannot be untied by communication technologies' (Hasanpour, 2003: 86–7). When faced, not with a minor issue of the balance between different kinds of cultural production, but with a challenge to what it perceived as its central interests, the state retained the resources to impose its will. A successor broadcaster, *Medya-TV*, was eventually licensed under French law and continues to broadcast. It abandoned the struggle for national independence and concentrated instead on cultural rights (Hasanpour 2003, 87).

This is a dramatic instance of the continued reality of state power, but there are numerous other instances we can cite, not all of them involving highly-charged political issues. The differences between obscenity regulations in the UK and some of its EU partners has prompted a number of entrepreneurs to try to establish pornographic subscription services, uplinked from more libertarian countries but aimed at the UK market. The British government has been able to defeat all of these efforts relatively easily through its use of the provisions of domestic British law, which make it possible for the relevant minister (the Secretary of State for Culture, Media and Sport) to 'proscribe' particular satellite services. When this provision is invoked, it becomes an offence to advertise with a service, to advertise the service, to sell decoding equipment, or to collect subscriptions. These measures make it impossible to run a profitable service, and in each case the company trying to run it was forced out of the business (ITC, n.d.).

There are two general lessons to be drawn from the actions of the ITC in these two sorts of cases. The first is that, although the technology of satellite broadcasting makes it possible to uplink from one country and downlink to another, there is no point on the surface of the earth that is outside the legal remit of one jurisdiction or another. The state within which the uplinking takes place retains effective control over the activities of the service in question. If it decides that it is not in its interest to permit such a service, and that it wishes to impose certain conditions upon the broadcasters, or intervene in any other way with the station, it retains the power, and the right, to do so, every bit as much as it does with the terrestrial services it has long regulated. These powers the state can exercise with impunity whether for economic or political motives.

The second lesson concerns economic issues alone. Commercial broadcasters, whether terrestrial, cable, or satellite, exist to make money, and if they fail to do so they will eventually be driven out of business. There are two ways in which it is possible to raise revenues: advertising and subscription. Both of these involve physical organizations and people who must be located within definite countries and subject to the legal codes of those countries. In order to run an advertising-funded service, you need to sell airtime and to collect revenues. These activities require offices, staff, bank accounts and so on. In order to run a subscription based service, you need to sell and renew subscriptions, distribute decoding devices, advertise your services, collect revenues, and so on. These activities require offices, staff, bank accounts and so on. Both of these revenue raising strategies are thus predicated upon the broadcaster having an organization that can work legally and uninterrupted within the target country, and can transfer funds, etc., in exactly the same way as any other business. It is thus every bit as much subject to the legal environment of the country within which its audience is located as is a terrestrial broadcaster.

The notorious example of these realities is provided by the activities of News Corporation in its efforts to enter the Chinese market. In order to do so, News Corporation has not only abided by Chinese law, but has made a number of important compromises with the sensibilities of the leadership of the Chinese Communist Party. The most notable examples were the decision to drop the BBC's world news from Star TV because its reporting of China was judged too critical by Beijing (Page and Crawley, 2001: 86). Another was the refusal of Random House, owned by News Corporation, to honour its contract with the last British governor of Hong Kong, Christopher Patten, because his projected volume was too critical of the Chinese leadership (Gleick, 1998). Liu Chang Le, the main shareholder, Chairman and CEO of Phoenix TV and News Corporation's main ally inside China, expanded these notorious tactical concessions into a strategic principle as the first point in his advice for media companies wishing to succeed in the Chinese markets:

> Foreign media companies need to develop a dialogue with the bureaucratic agencies
> that regulate the media and entertainment market. The purpose of this dialogue is on the
> one hand to enable the foreign company to understand the Chinese environment more
> clearly, and at the same time convince the Chinese side that foreign media organizations
> are not seeking to destabilize China, sow the seeds of social or political trouble, or
> weaken China's sense of cultural identity' (Liu, 2002: 4).

While China is an extreme case, the general condition for a commercial operator to work successfully in a particular territory is that they reach, at the very least, an agreement with the relevant political authorities. This applies whether what they are providing are terrestrial, cable or satellite delivered services.

The only broadcasters for whom these kinds of harsh realities do not apply are non-commercial services that enjoy subsidy from some interested party. These come in most cases from states that wish to pursue foreign policy agendas in a particular region and thus pay for more or less aggressive promotional broadcasting to be directed to the relevant audiences. Such state sponsored broadcasters are, if anything, on the increase, particularly in the Middle East. Apart from well established state-funded operations like the BBC World Service there are new ventures in this field like *Al Hurra*, which launched on February 14 2004. It is 'financed by the American people through the US Congress' (Al Hurra, 2004). This station joins many other state-funded broadcasters in the Middle East space, most notably *Al Jazeera*, which is dependent upon the goodwill and finance of the Qatari ruling family (Sakr, 2001).

The fact is that neither politically nor commercially are satellite broadcasters magically free of the constraints that are experienced by their terrestrial cousins. The belief that satellite broadcasting represents some form of 'extraterritoriality' that transcends the limits of the state system is simply false.

The nature of the local

If the evidence suggests that the state is not experiencing erosion 'from above' in any decisive way, a similar picture can be built up about the 'local'. It is true that there has been a crisis of the 'nation state', particularly in Europe, where there have been a number of major upheavals. Some states (notably the USSR, Czechoslovakia, Yugoslavia) have fragmented entirely. Others have been obliged to restructure and to offer national minorities a greater degree of autonomy (notably Spain and the UK). But what has replaced these failed states has been a series of new states, each with all of the trappings of the fully-fledged 'Westphalian State', and the drive for autonomy elsewhere (Scotland and the Basque Country for example) at the very least has an influential wing that wants independence and full statehood. The fit between 'nation' and 'state' has certainly proved an enduringly problematic one, but there is no evidence that it is leading to the erosion of the state as such, rather than to the weakening of particular states that are unable to legitimize themselves with a significant section of the population that identifies itself as a member of a different nationality. This, of course, is not a new development: attempting to align state borders with national aspirations was a major theme in nineteenth and early twentieth century international politics.

There are indeed 'local' media, in both of the senses that are in play in this debate, but their independence from the national state, and their links to global concerns, are much more contentious. A good example is the press, which in many countries has a primarily local circulation. The vast majority of the 1,476 daily newspapers in the USA in 2000 were local in circulation. The 'national' press is at most three or four titles (*USA Today, Wall Street Journal, New York Times*, possibly the *Washington Post*), all of which have become national within the last twenty years or so (World Association of Newspapers, 2001: 224–5). Even in the relatively unusual British case, in which daily newspaper circulation is dominated by national titles, in 2001 there were 94 regional and local dailies compared with 10 national papers (World Association of Newspapers, 2001: 220–1). A similar strength can be observed in developing markets: Brazil had five 'national' dailies as against 465 regional dailies; China claimed 70 national dailies as against 134 regional and 612 local dailies; India had 398 dailies, and of the top ten titles by circulation only *Times of India* and *The Hindu* could properly claim to be 'national' titles (World Association of Newspapers, 2001: 55, 68, 117). The local strength of newspapers is clearly evident both in the declining markets of the developed world and in the growing markets of the developing world.

The reasons for this local strength are well-known and obvious. The local press is heavily dependent upon advertising, and within that upon classified advertising, particularly for jobs, homes and cars. These are all primarily local in scope: it makes little sense to advertise the majority of homes in Washington State in Washington DC. The same is true for a great deal of the news that attracts an audience for the advertisers: a routine traffic accident in Washington DC is of little interest in Washington State. Finally, a physical newspaper appearing on a daily basis is difficult to transport long distance in bulk within its period of currency: it may make sense to transport a few copies of the *Washington Post* to Seattle by air every day, but it makes no sense to fly half a million copies across the continent to confront the *Seattle-Times* and *Post-Intelligencer* head on. Of course, satellite transmission and remote printing are altering this last factor, making physical distribution in a vast country like the USA much less of an insoluble problem. So *USA Today*, the *Wall Street Journal* and the *New York Times* are all significantly minor presences in the Seattle-Tacoma Designated Market Area (Seattle Times Company, 2003). These developments are, however, strengthening the national at the expense of the local, which is exactly contrary to the predictions of the globalization paradigm.

The social and economic functions of the local press are, not surprisingly, enduringly local. They are not, however, recent developments that represent a response to a new epoch of globalization. On the contrary, they are the same functions that were present at the birth of the modern newspaper 150 years or more ago. In economics, journalistic content, and circulation, the local press shows few marks of any recent transformation due to the impact of globalization. We might also note that in the case of India, the fastest-growing press over the last thirty years has been the necessarily local 'vernacular language' press, which is coming to replace the more 'global' English language press as the dominant form (Jeffrey, 2000).

The direction of development of this local press has been, over a very long time, towards the development of national chains, again for very well understood economic reasons. There is very little evidence of any direct relationship between local newspapers and global media. To the extent that there has been international ownership, this has tended to concentrate upon national chains, and sometimes upon national titles, or at least titles set in metropolitan areas. In the case of the newspaper press, then, the evidence appears directly to contradict the claim that the local is eroding the national. If anything, in the developed countries, the reverse is the case, with the readership of local newspapers shrinking faster than that of national titles.

Broadcasting presents a more complex case. Here, as again is well-known, the economic logic points towards chain ownership of stations and the construction of networks with the widest possible audience. Very often, this has been prevented by regulations laid down by the national state, as in the USA, where the FCC enforces a separation between the networks and the majority of local stations. Where this legally-enforced restriction upon the formation of chains has been lifted, the process of consolidation has been rapid and irresistible. In the UK, up until the 1990 Broadcasting Act, there was an enforced regionalization of commercial broadcasting, with 15 regional franchises each with specific local obligations. The Act began a process of relaxing restrictions on cross-ownership, which by the end of 2003, with the merger of Granada and Carlton, resulted in the emergence of a single dominant player in this market. The only example of a developed television market in which there was no effective regulation designed to enforce regionalization is that of Italy in the 1970s and 1980s. While this did indeed begin with a vast proliferation of local, indeed often micro-local stations, economic logic very quickly concentrated commercial broadcasting into the hands of Silvio Berlusconi. Even when regulation leads to the enforced survival of regional or local stations, commercial broadcasters tend to try to ensure that their commitment to regional programmes is as minimal as possible (Kleinsteuber and Thomass, 1995: 76).

In fact, rather than arising from the inner logic of the process of 'glocalization', the drive towards regional or local television has always been strongly political in nature and has focused on residual conflicts in the state system. If the intention of the modern state was to produce a uniform population, homogenous in language, culture, religion, ideology, ethnicity, and so on, more or less everywhere it failed. Contemporary states remain divided, sometimes bitterly, along all of these lines. Of Europe, de Moragas Spà and Garitaonandia remark that 'The regions of Europe are not the result of mere geographical or administrative divisions, but in many cases are the result of long historical processes, the legacy of feudal structures, of Romanization, or of even earlier times, which have created a profound and important diversity of culture and language in the continent' (1995: 5). These fissures find reflection in political struggles over broadcasting.

Such disputes led to a series of attempts to construct regional broadcasting systems that are responsive to these intra-state differences, particularly those based upon linguistic differences. From our point of view, what is interesting about these attempts is that they are most successful when based not upon the sorts of 'localities' posited by theorists like Ohmae that are the product of processes specific to the new epoch of globalization but upon differences that date from the pre-modern past (Garitaonandía, 1993: 290; Griffiths, 1993; Canova-Lamarque et al., 1995). What is more, they are very often linked with political aspirations that tend towards statehood for the social group (usually a nationality) in question. Where the attempt is made to construct regional or local broadcasters on patterns of locality that are not strongly marked in such traditional social realities they tend to find it hard to resist the pressures towards joining together on a national basis to achieve economies of scope and scale (Jauert and Prehn, 1997).

If the 'old' physical locality has proved an unresponsive ground for new forms of media, the 'new' localities that were so stridently proclaimed by Hall appear to offer more supportive evidence. There clearly are, in both the press and broadcasting, many examples of media directed towards such new localisms. Any of the large cities of the developed world, which have sucked in labour from across the globe, is full of newspapers, radio stations, cable channels and so on that cater to the cultural needs of these new localities. Very often, they define themselves in sharp opposition, through language and content, to the kinds of media available to the population as a whole. While the technologies involved in many of these channels are undoubtedly new, the issue is whether 'diasporic' media constitute a new phenomenon that is indicative of a qualitative change in the nature of social relations.

The evidence for novelty of mass migration is much less than conclusive, and on a global scale its character is different from that which is commonly supposed. The great centres of industrial production were sucking in workers from elsewhere more than two centuries ago, and while initially many of these people were from the surrounding countryside, from very early on the range of migration was international in scope. The majority of the current population of the USA is descended from Europeans who migrated across the Atlantic during the last few hundred years. Another substantial section is made up of the descendants of people forcibly traded across the Atlantic in the early modern epoch. In the UK, London, Manchester and Birmingham began to receive huge numbers of Irish and Jewish workers long before the *Empire Windrush* docked in Britain on June 22 1948, and there was a substantial black population in the UK from well before that date.

We can further ask how 'new' these new kinds of media are in the social, as opposed to the technical, sense. There were Irish and Jewish newspapers in nineteenth-century London, and when Robert Park examined the immigrant press in the USA at the end of the First World War he found that there were more than 2000 newspapers catering to the various language groups involved (Park, 1922). Most of these papers, of course, lost their readers and closed down in the years that followed. Immigrants, or at least their children, became Americans, and they mostly read the same newspapers as anyone else. It may be the case that the migrations of the current epoch are different in kind, and the diasporic media that they have produced will prove more enduring, but we cannot accept such an assertion without at least some supporting evidence. In its absence, it seems reasonable to see the diasporic media of today as important and interesting contemporary examples of a phenomenon that has been present in the history of migration and the media at least since the nineteenth century.

Considered overall, the argument for the weakening of the system of states 'from above' by international forces and 'from below' by their rise of different classes of local concern seems unconvincing. While it correctly identifies the fact that there is no longer any realistic prospect of autarchic national development, and demonstrates how the contemporary state is obliged to defer to the interests of capital, it mistakenly believes this represents an undermining of the state. With respect to its classical role as an instrument of force, both externally and internally, there is little sign that the state is at all threatened. On the contrary, by many measures, it is a more formidable force than ever it was before. In the mass media, the belief that satellite television presents a crisis to state authority is not borne out by the evidence. The stress upon the 'local' is even less convincing. While it is true that social life, and in particular large sections of the mass media, are local in the traditional sense, there is no evidence that this is leading to a weakening of the state. On the contrary, the logic of the media business has driven local outlets like newspapers and broadcasting stations into national chains. There is singularly little evidence that there is any direct link between global media business and local media. In the case of the new sense of the term local, the theorists of globalization have indeed identified an important trend in contemporary social life, but they have both misconstrued its dynamic and overstated its novelty. In reality, the evidence is that the modern diasporas are a relatively small part of a huge transformation of the working population that involves a shift from rural to urban, and which has been going on for some time now. The cultural phenomena that are stressed in theories of globalization in fact have a long history and it is not at all apparent that the current manifestations will have a different trajectory from their predecessors. The evidence from this strand of the globalization paradigm thus does not seem to support the view that we are living in a radically new epoch with a different social dynamic from that of preceding periods.

A world without a centre?

The sixth major claim made about the original character of globalization is that, unlike earlier epochs, the world is now without a centre. On the face of it, this is a quite incredible claim. The existence of competing centres of political and economic power, and competing forms of culture, was a commonplace in the twentieth century. The first half of the last century was dominated by a struggle principally between the incumbent British Empire and the emergent German Empire. The second half of the century, up to 1990, was dominated by the struggle principally between the dominant US and emergent Russians. Within those overall conflicts, there were numerous sub-conflicts, for example between Japan and Russia, and later between Japan and China, or between the European colonial empires and national liberation movements around the world. There was no single state that could claim to be the dominant economic and military power in the same way as Britain could in the preceding century.

If anything, it looks as though the period after the 1990s has been dominated by a single world superpower, the USA, which has faced no serious challenge to its will. Since the end of the 1980s, the USSR and its empire have collapsed and Japan has entered a prolonged period of stagnation that has meant that its once perceived challenge to the USA is no longer convincing. China and India are, of course, developing rapidly and changing the balances of power, but their assumption of equal status with the USA is still decades away. The US, as we saw above, dominates world arms spending, and as a consequence has by far the most fearsome military machine in the world. At this level, there is no other state that could possibly stand up to it, in the way that the USSR managed to do, at ruinous cost, for 45 years after 1945.

Country	GDP in Millions of US$
China	1,237,145
Eurozone+UK+Sweden+ Denmark	8,562,793
India	515,012
Japan	3,978,782
USA	10,415,820

Source: World Bank 2004

Figure 8.2   Comparison of the Scale of Major Economies 2002

But in 1945, as we saw in Chapter 1, military superiority rested very firmly upon crushing economic superiority. Today, the USA is still, by some way, the world's largest economy but, as Figure 8.2 shows, it is no longer enormously greater than any potential competitor, even allowing for the fact that exchange rate issues distort such comparisons. China, and still more India, both of which are routinely discussed as long term potential geopolitical competitors with the USA, remain far distant in terms of the scale of their economies although they have vast populations and thus, potentially, vast internal markets. Already, however, Japan and particularly Europe represent substantial competitors in terms of the scale of their economies. The overwhelming military preponderance of the USA is thus seriously out of step with its economic position.

It is impossible to see the world simply in terms of single, unipolar, US domination, but at the same time it is necessary to recognize the continued economic strength of the USA, as well as its enormous military and political strengths. Even with that important proviso, however, it is wrong to claim that the world is therefore completely without any dominant centre. Even allowing for the real conflicts that exist between the handful of large economies, which are in fact relatively modest by historical standards, it remains the case that what we might term the 'geopolitical west' has an immense superiority over any other grouping, either real or potential. It is correct to claim that the world has no single centre, but power in all its forms remains centred in the high-income countries. The various dimensions of power are not, it is true, mapped directly one upon the other. They exist in different mixes in different countries, but that group of countries is relatively small, and none of them is without a combination of political, military and economic power. Even Japan, rejoicing in a pacifist constitution dictated by the USA, has quite substantial military forces: the 'Japan Self Defence Forces' have the third largest military budget in the world, at market exchange rates (SIPRI, 2003).

This sense that power continues to reside in the high income countries, and particularly in the USA, is even more clearly the case if we look at the media industries. Figures 8.3, 8.4. and 8.5 give some figures on the geographical breakdown of the three large, perhaps global, media companies that we examined above. As can be clearly seen, the centre of gravity of each of these countries is very firmly in the developed world. More than that, it is clearly in the USA. Time-Warner, at the time of writing the largest media corporation in the world, obtains 85 per cent of its revenue from the US market, and perhaps 95 per cent from the high income countries. News International, which is often taken as the archetype of the global media corporation, and which has been the company that has been most active in both India and China, 'only' 76.5 per cent of revenue comes

	$A million in 2002			
	USA	UK[1]	Australasia[2]	Total[3]
Sales Revenue	22,194	4,418	2,402	29,014
Assets	48,491	7,918	6,895	56,429
SR/Assets	0.46	0.56	0.35	0.51

Source: News Corporation Form F20 for 2002.
Notes:
1.. UK includes operations conducted in Europe
2.. Australasia comprises Australia, Asia, Fiji, Papua New Guinea and New Zealand
3.. Includes A$8,137 millions of 'unallocated' assets

Figure 8.3   Breakdown of Assets and Sales Revenue for News Corporation 2002

	USA	International	Total
Turnover by market (US$m)	20,576.5	4,029.2	24,605.7
%	84%	16%	100%
Profit before tax by market (US$m)	3,372.7	361.5	3,734.2
%	90%	10%	100%
Total assets (US$m)	79,869.2	2,718.2	82,587.4
%	97%	3%	100%

Source: FT.com

Figure 8.4   Breakdown of Assets, Profits and Sales Revenue for Viacom 2002

Region	US$m	Rounded %
UK	1,173	3
Germany	588	1.5
France	368	1
European 'Big Three'	2129	5.5
USA	32,676	85
Canada	394	1
North America	33,070	86
Japan	653	1.7
Rest of the World	2,382	6.2
Total	38,234	100

Source: FT.com 2004.

Figure 8.5   Geographical Analysis of Turnover by Market for Time-Warner

from the US division, and at least 92 per cent comes from high-income countries. Viacom provides a similar picture, with 84 per cent of turnover coming from the USA. If we examine the only case of a 'global' media corporation whose centre of gravity is in a large market outside of the USA, namely Bertelsmann, we find that, in round figures in 2002, 31 per cent of its revenues came from Germany, 35 per cent from the rest of Europe, 28 per cent from the USA, and only 6 per cent from the rest of the world (Bertelsmann, 2002). This concentration upon the US, and upon the developed world, is not markedly lower in the media industries than in other areas of economic activity. To continue our earlier comparison, GM's turnover in 2003 was US$186,763 million of which 74 per cent came from the USA alone. Only 3.5 per cent came from the categories labelled 'Brazil', 'Latin America' and 'Rest of the World.' The remainder was from Europe and Canada (FT.com 2004). Very far from the media representing an avant-garde case of the globalization of capital and of markets, it seems that at least in these cases it is more firmly tied to the developed world, and particularly to its 'home' country than is warranted by the overall distribution of world production.

The balance of evidence suggests that, very far from the world lacking any recognizable centre, as the strong globalization paradigm claims, the USA is politically and militarily more powerful than at any time previously. The economic balance is not so decisive, but here the overwhelming weight of production is in the developed world, while the US economy remains clearly the largest in the world. This general picture of the world is reproduced, if anything even more clearly, in the case of media corporations. There are most certainly media corporations that operate on a global scale, but they are clearly centred in a single 'home' country, usually the USA. While it is not true to identify a single country as the only centre of power, even of media power, it is hard not to agree with Mohammadi and Ahsan when they write '... this information technology and global media system is almost exclusively owned by a set of Western corporations ... none of the corporations in the business and information and news diffusion come from Asia, Africa, South or Central America, or any of the developing countries' (2002: 123).

Multiple production centres

The seventh claim concerning globalization is, in many ways, the most important. It is argued that while there is an increasing flow of images around the world, and that these come from a range of different production centres. There are, instead, distinct regional markets in which intra-country trade is more important than that with the USA. It follows that these programme flows cannot be interpreted as 'Americanization'. On the contrary, they are no longer specific to a single country. Sometimes, indeed, they represent a genuinely 'global' cultural form that is freely available to all.

In response to this line of argument, we need to begin to distinguish between different aspects of the culture industries. Although an enormous amount of cultural production in many countries is today subjected to the logic of capital, and ownership in many aspects of the cultural industries is extremely concentrated, the internal dynamics of different sectors is not necessarily the same. We can illustrate these differences if we compare the film, television broadcasting, and music industries.

Film production is certainly not concentrated in Hollywood, although few would deny that this is an important, if not the most important, centre. It is true that some of the major studios are owned by Japanese companies, but the commercial logic of revenue sources forces them to behave as though they were US companies. There can be no question that the films they produce are primarily aimed at the US market, which as we saw above is vital to the functioning of any large media company. On the back of this huge home market, US movies are sold around the world. It is, however, often claimed that other national cinemas, most notably the Indian cinema, represents a serious challenge to the international dominance of US movies. If indeed there is the development of a genuinely cinematic global culture, one index would indeed presumably be that movies produced in a variety of different countries circulated on equal terms around the world could expect to enjoy equal success with audiences in different countries. The crude numbers of films produced in leading countries suggests a rather more complex picture, as Figure 8.6 demonstrates.

In numerical terms, the Indian film industry is indeed more than a challenger for the USA, and its proportion of world production is growing more rapidly. In 1970, the USA accounted for nearly seven per cent of global production, but in 2000 this had risen to around 18.5 per cent of the total. India, on the other hand, went from just over 11 per cent in 1970 to just over 23 per cent in 2000.

There are many problems with these figures, since they do not rest upon a definition of what might make a 'national' film. This is clear in Figure 8.7,

Country	1970	1980	1990	2000
France	138	189	146	171
Italy	231	163	119	103
Spain	105	118	42	98
UK	97	31	47	90
USA	231	222	477	683
Mexico	--	108	72	29
Canada	46	54	42	55
India	397	739	948	855
China	2	82	134	91
Japan	423	320	239	283
World total	3512	3710	4445	3683

Source: Screen Digest July 2003, 202-203.

Figure 8.6   Feature Films Produced in Selected Countries 1970–2000

Country	Investment in $US million	% of World total
France	813.4	4%
Italy	261.9	1.3%
Spain	304.3	1.5%
UK	851.6	4.2%
USA	14,661.0	72.3%
Canada	133.1	0.7%
Mexico	21.0	0.1%
India	192.0	0.95%
China	50.0	0.25%
Japan	1,292.1	6.4%
World total	20,270.4	

Source: Screen Digest 2003, 204 (figures rounded)

Figure 8.7   Investment in Film Production 2002

where the high total for UK film industry investment includes figures for the production of several Hollywood movies, all or some parts of which were produced in the UK. The figures also vary considerably from year to year. The most recent figures in this series, for 2002, differ considerably in detail, but they do not contradict the general trends. On the basis of these imperfect figures, therefore, it would seem that while the USA is indeed increasing its share of the number of films produced, the rise of challengers like India, and the continuing vitality of other centres like France means that it is less true than before that the industry is dominated today by one country than it was thirty years ago.

While it is true that today, as in the past, many countries produce movies, the amount invested in film production varies enormously from country to country, as Figure 8.7 demonstrates, and here the US has a massive dominance. The average investment in a cinema film in the USA in 2002 was $34 million, while in India, the average was $1.5 million. What this means is that while it is correct that there are flourishing national film industries in many countries (often, like the French, dependent upon state policy for their investment) other than the USA, the global film industry is dominated by Hollywood, which accounts for around 72 per cent of the total investment in new products. The consequence of this is that, although there are certainly many films showing in the world at any one time, the largest audiences, and the largest incomes, are invariably for Hollywood movies: in both 2001 and 2002 the list of 100 top-grossing movies in the world is completely dominated by US products (*Variety*, 2004a, b). We can see the obverse of that domination if we look at the box office share of domestic production in a range of countries that have indigenous film industries. Figure 8.8 demonstrates that while domestic films enjoy a healthy, albeit minority, market in many countries, the US is completely dominated by its own product. If we look at the country of origin of the foreign movies that dominate these markets, then it turns out that they are mostly from the USA. So far as I can determine, in none of the countries in Figure 8.8 were the top foreign movies from anywhere other than the USA (*Variety*, 2004c). There is no two-way street in movie production, and if we took only the film industry as our embodiment of the global dynamics of the culture industries we would be obliged to say that the US is massively dominant.

We obtain a contrasting picture if we look at the music industry. It is very hard to sustain the notion of the complete dominance of the creative impetus of the US, or of the Anglo-Saxon, music companies in this field. It is hard not to agree with Aggrey Brown, when he wrote of the Caribbean that 'the region's international success in music in particular (reggae, socca, calypso), as well as in dance and drama, demonstrate the obvious, namely that no nationality has a monopoly on creative imagination' (Brown, 1995: 43). More generally, the contemporary musical scene welcomes performers from

Country	Box Office Share %
France	34.80
Italy	22.20
Spain	13.60
USA	96.30
Japan	27.00

Source: Screen Digest July 2003, 208.

Figure 8.8   Box Office Share of Domestically Produced Films in 2002

all around the globe, and there is even a category 'world music' that reflects that reality. The reason for this apparent difference with the film industry is the difference in economic scale. Producing music can be done with very few resources indeed. The dominant western form of the professional musician contracted to, or aspiring to be contracted to, a large company is not the only available model. In many parts of the world, including the developed world, a vigorous musical culture is possible without professional musicians, let alone recording companies. The possibility of human creative potential being embodied in artefacts is thus far greater in this field than in the cinema, where even the most modest effort requires substantial resources.

Recording that music, and still more distributing it around the world, are much more expensive businesses than simply producing it. To the extent that any music circulates around the world, its recording, marketing and distribution are subject to a similar logic to that of the cinema. The largest and richest markets, by far, are those of the developed world, and commercial success depends upon selling into those markets. In order to do this, the 'authentic' dimension of music other than that of the dominant western forms undergoes a subtle process of alteration to make it more marketable (Frith, 2000: 309). Thus, despite the diversity of origins, and the very marketability of the differences that it embodies, music from outside the west is taken up and valued only so far as it fits into spaces existing in the developed world: '... the logic of capitalist production has developed such that there are enormous problems of access to the world market for musicians, producers and companies who want to root their work in local experience or language, especially if these are experiences alien to the people who work for the major companies in London, New York and Los Angeles' (Hesmondhalgh, 1998: 179). Thus, in the case of music, while there is much greater diversity in the origins of different musical styles, the logic of the industry pressures towards a standardization and uniformity that results in the domination of the tastes of the developed world every bit as much as is the case in the cinema.

The case of television lies somewhere between these two cases. Although the USA is by far the largest and richest market, and by far the largest producer, it is certainly not the sole producer. There exist many other strong and well-developed broadcasters in other countries. Many of them are state or public broadcasters, like the BBC, NHK, ARD, CCTV and so on. They all pursue a policy of attempting to provide a full range of broadcasting covering most, if not all, of the major popular genres, notably drama and news.

On the other hand, there are many broadcasters whose resources do not permit such an ambitious strategy, and who are forced to import important parts of their programme material. This is the case in smaller developed countries like Ireland, where the size of the revenue base means that, despite strong audiences, the national broadcaster is unable to compete across the range of programming (Corcoran, 2004: 94ff). It is also the case in smaller, less developed countries where the revenue base is similarly restricted. It is even the case in large, rich, developed broadcasting markets like the UK, where the introduction of multi-channel television greatly increased demand for programming without generating a proportionate increase in the available revenues, and the consequence was a great increase in imports.

We can see the effect that this has on the balance of programming by looking at the impact of satellite broadcasting upon the trade in television programmes in the UK. The UK has a strong and well-regarded television industry that has a long record of substantial local production. In the UK, as almost everywhere in the world, audience preferences are for domestic products. For many years up to the 1990s, the UK imported and exported television programmes of roughly equal value (Shew, 1992: 79). In the 1990s, however, the growth of niche channel satellite broadcasting, which is permitted to avoid European Union indigenous content regulations and imports most of its programming, has led to a sharp deterioration in the balance of trade in this sector, which meant a much faster growth in imports than in exports. By 2002, the UK was in deficit on the trade in television programmes to the tune of £553 million (Pollard, 2003: 10).

Overall, then, the evidence from film, music and television is that while there are strong national centres of production outside of the USA, very few if any of them are able to generate sufficient material to satisfy their home market entirely with indigenous products. In the case of television, despite the existence of strong national broadcasters, and known audience preferences for local programming, the proliferation of channels has led to an increase in imports.

Regional markets

Given the existence of the need for programme imports even in large and rich countries, and the existence of multiple production centres, the conditions certainly exist for the kinds of regional markets that are said to constitute an important argument for globalization.

Some of the evidence for the UK balance of trade in television programmes that we mentioned above seems to suggest this. In the years 1985 to 1990, imports from North America fell from 68 per cent to 61 per cent of the total, although they rose in value from £59 million to £129 million. At the same time, imports from the EC rose from 16 per cent to 22 per cent of the total. Other developed countries accounted for shares changing from 9 per cent to 14 per cent. Imports from the developing world fell from about 7 per cent to around 3 per cent of the total (Shew, 1992: 79). This trend, however, did not continue as the full impact of multi-channel broadcasting became apparent. By 2002, imports from the USA accounted for 60 per cent of the total by value. The next large source of programming was the Netherlands, at 9 per cent. The European Union together accounted for 24 per cent and the whole of Europe for 35 per cent of the total. The whole of Asia other than Japan and Israel, Latin America and Africa accounted for just 2 per cent of the total (Pollard, 2003: 10). What this data clearly indicates is that the US was and remains the dominant exporter of television programming to the United Kingdom.

The domination of UK programming imports by products from the USA might be thought to be a function of the fact that the two countries share some social and political dimensions, not to mention a common language, but as Figure 8.9 shows, the percentage is high in all European countries. All of these countries have well-developed national television systems capable of

Market	% from USA
Australia	71
Canada	87
France	72
Germany	87
Italy	66
Japan	83
Netherlands	74
Spain	69

Source: Graham and Associates 1999: 17.

Figure 8.9   Market Share of US Programmes as a Percentage of Total Programming in 1997

Market	% from USA	% from UK	%f from France	% from Germany
France	72	8	–	9
Germany	87	3	1	–
Italy	66	1	3	3
Netherlands	74	9	3	2
Spain	69	3	3	0
Sweden	64	12	1	0
(UK	60	–	5	2)

Source: Graham and Associates 1999: 17. (Time measures? For 1997)
(UK figures for 2002. Value measures. National Statistics October 2003)

Figure 8.10   Market Share of Imports in Europe

producing high-quality programmes, so there is clearly a diversity of supply with the region. There is certainly some exchange between the different countries, so we may say that a regional market does exist. The amount of exchange within the region is, however, tiny compared with the amount coming in to all of the countries from the USA. In this case at least, the regional market does exist, but it is marginal as opposed to the flow of programmes from the US.

The predominance of US imports is true for other developed countries, at least in volume terms, as Figure 8.10 demonstrates. We would expect to find that in some of the markets in the developing world, for which we do not have the same kind of data, the percentage of US programmes is lower than it is for the developed world – according to one relatively recent report 'the West' accounts for 30 per cent of programming in the Chinese market, for example (Brennan, 2003). We should, however, remember that North America and Europe account for approximately 75 per cent of the world spending on advertising and therefore the absolute size of the markets in the developing world is small. Economically speaking, therefore, it is almost certain that the US is the dominant player in the international trade in television products and that regional markets, even in rich areas like Europe, are relatively small by comparison.

Global media products

We can generalize this set of relations between the forms of cultural production that are dominant on a world scale and those that flourish alongside them in terms of a double movement. The simplest dimension to understand is the process of what is sometimes known as 'creolization' (Hannerz, 1996: 67ff). This is a process whereby a cultural artefact produced in the developed world is appropriated and changed, if not transformed, by cultural producers in 'the periphery', who adapt the standardized product in ways that fit in better with local tastes. While we might suspect that this separation of centre and periphery obscures a similar dynamic between 'official' and 'unofficial' cultural institutions within the developed world itself, the stress upon inequality, and the creative primacy of cultural production in the rich and developed world, is clearly correct.

The other side of the issue is the process whereby a 'local' cultural artefact is taken up and becomes a global cultural commodity. This is the issue that we discussed in the context of *Mulan* in the last chapter. While this example is very illuminating, it is far from conclusive: as Joseph Man Chan himself put it, the spin that Disney put upon it is 'universal or American', which is an extremely suggestive elision. The difficulty is partly because the story is one that exists in several different versions independent of its use by Disney, but also because taking a traditional story raises issues of translation, not only from the original language, but also from the original cultural setting and form. One inevitably becomes involved in important but tangential arguments about authenticity and commercialization, not to mention much larger questions like historical epochs and creative genres. The general processes are better understood, perhaps, through looking at what happens when a cultural artefact produced entirely for the market in a developed country becomes a genuinely global commodity. In the latter case, there are no problems about what is the original form, or about how far we are discussing a process of transition from pre-capitalist to capitalist cultural production, or even how far the culture of an historically-oppressed people is being mined and exploited by a global media giant located in an oppressor country.

The example that illustrates these points very well is Winnie-the-Pooh. The two original books, *Winnie-the-Pooh* and *The House at Pooh Corner*, were published in London (in the heart of what was then the world's largest empire) in 1926 and 1928 respectively. Contrary to popular belief, these were not originally stories told in private by a doting parent to a drowsy child. They were from the first commercial fiction produced by a career writer (A.A. Milne) and a career illustrator (E.H. Shepard). They produced the works as the result of a careful and entirely professional collaboration that was aimed at a market that both originators understood from extensive prior experience. The books were an immediate success, in both the UK and the USA, and were constantly reprinted. By 1992, they had been translated into 32 languages, including Esperanto and Latin (Thwaite, 1992: 109). The authors were quick to exploit the success, in radio, Christmas cards, nursery prints, birthday books, project books and so on (Thwaite, 1990: 295ff). In order to make them more marketable commodities, both Milne and Shepard were happy to make changes to their originals. These were, from the start, thoroughly commercial artefacts that were exploited in a huge variety of ways and which sold around the globe. There are no issues of 'authenticity' or of 'exploitation' to concern us in this case.

In the 1960s, Disney acquired most of the rights to these two books in a process that was the subject of a recent major legal battle in the USA, and proceeded to integrate the material into the work of his company. Since the 1960s, there have been five theatrical release films, a television series using new narrative material, and a deluge of Pooh-related merchandising. From our point of view, the significant facts concern not the change in the owner and manner of exploitation of the same intellectual property, but the transformations it underwent in the process. In fact, Disney's Pooh is different from Milne's Pooh in at least six ways, which are clearly apparent to the dedicated (adult) fans of this imaginary world (Sparks, 1998b). The change from Shepard to Disney is a visual change. Disney's Pooh is cartoonized, clothed, anthropomorphized (his nose and eyebrows particularly) and made into a figure recognizably in the US cinematic animation tradition. The sound is distinctive as well. The books, of course, had no accent, but most of the characters in Disney's version have US accents, notably Pooh and Tigger but also, at least in some films, Christopher Robin. The director, Wolfgang Reitherman, told the *Daily Mail*, which was leading a xenophobic campaign against the first animated feature: 'The Mid-West accent is the generally accepted neutral accent at which we aim as it is acceptable to the whole American market' (quoted in Thwaite, 1992: 165). The place is shifted from a weakly marked UK to a strongly marked US suburbia, particularly in the short video animations. In one, Christopher Robin plays with a football. Guess which sort of football? The language is altered, too. The original version was famously cavalier about language: Christopher Robin was 'bisy' and would be 'backson'. The Disney version is ferociously educationally correct – culminating in an 18 volume 'Grow and Learn' library of texts based on the characters and aimed at improving literacy. Disney also plays havoc with the narrative structure. The most notable of numerous alterations is that Tigger does not appear in the original until the second story in the second book, but in the Disney version he is present from the start; the stories are often billed as 'Winnie the Pooh and Tigger Too'. Closely aligned with these narrative changes are changes in character. The most obvious is the introduction of Gopher, whose opening words are 'I'm not in the book', but the shift of the central relationship from that between Pooh and Piglet to that between Pooh and Tigger is the most significant shift. Gender, almost invisible in the original, is very strongly marked in Disney: Tigger clearly fancies Kanga.

It is possible to continue cataloguing the changes at length, but it is quite clear that there has been a shift in what we might call the underlying cultural unconscious that informs the whole. The original books are, unquestionably, straight out of the comfortable world of the British middle classes. The sensibility at play is that of the magazine *Punch* for which both original creators regularly worked. The films, videos and mountain of merchandise are, equally unquestionably, straight out of Middle America. We can illustrate the extent to which the new versions are the product of an American sensibility very simply: one of the books spun off from the videos is *Winnie the Pooh's Thanksgiving*. This transformation has been central to the way in which Disney's Pooh has become a global cultural commodity. It is a different artefact from the (unquestionably imperialist) English original.

Further evidence as to the extent to which the world media are closely mapped on to the centres of power in the wider world comes from a study of the case of a small media corporation that, on the face of it, did seem to have much less of a 'home country' than any of the major players we have just examined. After the collapse of Communism in Central and Eastern Europe, most countries began the process of opening their media systems more fully to the world market (Sparks, 1998a). In particular, they changed the laws to allow commercial broadcasters to win licences for radio and television. One of the most active companies was Central European Media Enterprises (CME). It has its headquarters in Hamilton, Bermuda, but its business address is in London. CME's Chairman, Ronald S. Lauder (of the cosmetics fortune) resides in New York. By March 1999, it was traded on the US NASDAQ stock exchange and had 41 subsidiaries in 13 different countries, including the Netherlands Antilles (Sparks, 1999). Its main businesses, however, were located in the Czech Republic, Slovakia, Slovenia, Romania, Ukraine and Hungary. In each of these countries, it had formed an alliance with local businessmen and politically influential individuals to set up TV stations whose main content was imported programming, largely from the USA but also some from Western Europe.

This sounds like a text-book case of globalization. While one might convincingly argue that, however big its international operations, a company like Time-Warner is in the end primarily a US company because that, as we saw, is where the vast majority of its assets reside and where the bulk of its revenues come from, CME does not seem to have any such 'home' state. It looks exactly like global capital making links with local agents to exploit market opportunities following from the collapse of the attempt to develop autarchic economies.

This was not, in fact, the case. In practice, CME is a US company. Its capital base was provided initially by Lauder's US fortune, and regular injections from him have been necessary to sustain what turned out to be a very problematic and unprofitable business. Its chief executives have been US citizens and the company's contracts specified that disputes would be settled under the laws of New York. It is, of course, incorporated in Delaware. When, in 1999, a crisis and split arose, the dependence of even a multinational operation like CME upon a state was starkly demonstrated. The Czech partner, Vladimir Zelezny, effectively seized control of the profitable TV Nova subsidiary and in this he was defended by the Czech courts. Lauder's response was to use his very considerable contacts with the US political establishment to get them to put pressure on the Czech government. Madeleine Albright, then US Secretary of State, allegedly raised the issue in personal conversation with Czech President Vaclav Havel and other US politicians lobbied the Czech government hard on behalf of Lauder's interests (BHHRG, 2002). Although it has been unable to obtain redress from the individual involved, in the event CME, through its Dutch subsidiary, was, in May 2003, able to obtain $358.6 million from the Czech taxpayers, via their government, under international trade arbitration rules (CME, 2004: 29). In this context, 'global' has effectively meant 'US' and 'local' meant Czech.

Conclusions

Of the ten main propositions that we argued defined the globalization paradigm, most of them appear not to be supported by the evidence, at least with regard to the mass media. Indeed, a number of them are directly contradicted by the examination of easily available material. Much more than any of the earlier paradigms we reviewed in this book, the globalization paradigm appears to be more a popular rhetoric than a guide to serious analysis. We may summarize the findings above in the following manner:

- The claim that culture in general, and the mass media in general, are today driven much more by an autonomous logic that cannot be analysed in terms of economic factors is contrary to the most obvious evidence about broadcasting systems around the world, and ignores the fact that the main site of international discussion about culture and the media today has shifted from the culturally-oriented UNESCO to the unequivocally economic WTO.
- It is correct to say that the globalization paradigm does not lead to any clear practical commitments. Although many proponents of globalization have indeed engaged in practical activities, these differ widely in their content. The most prominent strand, accepting the logic of global markets, stands on the right and centre of the political spectrum. Others, more critical of the operations of the market, stand on the left.
- There is little evidence that the media are more central to economic and social life today than in the past. It is difficult to find a way of measuring their importance on a global scale, but if we look at the largest media corporations it is clear that they are substantial enterprises in terms of capital employed, revenues and number of employees, but they are not larger than iconic examples of an earlier, 'Fordist', epoch. Neither is it the case that their production is more globalized. On the contrary, things like cars, aeroplanes and petroleum products are much more globally homogenous than newspapers and TV programmes.
- The claim that the powers of the state are being eroded by supranational organizations cannot be sustained. It is true that some states have 'failed', but

others, notably the largest and richest states, remain in rude health, and continue to exercise the traditional, central, Westphalian rights of controlling their denizens and waging war upon other states. In terms of their internally repressive capacity, major states are today stronger than before. In terms of their aggressive capacity, after a fall at the end of the Cold War, armament expenditure is firmly on the rise again. In the case of the media, the development of new technologies, notably satellite television, does not abolish national boundaries, since states, business and audiences remain firmly rooted in terrestrial realities.

- There are powerful trends towards more local forms of political and media organization. In political terms, the most successful of these have established traditional states. In media terms, there is a long and established tradition of localism in the press, although the development of national chains is a marked phenomenon. Broadcasting tends very quickly to concentrate at the national level unless checked by legislation. To the extent that global media corporations relate to national media, they tend to focus on national markets rather than local ones. There are 'new localities', but these are hardly novelties and their media do not follow distinctive rules.

- In media, there are indeed multiple production centres, and the degree to which production is distributed varies from medium to medium. On the other hand, the media systems in the advanced world, and notably in the USA, are far larger in terms of resources and reach than those of the rest of the world. In the case of television, even in the richer countries with strong, well-established and adequately funded broadcasters, the proliferation of channels has led to a sharp rise in the volume and value of imports. These originate, overwhelmingly, in the USA.

- There are, indeed, regional markets in broadcasting products. There is one, for example, in Europe. It is, however, tiny and marginal in terms of the trade between regional partners. The vast majority of the import of programmes comes from the United States of America.

- Global media products do exist, but their character is dependent upon markets in the rich nations. When they originate in poorer countries, they are changed where necessary to suit the tastes of richer nations before they become global products. The same process takes place even when a product originates in one rich nation and is taken up and globalized by another: in order to undergo that spread it is first modified to suit the tastes of the globalizer's home market. Even apparently 'homeless' media capital in the end rests upon the legal and political powers of particular states.

- Overall, there is extremely little evidence that globalization constitutes a new epoch in human history. Many of the factors identified as central to its novelty do not in reality exist. Others are familiar from the earlier history of capitalism. So many of these factors are absent or not distinctive to the present that the claim that it is their combination that constitutes the novelty of the current epoch cannot be sustained.

The problem with globalization is not that it is simply bad social science. Like all theories, it directs attention to certain phenomena and neglects others. In the case of globalization, the theory directs attention towards international displacement and transnational exchange. These are real phenomena, and to the extent that is has sensitized us to these issues, particularly in the realm of economics, it has played a valuable role. But this focus has been at the expense of considerations of power and of inequality, which are traditional themes of social sciences and which were central to the earlier paradigms we examined. Neglect of these factors leads to a very distorted picture of the contemporary world.

We can illustrate this by looking at one of the areas in which theories of globalization have informed research that has led to very illuminating work: namely, that concerned with diasporas and with diasporic media. This has led to a large number of very interesting studies, and we do not wish to disparage their particular interest, but they are only telling, albeit brilliantly, one small part of contemporary human experience.

Migration across borders remains a central social and political reality in the contemporary world. Half a million people migrated (i.e. moved to live for at least one year) internationally into the UK in 2001, and between 1991 and 2002 more than 3.5 million made the same move. Incomings, of course, must be balanced against outgoings to get some sense of contemporary international shifts in population. In the UK case, in the decade 1993–2002, 3.9 million people entered the country and 2.8 million left, giving a net inflow of just over one million people (National Statistics, 2004). These are substantial movements of population, and the figures for the USA are, of course, much greater. As Figure 8.11 shows, globally, the figures are much larger, and increasing. Clearly, international migration is a significant feature of the contemporary world.

	Numbers in Millions		As percentage of the population	
	1980	2000		
World	99.8	174.9	2.3	2.9
Africa	14.1	16.3	3.0	2.0
Asia	32.3	43.8	1.3	1.2
Latin America and Caribbean	6.1	5.9	1.7	1.1
Northern America	18.1	40.8	7.1	12.9
Oceania	3.8	5.8	16.4	18.8
Europe	22.2	32.8	4.6	6.4
USSR (former)	3.3	29.5	1.2	10.5

Source: United Nations Population Division *Trends in Total Migrant Stock: The 2003 Revision*

Figure 8.11   Numbers of international migrants in the world

	1980		2001	
	Urban population	Percent of total	Urban population	Percent of total
China	192.8m	20	466.7m	37
Brazil	81.2m	67	140.8m	82
South Korea	21.7m	57	39m	82
Low and middle income countries	1,136.6m	32	2,148.5m	42
Globally	1,741.8m	39	2,890.5m	47

Source: World Bank 2003

Figure 8.12   Recent mass internal population movements

It is a mistake, however, to think that such movements, though important in themselves, represent the typical or most significant population movements of the current epoch. The truly gigantic population shifts of the last quarter century are the same as those that dominated nineteenth century Britain. They are movements within a state from the countryside to the town. As Figure 8.12 shows, hundreds of millions of people are on the move, but their movements are predominantly within states rather than between them, and represent the continuation of a process that has been going on at least since the eighteenth century.

These movements within countries, between people who may be very different from each other but who do not have to cross geopolitical boundaries, dwarf the scale of international migration. While the media of the new localities are therefore significant, and very much brilliant and illuminating work has been done upon them and their audiences, their overall importance needs to be kept in proportion with respect to the very much larger changes that are going on inside the state system. There is no reason to believe that the media patterns of cities across the developing world that have exploded in size due to huge internal migration would be any less interesting as objects of study, or produce insights less valuable for our understanding of human experience.

It is an astonishing fact that while a great deal of energy and effort has been devoted to studying the cultural life of cross-border migrations, relatively little has been spent on these much larger phenomena. There are two reasons for this gross neglect. The first is that if one looks at the destination to which international migration has mostly taken place in the last 20 years, it is within the developed world: notably, Australia, North America and Europe. In much of the developing world, it has actually fallen as a proportion of the population even when the numbers have risen. This is clearly not a new development in Australia or the USA, or even much of Europe, but it is an increasingly evident one. The reason scholars have focused on this, and not the changes taking place on a larger scale in Asia and elsewhere is simply parochialism: they have looked out of their own front doors and imagined what they could see there was typical of what was going on in the world.

The second reason is that this march into the cities is evidence of the failure of the globalization paradigm to account for the starkest features of the contemporary world. Once it is recognized as the central migratory experience of the contemporary world, this huge population movement forces us to reconsider the social system within which it takes place. Very far from being some novel process with a unique and unprecedented dynamic, this phenomenon is extremely familiar. The move from the countryside to the city, from peasant to proletarian, is one of the well-established consequences of the development of capitalism. It emptied Goldsmith's village. It crammed Engels's Manchester. It filled the boats from Ireland, Germany, Italy and the rest of Europe to New York. More grimly, it filled the slave ships from Africa to the Americas. Today, it drives migrants across the Rio Grande, suffocates them in container lorries in Dover, and drowns them in the quicksands of Morecambe Bay.

The same is true of all of the other phenomena we have examined. Many are very familiar to anyone with any historical sense at all. To the extent that they are new, they are clearly part of a much longer and deeper process than the last quarter century or so. The master category that explains them all is not globalization but capitalism, in its most recent and expansive phase.

9

TOWARDS A NEW PARADIGM

In reviewing theories of development communication and international communication, we have covered a very wide range of topics and, as we bring this investigation to a conclusion, it is important to recall our starting point. We began by identifying the huge disparities that are a central feature of the contemporary world. Some of these disparities are in material circumstances: income, life expectancy and infant mortality are the most obvious measures of the ways in which accidents of birth determine the kinds of future people can expect. Others are less tangible but nonetheless real. There are differences in social status, in cultural esteem, in self-determination and in access to the means of self-expression that are felt just as acutely, although in quite different ways, as needs that are more fundamental in the Maslovian sense. We were concerned to examine what contributions communication, and particularly the mass media, could bring to alleviating these inequalities and particularly to alleviating the very real misery in which millions today are still forced to try to survive.

We found several ways in which it has been argued that communication could help change the situation for the better. The dominant paradigm began from more or less exactly the same starting point as us, and it gave a clear answer: the media could be used to change people's minds so that they became 'modern' and learnt to live differently and better. Its participatory descendant gave a different answer, at least in its more radical versions: the task of the mass media is to help give a voice to the poor themselves so that they can claim the rights that they are today denied. The imperialism paradigm recognized similar problems of systematic disadvantage but argued that these arose not from the failings of individuals or social groups but from the international structures of domination. Until these were addressed, little could be expected from efforts to solve this or that local problem. In media terms, this meant that the key task was for states to seize control of their own communication spaces and use them to articulate nationally defined goals. The globalization paradigm was, and still is, very much more optimistic. Its starting point is not a critique of inequality but a celebration of exchange between nations, firms and individuals. In our special area of interest, this translates into exchanges between broadcasters and between broadcasters and their audiences in which there is all of the freedom and equality of the market. Arguments about states and about domination are, it is claimed, now obsolete and the invisible hand of the world market in images will ensure that everybody gets just what they want, rather than what development experts or state bureaucrats think it would be good for them to get.

We have seen that there are objections, theoretical and practical, to the complete programmes articulated by the proponents of each of these positions. Each of them, however, also has real strengths. They have all identified features of the contemporary world that are important and valuable and they have helped us better to understand what is happening, and what can happen, in the media today. It is these real strengths that have convinced quite large numbers of people that one or other of the paradigms is worth taking seriously. Any critical account that wishes to be taken seriously in turn needs to give due recognition to these strengths as much as to the objections.

Are we at a theoretical turning point?

The globalization paradigm is today still far and away the most popular and influential way of thinking about the world, and the world of media and communication in particular. Politicians still make speeches praising or blaming globalization, and using it as an alibi for whatever measures they wish to enact. Academics still churn out torrents of books on this or that aspect of globalization. Graduate students endlessly repeat what they believe to be the latest in revealed truth about the world. There are some critical voices, but there can be no doubt whatsoever that the globalization paradigm has the status of orthodoxy.

The high tide of the globalization paradigm was in the 1990s and the conditions that led to the predominance of a theory with these particular characteristics were, fairly clearly, those prevailing in the decade after the fall of the Berlin Wall and the end of European communism. The concept of a new stage of society, free of the conflicts of capitalism and imperialism, seemed to fit the world very well after the collapse of communism and the sharp reduction of military spending in the advanced world. Certainly, there remained conflicts of an extremely murderous kind – notably in the former Yugoslavia and in various parts of Africa – but these could be seen as the residues of earlier forms of social organization rather than endemic to the prevailing order. The nightmare of the imminent outbreak of a catastrophic third world war, which had haunted the minds of a generation, was lifted. There was now no real clash of systems. In the advanced world, the moves towards an information society and the triumph of free trade were seen to have removed the tensions that had led to earlier conflicts. The rapid development of the internet made international networks, rather than geo-political spaces, the centre of contemporary enthusiasm, for example in the work of writers like Castells.

Development, and the relations between centre and periphery, now also appeared in a new light. Countries that had previously attempted to insulate themselves from the world market now increasingly abandoned the attempt at economic autarchy and import substitution in favour of integration into world trade. China is the most important instance, but many other countries with quite different political and economic trajectories, like Brazil and India, adopted a similar strategy, albeit with many hesitations. The reasons for this new openness varied. Sometimes it was the result of a strategic decision by the government and sometimes it was imposed in the form of a Structural Adjustment Programme as the price of international aid. Outcomes varied, too, from stagnation in much of Africa to extremely rapid growth in parts of Asia, but apart from some isolated hold-outs like North Korea and Cuba, the process seemed irresistible. At the economic level at least, the world did seem to be reversing the trend of the previous epoch and transforming itself into a single global unit. Whatever else might be said in criticism of the globalization paradigm, there were clearly some important changes going on that demanded explanation.

Even during its high period, however, there were always dissenting voices. The background noise of continual turmoil in the Balkans and Africa gave a basis for critics who questioned whether globalization was the best way to theorize the new realities. The orthodox left retained a stubborn insistence on the continuing utility of the concept of imperialism at the level of general theory (Callinicos, 1994). In the study of media and communication, as we have seen, the 'weak globalization' approach of writers like Herman and McChesney (1997) and Hamelink (1994) retained many of the central features of the old imperialism paradigm, despite adopting some of the language of globalization.

Much more important, in terms of immediate impact at least, was the developing anti-globalization current of thought and action. Very often, writers adopting this perspective accept that there is indeed a process of globalization, which they see as distinct and novel, but mount a critique of the optimistic conclusions drawn by its proponents. The main theoretical framework remains the same but in this version the emphasis is placed upon the negative and destructive features of globalization rather than on celebration of the new opportunities.

Anti-globalization became a major public force with the 'Battle of Seattle' in 2000. The protest against the straightforward globalizing agenda of the World Trade Organization brought together a wide range of social forces that have, over the following years, continued to mount protests against the gatherings of those it sees as the agents of destruction for jobs and ways of life ranging from the industrial heartlands of the USA to the indigenous communities of the tropical rainforests. The various manifestations of the World Social Forum have provided an organizational and theoretical focus for this new movement. The challenge to the rosy assumptions of globalization theory has called forth a sharp reaction, from repressive policing of subsequent protests to firm theoretical restatements of the benefits of global capitalism and free trade in terms of jobs and living standards.

Taken together, the disparate collection of writers and activists who gather in the successive World Social Forums can be said to constitute a continued alternative intellectual and practical pole of attraction to that provided by theories of globalization. In the new century, contingent factors rendered the salience of this alternative increasingly obvious. Of these developments, by far the most important was the sudden change in US foreign policy that followed the terrible atrocity of September 11 2001. Whether this attack was the reason for a sudden change in US policy or whether, as some claim, it provided the horrible catalyst for a project that had long been maturing in think tanks with influence in the US administration, is not a matter upon which we are called to speculate. We need only note the incontestable reality that the USA, supported by some of its more loyal allies, has subsequently adopted a much more aggressive foreign policy, which includes the willingness to use military force in order to establish US influence in foreign countries. Such initiatives fit very poorly with, for example, the claims of globalization paradigms that the state is no longer a significant actor in world affairs. Although these methods appear strikingly new to some observers, an older way of thinking about the world seemed more appropriate to others. Sebastian Mallaby, for example, wrote that: '... a new imperial moment has arrived, and by virtue of its power America is bound to play the leading role' (Mallaby, 2002).

The nature of this new foreign policy, and whether it can properly be compared with earlier imperial ventures like that of the UK, is hotly contested, but the debate has certainly highlighted the continued relevance of the concept of imperialism. Some writers are unashamedly and enthusiastically in favour of the practice, and indeed even the language, of imperialism. One of the best known of these is Max Boot, who wrote in *USA Today* that: 'Given the historical baggage that 'imperialism' carries, there's no need for the U.S. government to embrace the term. But it should definitely embrace the practice' (Boot, 2003). To be sure, for Boot, the liberal empire that the US has been constructing since the Louisiana Purchase differs from the older and more rapacious kinds in being concerned primarily to spread freedom and democracy, but it remains an empire nonetheless. It is a mechanism for imposing the will of the USA upon the population of other countries, every bit as much as was the British Raj. Other writers take a more nuanced view, but in discussion of US policy in Afghanistan or Iraq it is seldom or never that the concept of globalization is invoked to describe the new realities. Rather, the debate is to whether it is proper to label current US policy as 'imperialist', as one author in *Foreign Affairs* put it: 'Any realistic discussion of U.S. foreign policy must begin with the recognition that, notwithstanding Americans' views and preferences, most of the world sees the United States as a nascent imperial power' (Simes, 2003). Articles and books propounding similar views, or arguing robustly that the US is not an imperial power but a benign force whose actions are aimed at spreading peace, justice and democracy, appear in bookshops and newsagents around the world (Mann, 2003: 9–11; Panitch and Gindin, 2004: 7–12; Ferguson, 2003, 2004).

It is much too early to speak of a crisis of the globalization paradigm, but it is certainly the case today that the paradigm faces many more, more vocal and more persuasive, critics than it did a decade ago. It is therefore quite appropriate and timely to attempt to sketch the outlines of a new paradigm. Any new intellectual project is based, even if negatively, on the foundations of early theorizations and this case is not an exception. All of the previous paradigms have provided some insights that retain their value today, although as is perhaps already obvious the approach adopted here is much more indebted to the participatory and imperialism paradigms than to the two alternatives. In the remainder of this chapter, we therefore review briefly the main points that can be taken from the dominant paradigm and the globalization paradigm before discussing the strengths and limits of the other two in more detail.

One major problem with all four of these theories, which we noted in the first chapter, is that none of them adequately addressed the relationships between small-scale local issues and the larger questions of power and domination. In the case of the dominant paradigm, the state and other power structures were certainly present as the patrons of local development initiatives, but the assumption that such problems could be resolved without questioning the existing distribution of resources proved untenable. In fact, the paradigm was particularly sensitive to the danger that the kinds of micro-social changes it advocated would have destabilizing effects on the larger power structure. The participatory paradigm, on the other hand, recognized the existence of large power structures but either consciously limited itself to 'safe' activities or did not elaborate on how to confront them. The imperialism paradigm, on the other hand, was very much concerned with macro-structures of power, but in practice it concentrated on relations between states, and remained silent about the distribution of power inside societies. There was a certain overlap in terms of personnel between the participatory and the imperialism paradigms, but no attempt was ever made to theorize their relationship. The globalization paradigm, for its part, concerns itself with large-scale developments and assumes that relations between the global and the local are more or less unproblematic interactions.

Any satisfactory theory must provide an adequate account of both levels of social action. The example of the ways in which neglect of intra-state power relations helped to cripple the imperialism paradigm's critique of inter-state power relations is a salutary one. One of the major tasks of this chapter is to try to address this disjuncture in existing theories.

Development communication

The first part of this book was concerned with the various ways in which the relationship between communication and development has been theorized. We saw that there are quite serious criticisms to be made of all of the versions of this approach, but we should say at once that all have the very great strength of starting from the right point. All of them begin by recognizing that the world in which we live has deep wells of poverty and its attendant ills. Despite the huge improvements of the last decade or so, there are still hundreds of millions of people who survive on less than a dollar a day, who have no access to electricity, for whom obtaining clean fresh water is a constant struggle and for whom the barest minimum of health care is scarcely available. All of the versions of development communication recognize these as serious problems that need urgent remedies, and their concern with communication is designed to help solve them.

Having said that, however, we must also recognize that writers within this tradition have given very different answers. In our analysis, we made a distinction between the dominant paradigm proper, and its close descendant the continuity variant, on the one hand and the participatory paradigm on the other. The problems with the two groups are rather different, and we need to deal with them separately. Here, the dominant paradigm is addressed. This has been very heavily criticized since at least the late 1960s, and it has usually been thought to be both entirely discredited and obsolete, but we saw how in its continuity variant it remains an important source of legitimization for many communication projects around the world. There is little need to repeat the central critique of the dominant paradigm in detail: it is widely accepted today that the attempt to inject modernity (or for that matter, postmodernity) into societies through the use of mass communication is neither possible nor desirable. There is, however, a danger that an entirely correct critique of the pretensions of western modernity to represent a superior way of life will obscure the fact that it has produced the knowledge and techniques that can help improve the lives of people around the world.

We can elaborate on our discussion of health communication and draw a distinction between what we may term technical and political modernity. Technical modernity refers to those ways in which western capitalism developed human control over nature, notably by the development of scientific practices. Political modernity, on the other hand, refers to economic, social and political arrangements that are characteristic of developed western societies, and notably of the USA. Technical modernity has unquestionably been responsible for improving the human lot in a multitude of ways. Of course, we have to recognize the force of the critique that notes that the west has devoted far more energy and ingenuity to using this knowledge to develop ever more terrible weapons than it has to promoting human happiness. There are numerous recent critiques of the Enlightenment, most famously that of Foucault, which point out in detail that it has a dark side. On the other hand, if it has a dark side, it also has a bright side. Scientific methods can be used for other ends as well as slaughtering, dominating, controlling and exploiting. About 1,000,000 children a year recover from potentially fatal diarrhoea, and a major contributor to that success is rehydration therapy, which although a relatively simple procedure is the product of scientific investigation. Perhaps the scientists and doctors who developed it were arrogant. They certainly did not fully understand the processes involved as recently as a decade ago, and probably there is still much to be discovered. Perhaps the efficacy of the treatment itself has provided an excuse for not undertaking the more difficult task of providing potable water in poor countries. But it is a poor philosophy that says that because knowledge is imperfect, or that it is sometimes misused, or that its proponents have overweening pretensions to omnipotence, then we should abandon the attempt to understand and improve the world.

The communication of technical modernity remains valuable, and to the extent that contemporary exponents of the continuity variant are engaged in this they are undertaking worthwhile and positive projects. There are, however, real limits to the value of this work. As the dominant paradigm discovered long ago, it is very difficult indeed to alter deep-rooted patterns of human behaviour, and it is often unrealistic to expect communication to do that on its own. Very often, the communication project requires, as a condition for its success, other substantial social changes as well, and without them it will likely prove ineffective. The process of change can rarely be restricted simply to technical change.

Although we can draw a conceptual distinction between technical and political modernity, in reality the two are almost always closely intertwined. The objectives of the technical project are often defined by political forces. The resources needed, and even the methods that are acceptable, are decided on political grounds. The limits of social change are prescribed by political rather than technical considerations. It is the ready acceptance of the limits posed by the existing structures of power that marks one failure of the continuity paradigm. Despite the talk of participation in this school of thought, the model is often close to that of marketing communication designed to sell a pre-determined product to a given population rather than to ask what are its needs and aspirations. Nevertheless, in its stubborn insistence that there are ideas and practices produced by modern societies that can be of great assistance in alleviating contemporary problems, the classical paradigm retains a claim to our attention. One of the starting points of any serious attempt to use communication for the tasks of human betterment must be the clear recognition that in some aspects of human life the 'modern' scientific world view is able to provide better answers to pressing problems than any alternative, and that the media have a role to play in propagating the ideas and practices that are likely to achieve the desired outcomes.

The globalization paradigm

The utility of the globalization paradigm for the development of a strategy capable of confronting the continuing reality of poverty and inequality is considerably less than for any of the other theories considered in this book. In their very different ways, the development and imperialism paradigms began from recognition of the fact that the world was structured into disparities of wealth and power. Globalization has no such precise focus. Only in its economic form does it claim that it can address and remedy these problems through the universal application of free trade and free markets. The earlier theories were guides to action. Globalization has no such pretensions, except its secret guilty belief that Gates and Ellison and Murdoch and Redstone and the rest are pushing forward the new world.

This does not mean that the globalization paradigm is of no use whatsoever. On the contrary, its critique of the approach which concentrated upon the existing state system and its organizations, which was so marked in the imperialism paradigm, was invaluable. In our own field, this is obviously true in its deconstruction of the category of 'national culture'. It is clearly correct that 'national culture' is the culture of the dominant group, and the defence of such unitary constructs is always at the expense of the complexity and diversity of the cultures of any real, living population in which the less powerful and the powerless will have their own distinctive cultural patterns. The circulation of cultural commodities is a reality even if its extent and impact is grossly exaggerated by the globalization paradigm. The stress upon diasporas, however much it may have distorted the overall analysis of the shape of population movements in the contemporary world, had the enormous strength of demonstrating that products produced for quite different audiences in one society could satisfy cultural needs for people living in countries far from the point of production much better than did material produced more or less next door. Faced with the evidence as to what the populations of the great cities of the developed world actually do watch, read and listen to, and with the various ways in which they make sense of the material available to them, it is impossible not to recognize the more general truth that the state is not the sole and only guarantor of a living culture.

It follows more or less directly from this that a cultural or media policy that consists exclusively of defending a 'national' culture and 'national' broadcasters, whether state or privately owned, is unsustainable. Whatever the good intentions of the policy, the reality is that broadcasters, however they are owned, will tend to be captured by elite groups (in just the same way as any other powerful institution in a divided society) and turn either into a sclerotic bureaucracy subject to political whim or a private fiefdom organized solely to maximize profit. Sometimes, as in Berlusconi's Italy, a whole broadcasting system can display both vices at once. The way that big broadcasters define and articulate the 'national culture' will tend predominantly to reflect the beliefs and values of the dominant group rather than society as a whole. It will certainly not be the vehicle for the enormous variety of cultural experiences that are present in any society.

The other main contribution of the globalization paradigm is rather more abstract, but arises from precisely the same break with the state-centred approaches of earlier theories. The theory of imperialism has the benefit of describing fairly accurately the first three quarters of the last century, but a confrontation with globalization theory suggests that the final years of the last century, and the early years of this century, require a new approach. The last quarter of the last century saw the collapse of the autarchic model and its replacement by ever greater economic integration. As we shall see, the decisive moment of crisis for the classical theory of imperialism is not 1945 but 1989. At the very least, the insights of globalization theory mean that a fresh look at the assumptions upon which the theory of imperialism rested became unavoidable.

Imperialism and participation as strange bedfellows

Although our debt to the other two paradigms is much greater, we cannot simply adopt one or the other of them wholesale. For one thing, although not all of the critical points we discussed in earlier chapters are entirely persuasive, enough of them are to suggest that both paradigms need, at the very least, serious revision in order to be credible. Secondly, and perhaps more importantly, although the proponents of the two paradigms were and often are allies, and individuals were and are active proponents of both of them depending on where they were located, the two had different, indeed ultimately contradictory, elements in their theorization. The imperialism paradigm, as we have argued, was markedly state-centric in its view of the world, while the participatory paradigm was and is oriented very much on the grass roots. It has little to say about the state. Those versions of the paradigm that do address the problem are the most 'moderate' ones, which tend to counsel caution and the acceptance of the limits imposed by state power, thus opening themselves to exactly the same limitations that cripple the dominant paradigm itself. The more radical versions of the participatory paradigm have clear implications for politics but they are rarely clearly articulated, let alone interrogated.

It is to the credit of both of these paradigms that they aim to provide more than simply an academic account of the world, and to furnish at least the basis for social action that will solve pressing social, economic and cultural problems faced by the world's poorest people. At the strategic level, however, both paradigms propose different ways of achieving this.

For the imperialism paradigm, the main actors were states and their governments, organized in international bodies like UNESCO, and today in the World Summit on the Information Society (WSIS) (Padovani, 2005; Preston, 2005; Mastrini and Charras, 2005). Over the last few years many of the surviving activists from the NWICO years have devoted their time and energy to attempting to influence the outcomes of the WSIS, which has been animated by the International Telecommunications Union (ITU). These efforts have been directed towards entirely worthy goals. While new information and communication technologies are no more 'magical' than was radio fifty years ago, they do, particularly in the form of the Internet, provide an important tool which is usable by radical movements as part of their drive towards self-organization. The distribution of such resources, particularly access to the Internet, are notoriously unequal and the 'digital divide' maps very closely on to the main social and economic divisions in the world. What is more, the decision-making process within the Internet is highly undemocratic, with a controlling interest being held by one country (the USA). Clearly, these are issues which are of some importance, but in reality the limited resources available outside of the official world mean that a decision to participate fully in such a process inevitably detracts from the effort that can be put in to other, more productive, fields. It can be argued that, in comparison with the NWICO phase of activism, the debates around the WSIS represented an advance, since at least NGOs were admitted to the process, although their direct financial contribution of 1,729 Swiss francs out of a total of 4,309,289 Swiss francs with the balance coming from governments and industry, demonstrates their marginality in terms of resources (ITU, 2005). An orientation upon states as actors requires devoting time and resources to international meetings and seminars, to lobbying and writing briefing papers aimed at politicians and civil servants, and to what can only really be described as a form of cultural diplomacy. In terms of the outcomes, even some of the more enthusiastic participants today recognize that the terrain was not favourable to the sorts of issues of inequality and domination that they wished to raise (Hamelink, 2006; Raboy, 2006).

The orientation of the participatory paradigm upon helping in the articulation of the demands of the poor means meeting different people in different locations, to producing different materials in different languages, and to what some writers more or less state is a form of cultural agitation. While some protean individuals may manage to straddle this divide, it is difficult to see how organizations can follow both of these paths simultaneously even in the best of circumstances. Circumstances are not always of the best, however, particularly since many of the states that are to be wooed are also engaged in fierce repression of any expressions of internal dissent, the encouragement of which is one of the main aims of the more radical versions of the participatory paradigm.

The task, then, is to construct a new paradigm that retains the strengths of the two approaches but achieves a synthesis between the two at the level of the kinds of political action which is embedded in the concrete policy for communication. The imperialism paradigm clearly identified the fact that the problems of the world were structural in origin, and that these structures were not to be explained in terms of the psychology of individuals or social classes but were embedded in the economics and politics of the world market. The participatory paradigm, on the other hand, recognizes that self-emancipation is the only path to human freedom and that this requires conscious action on the part of communicators concerned with achieving that goal.

In order to bring these two separate insights, each valid in its own sphere, together we need to be precise about the ways in which terms are being used. This is not a serious problem with the participatory paradigm, where the radical variant is rather precise about its starting point, and clearly differentiated from the other versions that are more limited in their ambitions. For the radical version of the participatory paradigm, it is 'power participation' that is at stake. It argues that 'participation as a process of empowerment, through politically quite risky, is our favoured approach' (Melkote and Steevers, 2001: 337). Cultural and media imperialism, on the other hand, are notoriously ill-defined concepts that are used in different ways by different writers, and the situation with regard to the underlying concept of imperialism itself is even worse. There are radically different views of what the term 'imperialism' might mean held by different authors. Since one of our problems with the globalization paradigm was precisely that it existed in a bewildering variety of contradictory forms, we cannot expect credibility for our own ideas unless the exact way in which the term is being used is stated very clearly.

As a consequence, we intend to discuss the general theory of imperialism, both in some of its more important historical manifestations as well as in contemporary discussions. We will then consider the concept of 'cultural imperialism' and 'media imperialism', which are the subject of further contestation and confusions. Once we have done that, we will show how these revised categories fit together with the insights of the participatory paradigm.

The theory of imperialism

The main writers of the imperialism paradigm did not devote much space to spelling out exactly what they meant by the concept. Schiller, for example, does not give much space to a discussion of what he means by imperialism, although his general sense is quite clear in passages like: 'The nation's electronic sophistication, a product of massive research and development supported by huge federal expenditures, has been commissioned to oversee and sometime to overpower primitive economies steeped in social misery if they give any signs of rebellion' (Schiller, 1970: 65). Mattelart, similarly, operated with an unexplicated concept of imperialism but a real and definite sense, borne from personal experiences, of the way in which it involved ideological, economic and coercive dimensions (Matterlart, 1979, 1980). Perhaps in the press of events, the reality of imperialism seemed so obvious to these writers that there was no need to theorize it elaborately. For us, however, it is important to be clear about the theory that informed their writings, so that we can form a better picture of how it might fit the contemporary world.

Schiller, Mattelart, Smythe and their co-thinkers were, of course, working within the Marxist tradition of analysing imperialism, which sharply distinguishes between modern imperialism and earlier empires. The classical 'briefest possible definition ... [of modern] imperialism is the monopoly stage of capitalism' (Lenin, 1917/1964: 266). This view of imperialism, although inalienably associated with Marxism, was partly built on the work of liberal anti-imperialist writers like Hobson. As theorized by Lenin, and more systematically by Bukharin, the theory ran that the development of capitalism led to the increasing scale and concentration of the means of production, and a fusion between banks (finance capital) and industry (manufacturing capital) (Bukharin, 1972). Within national markets, there was a marked tendency towards monopoly, and a shift towards international competition between capitalists located in different countries. In consequence, capitalists turned to 'their' state to help them win the competitive struggle: 'it is not too much to say that the modern foreign policy of Great Britain has been primarily a struggle for profitable markets of investment' (Hobson 1902/1938: 53). In Bukharin's bold formulation there was a fusion between capital and the state: 'into one gigantic combine enterprise under the tutelage of the financial kings and the capitalist state, an enterprise which monopolizes the national market' (Bukharin, 1972: 72–3).

This fusion of the capital residing in a particular country with the state machine confronted a world market in which there were other capitals that had undergone a similar process of evolution. The natural competitive struggle between capitals, which had produced this concentration on the national scale, was thus transferred to the international plane, and because it involved the fusion of state and capital also implied the fusion of economic and military competition: 'the more strained the situation in the world sphere of struggle – and our epoch is characterized by the greatest intensity of competition between 'national' groups of finance capital – the oftener an appeal is made to the mailed fist of state power' (Bukharin, 1972: 124).

There were, however, other theories of imperialism. The most important division was between those who saw imperialism as primarily 'economic' and those who saw it as 'political' in origin (Kemp, 1972: 22). On both sides of the debate there were Liberals and Marxists. The basic idea of the 'political' interpretation of imperialism was an eerie precursor of globalization theories, arguing that capitalism is an international system that desires open and regular exchange between different parts of the world, and which is thus so integrated that it needs peace rather than war. The idea that imperialism was an optional policy for a state, and that capitalist development might require international peace was taken up by some Marxist writers, notably Kautsky (1983: 88–9; Salvadori, 1979: 190ff). The clearest expression, however, was that given by Schumpeter, for whom 'imperialism is ... atavistic in character' and is a product of the continued influence of pre-capitalist social groups within capitalist society and 'stems from the living conditions, not of the present, but of the past' (Schumpeter, 1919/1951: 84). In particular, the powerful hold that the remains of the feudal aristocracy held over the state and notably its military arms, which was especially prominent in the case of Prussia, meant that national policies were not conducted according to rational, peaceful, capitalist principles but rather the warlike and aggressive methods appropriate to feudal barons. Imperialism was a function of incomplete capitalism and represented the political–economic expression of the surviving pre-capitalist elements in society: 'a purely capitalist world ... can offer no fertile soil to imperialist impulses' (Schumpeter, 1919/1951: 90). The attempt to carve up the world into distinct economic zones which were protected from each other by economic tariffs does not follow from the nature of the economic system and: 'it is a basic fallacy to describe imperialism as a necessary phase of capitalism, or even to speak of the development of capitalism into imperialism' (Schumpeter, 1919/1951: 118).

These divisions, we shall see below, find remarkable echoes in contemporary discussions of imperialism, but the world has changed a great deal since the depths of the First World War. None of the accounts from that period can be accepted uncritically as explaining the whole of the twentieth century, let alone the nature of the contemporary world. We can identify a number of problems with all of the theories long before the difficulties of understanding the present were apparent.

Schumpeter's account, despite its brilliance, has become increasingly unconvincing as a general theory of imperialism. Even when he wrote, it was difficult to see the hand of a pre-capitalist aristocracy in the policies of many of the major protagonists of the First World War. Clemenceau, for instance, possessed impeccable republican credentials and Lloyd George had made his reputation attacking the House of Lords. In the longer term, the rise of the USA has made the position quite untenable. It is true, as Innis once observed, that military men have had a strong influence on US politics (2004: 21–39, 118). This has continued since his day, through figures like Eisenhower and Powell, and a host of others. It is also true that the USA has a strong dynastic current in its politics (Kennedys, Bushes, perhaps tomorrow Clintons). It is however, ridiculous to see US foreign policy as dominated by 'feudal remants'.

Another obvious point is that all parties in the earlier debate, but particularly the Marxists, took it for granted, because of the examples before their eyes, that the concept of empire was linked not simply with military conflicts between great powers but also with the possession of colonies. The First World War appeared to confirm this view, since it undoubtedly resulted in exactly the re-division of the world that the theory of imperialism predicted. The Second World War can be seen, at least in part, as an attempt to revise the outcome of the First and bring it more in to line with the realities of economic and political power. The period after 1945, however, did not fit this view. One of the major features of international relations during those years was the long and bitter struggle for liberation from colonial rule. The struggle against imperial rule was not a new one, and it had had its first major success in Ireland in 1921, but it only became a general phenomenon twenty-five years later, and is still not quite completed today. During the period after 1945, the people of the major colonial empires managed to free themselves from their foreign rulers and establish independent states. This forced a modification of the theory. Logically, the theory of imperialism as a struggle over the control of the political and economic life of a country does not necessitate formal occupation, and it turned out to be quite possible to have 'imperialism without colonies' (Magdoff, 1972, 2003). This new form of non-colonial imperialism was an important part of the background to the media imperialism paradigm. The media were seen as being of central importance to the maintenance and extension of imperial power precisely because the direct mechanisms of colonial rule had given way to indirect means of influence.

The third major issue that required analysis was the changing shape of international rivalries. When all of these theories were first articulated, it was clear that there were several competing empires. As Hobson put it, 'the novelty of recent Imperialism ... consists chiefly in its adoption by several nations. The notion of a number of competing empires is essentially modern.' (1902/1938: 8). This worked well as a description of the world until the end of the Second World War. After that point, however, 'inter-imperialist rivalry' more or less disappeared from the discussion. The concept of media imperialism is a case in point. Although there are some echoes in Schiller's discussion of the struggle for control of global communication between the US and the UK, most of the time the case was argued more or less exclusively in terms of 'US imperialism'. This was the theoretical weakness that allowed writers critical of the imperialism paradigm to point to other centres of production as evidence of the inadequacy of its account.

The main reason why the theorists of the media and cultural imperialism paradigm were reluctant to accept the centrality of rivalry between the major powers as the defining feature of imperialism during the last half of the twentieth century was that the manifest conflict, which dominated global politics during that era, was the struggle between the USA and the USSR. Since most of the proponents of cultural imperialism accepted, more or less explicitly, that the USSR was a socialist or communist country, and therefore on their account not capable of imperialism, it followed that the main feature of imperialism was the fact that the USA, and to a much lesser extent its allies amongst the developed countries, dominated the rest of the world, and threatened the socialist countries. There could not be a clearer case of how holding fast to a particular paradigm leads one to discount an overwhelming mountain of evidence that contradicts one's views. Holding that the USA was the sole significant imperialist power, and that together with its minor allies it exerted domination over the rest of the world, led the theorists of cultural imperialism to lay much too heavy a stress on the media and cultural products of that country. And in defining statist autarchic solutions as an alternative, rather than a complement, to US capitalism these theorists logically came to the conclusion that state policy, even the policies of actually existing and very unpleasant states, represented a better model for human organization. When the theorists of cultural imperialism made their compromises with the state system they were simply pursuing the line suggested to them by their overall understanding of imperialism.

There is an alternative to this view. The logic of Bukharin's analysis of the fusion between capital and the state is that we can see the 'soviet communist' model of social organization as the extreme form of this process. If at one end of the spectrum there is the relative disarticulation of state and capital, as in the USA, there are many other examples of societies in which there has been a much greater degree of fusion (Brazil, South Africa, Japan, France, for example). At the other end of the spectrum lie those societies in which the fusion of state and industry, of economics and politics, was most completely achieved. We can locate countries like Britain somewhere in the middle of this spectrum and understand the need to fuse the state and industry as a consequence of the struggle between rival empires. Eric Hobsbawm wrote that Britain during the Second World War was forced 'in the interests of survival, into the most state-planned and state-managed economy ever introduced outside a frankly socialist country' (1968: 208).

From this perspective, the conflict between the USA and the USSR can be seen as a struggle between different forms of empire, in which both sides used a gamut of techniques, from economic means through proxy wars up to the threat of outright nuclear confrontation, to advance their particular interests. Both of these major powers ran 'alliances' in which they were overwhelmingly the dominant force. Sometimes there were clashes of interest, as between the USA on the one hand and Britain and France on the other, over Suez, or between Russia and China in 1959. These conflicts, however, were subordinate to a central confrontation between rival imperial systems. Even during the period of its wide dissemination, theorists of cultural imperialism like Dallas Smythe failed to recognize the nature of the central conflict in the world. It is 1991, not 1945, that the classical theory of inter-imperialist rivalry is thrown into crisis by the collapse of the USSR. From that point up to the present there is only really one significant power in the world, and contemporary theories of imperialism have to be reconstructed to consider what the implications of that fact might be.

Debates over imperialism today

Since the invasion and occupation of foreign countries is now an accepted part of the foreign policy of the world's strongest state, not to mention its willing allies, clarification of the theory of imperialism might seem otiose. Even the most superficial observer is bound at least to consider comparisons with earlier empires. The inevitable parallel that has been drawn is with the period of the Vietnam War, which was the last time that the concept of imperialism attracted substantial interest. Alongside this changed political reality, the new millennium has seen a much higher degree of general recognition of the continued importance of those pervasive unequal distributions of wealth and power that theorists of globalization, with the honourable exception of Bauman, have tended to marginalize. The times are much better suited to a theory that recognizes those factors as central to social and political behaviour both in the rich and dominant countries of the North as well as the in the much more impoverished South.

The times, however, are very different from those in which the classical theory of imperialism was formulated, or indeed from those in which the theory of cultural imperialism became influential. Even if we agree that the present period is best characterized as 'imperialism', we are very far from a clear understanding of what is meant by that term. There are debates about the exact meaning of the term that are every bit as sharp as those of the classical period, and which reproduce to a surprising degree some of their central features. Before embarking on an examination of these debates, we should be clearer about which changes are of most interest for current theory.

One aspect of the classical theory retains its vitality. We most certainly live in a world dominated by large scale capital, and by the international circulation of capital, which today is at least as pronounced as it was in 1914 (Harman 2003: 57–66). The major change is that capital is much less closely integrated with the state machine than it was in the immediately preceding periods. The autarchic road to national development was closed off permanently in 1989 and the neo-liberal project in the west led to the state withdrawing at least partly from economic life. This does not mean that the state is no longer a central actor, nor that it has renounced violence for economic and political ends. Those states with political power, and most notably the USA, seek to use it to strengthen their own economic position and to ensure that they remain in a position to play a dominant role in the future when the balance of economic power is shifted even further against them. As David Harvey put it, 'whoever controls the Middle East controls the global oil spigot, and whoever controls the global oil spigot can control the global economy, at least for the near future' (2003, 19). The contemporary debate revolves around how best to understand this new role of the state.

There are, essentially, four major ways of thinking about what the role of the state in the present period is, and what its relationship to capital is. All of these theories focus on the US state, since that is by far the strongest state from the military point of view, and its actions are central to understanding international relations in the present period. They differ not only in their assessment of the importance of this state and its international role but also on the role of the other states in the world.

The first set of theorists form what we might term the positive imperialist school. This view has a considerable history, but their best known contemporary theorist is Niall Ferguson. In two popular works he argues that empire is the establishment by force of 'the free movement of goods, capital and labour' and his history of the British Empire is 'the history of globalization as it was promoted by Great Britain and its colonies' (2003: xxi, xxiii). With this definition, the US is both an imperial power and the natural inheritor of the UK's international role (2004: 286–7). US policy is to use its military force to establish the rule of liberal capitalism around the world, and from that will flow positive developments in terms of human happiness. This view, which is obviously close to the views expressed by leading foreign policy intellectuals in the USA, is one that sees the state as functional for liberal capitalism. In many ways it is the equivalent of some of the cruder Marxist theories, albeit with a positive rather than a negative assessment of the outcomes.

The second position is that associated with Negri and Hardt in their influential book *Empire* (2000). Their view is that the age of competing state bound empires is passed and that today a placeless capital and its stateless empire confront a declassified multitude. Their work has provoked considerable interest and much commentary, positive and negative (Balakrishnan, 2003; Boron, 2005; Passavant and Dean, 2004). As has often been remarked, history has not been kind to Hardt and Negri: no sooner had they published their claim for the withering away of the imperialist state than the US state began to demonstrate many signs of its continuing imperialist vitality.

The other two sets of theories share a common sense that it is not possible to reduce the actions of the state to the expression, conscious or otherwise, of the needs of capital. They tend to follow Arrighi and David Harvey in distinguishing between the 'territorial' and the 'capitalist' logics of power (Harvey, 2003: 26–31). Both recognize that the actions of states cannot be explained solely in the pursuit of the economic interests of the group of capitalists that are primarily located within its geographical boundaries.

One view, expressed by Panitch and Gindin, is that the US state is the only one capable of acting autonomously. All other contemporary states are in effect subordinate to the demands of the US state. This latter has an indirect empire to which there is no serious international challenge (Panitch and Gindin, 2006: 196–8). As they put it, 'the crisis that has produced an unconcealed American empire today lies, then, not in overaccumulation leading back to anything like inter-imperialist rivalry but in the limits [of] an informal empire based on ruling through other states' (Panitch and Gindin, 2004: 62). The struggles that are taking place today are thus a new version of the struggle of the centre to dominate and exploit the periphery and US neo-conservatism is 'a doctrine that expresses the broader aim of securing a neo-liberal capitalist order on a global scale' (ibid., 75).

The fourth main view concentrates mostly on the disjuncture between the economic and military strength of the US state, and sees its current activities as attempts to barter its overwhelming military preponderance for economic advantage (Rees, 2001: 18). In this account, there remain other states capable of independent action, which pursue different interests from that of the US state. They identify not a single imperialism personified in the USA but a plurality of existing and would-be imperial states or groupings of states. At the military level, it is true that there is today only one imperial state, but it does not 'act through' other states. On the contrary, these sometimes ally with the US and sometimes oppose it. None are today strong enough to reproduce the classic 'inter-imperialist rivalry' that led to the two World Wars, but they certainly lead to political conflicts and to trade disputes. In the very long term, the changing geopolitics of the world mean that, in the shapes of China and India, and conceivably a revitalized

Europe, there might be centres of economic and political power sufficiently strong and coherent as to mount a military challenge to the USA, but today there are no such contenders. We might therefore conclude that the distinguishing characteristic of contemporary imperialism is sharp economic rivalry accompanied by geopolitical paralysis.

In terms of the media, the logic of the first three positions is similar. All concentrate on the notion of a single world power which is overwhelmingly dominant politically and militarily. In the case of both Ferguson and Panitch and Gindin that power is the USA. In the case of Negri and Hardt power is de-territorialized but definitely unitary. Following these theorists, we would expect to find a single centre of media power, most likely in the USA. On the fourth interpretation, we would expect to find a number of centres of cultural production capable of functioning in the global market, and we would expect that they would display the same kinds of competitive behaviour, and look for the same kinds of state support, as do other industries like shoes and steel and automobiles. International conflicts over the sale of television programmes, or more recently over internet governance, would thus find echoes in state policy and state conflicts, albeit of a pacific nature.

On the basis of the evidence we have considered here, the fourth position is clearly the best fit for the contemporary world. The US is by far the largest producer, and exporter, of television programmes and many other media products, but it is certainly not the only centre. There are other centres of production that are both able to provide attractive media products for their own society and to sell some of them internationally. Everywhere, these industries seek to influence the government to improve their competitive position both internally and internationally. International competition, in particular, is a field in which the state is often active, and in which there are conflicts between states. To the extent that contemporary media have to be discussed in the context of imperialism, it is in terms of competing centres and competing states.

What's really wrong with the cultural and media imperialism paradigm?

If we accept the continued utility of the theory of imperialism to explain aspects of the media, we need to consider whether this situation can be considered as an aspect of either cultural or media imperialism. Some of the well-known critiques of the cultural and media imperialism paradigms were mistaken, others were perhaps overstated, and some were accurate. In order to decide whether we can continue to employ such terms we need to reconsider some aspects of the debate.

The claim that there was substantial 'contra-flow', that the US dominance of the global media market was seriously challenged by other producers of audio-visual artefacts, and the importance of regional markets, were all seriously overstated. In a number of cases – the import of Spanish language programmes into the US market for example – the earlier claims of contra-flow were premature. The developing market has resulted in US based media corporations gaining control of this sector and beginning to dominate the continental trade. To say that the flow of programmes is more complex than simply a flow from the USA to the rest of the world is true but not very illuminating. To claim that the USA dominates the world trade in media artefacts is, of course, a gross over-simplification of reality, but it contains an essential truth. The flow of material is, however, predominantly from the USA to the rest of the world. Consistent with the theory of imperialism, there are other important programme makers and programme exporters, mostly in the developed world. Companies based in the UK dominate the world trade in formats, and total UK TV exports are around $1 billion, for example (DCMS, 2004; Smith 2005). The scale of these operations, however, is very much smaller than that of the US giants.

A more serious criticism of the media imperialism paradigm is the way in which it argued for an effective fusion between media companies and the 'military industrial complex'. As we have seen, any satisfactory account of contemporary imperialism needs to distinguish between what is the logic of capital (i.e. the sphere of action of the capitalist enterprise) and the logic of territory (i.e. the sphere of action of the capitalist state). In the longer term, the dynamics of the media and culture industries, while sharing a capitalist logic with other industries like those of telecommunications and defence, remain distinctive. NBC is indeed a division of General Electric, but it is an exception: none of the other major global media companies are the direct extension of other units of capital. Although there is undoubtedly a process of concentration of capital going on in the media industries, both nationally and internationally, this is mostly a concentration within the industry rather than a takeover of the industry by capital from outside.

Given this lack of close articulation of different units of capital, it follows that the unity of purpose in imperial planning that writers like Schiller detected are not likely to be present. A better description of reality is that there are numerous different and competing economic interests, one minor part of which are the interests of media corporations. Certainly, there are organizations like the MPAA that seek to give the industry a united voice, but they are far from constituting a controlling centre that directs the activities of its subordinates. Such organizations may succeed in influencing state policy (the MPAA proclaims itself to have been particularly successful in that area) but they also may not. So, too, the state planners, when pursuing their own foreign policy designs, may work closely with the existing media corporations, or they may chose to employ some other grouping. The reconstruction of Iraqi media, for example, was paid for by the US government but was not undertaken by the large US media corporations but by companies only some of which have any media track record. The key personnel were British, and what they tried to establish was not an FCC and private networks but an 'Ofcom and BBC' style set-up. They initially operated under quite tight control from the Coalition Provisional Authority and then from the appointed Iraqi Interim Governing Council. These restrictions were apparently sufficiently tight as to restrain some obvious bidders, for example the BBC, from entering the competition to run the services (Peckham and Chaffin, 2004; Sakr, 2006: 244–6).

Given this state of conflicting interests, it follows that to the extent that theories of cultural and media imperialism claimed that there is a conscious policy on the part of the USA to export its media products in order to facilitate its imperial control of the rest of the world, as is often alleged without any known textual support against theorists of cultural imperialism, they would likely be mistaken. Certainly, the companies themselves have conscious goals to expand their market share, both at home and internationally. There are very often specialized units of government that are charged with assisting the international operations of media companies. Sometimes, as in the case of the struggle against the NWICO, media organizations may find themselves working very closely with their own governments, but this is not necessarily the case, and there are certainly no grounds for claiming that such collaboration is a distinguishing feature of the present epoch.

The next obvious error of these theories was in assuming that there is a fixed meaning in a television programme or film that is transmitted more or less directly to the mind of the viewers. Research, both on international and on national consumption of media, has shown that there are variant readings, depending upon a range of different variables. It does not, however, follow from this well-established reality that the issue of the trade in cultural artefacts is as devoid of issues of meaning as the trade in iron ore. In the first place, no one seriously imagines that the highly coded texts that are traded across the world are completely polysemic. On the contrary, although they are clearly open to different interpretations depending upon the characteristics of their audiences, it is universally agreed that there are in practice limits to the ways in which these texts can be interpreted; we can argue endlessly about the meanings of *King Lear* but if we want to give it a happy ending we are obliged, as were the theatre owners of the eighteenth century, to rewrite it so that Cordelia and Lear survive to be re-united and live happily ever after.

We should be careful not to overstate the degree of reinterpretation that is possible for any audience. In practice, while studies of individual programmes or series have tended to show that there is quite a range of responses possible, more systematic accounts of countries in which television is dominated by imports suggest that there is a strong tendency towards a single cultural effect. There is, it is suggested, a version of what cultivation theory would call 'mainstreaming' observed in some Caribbean countries or in Morocco, but the mainstream of values and beliefs towards which people are directed is that of another country or countries (Brown, A., 1995; Lashley, 1995; Sabry, 2003).

Secondly, the consumption of texts is only one side of the coin. There is also the issue of the production of texts. A complex symbolic structure like a television programme is inevitably dependent upon the circumstances of its production. Different persons, in different situations, with different experiences and histories, having different generic and dramatic assumptions, make different kinds of artefacts. It is widely recognized within societies that it is not desirable to have a media industry that is dominated by one kind of person. In countries with diverse populations, like the USA or the UK, very considerable efforts have been made to try, often unsuccessfully, to ensure that white men educated in elite institutions do not dominate the production of TV programmes and other major media. An exactly similar case can be made out for nationality. Hollywood is undoubtedly the capital of the world's imagination and it produces first and foremost for the US market. It is a limit on the representation of the range and diversity of human experience that internationally-traded TV programmes are largely produced by companies based in the developed world, indeed in one particular city in one country in the developed world.

Thirdly, even though it is well-established that audiences offered a choice between entertainment originating in their own culture and imported material tend to prefer that which is closer to their experiences, the realities of differential market power mean that they will very often be exposed to programmes that have been produced with the tastes and interests of the audience of a particular developed country in mind. In other words, the limits placed upon the range of human experience that is articulated in media artefacts available on the international stage will not only be the result of the nationality of the producing units but also of the fact that these organizations, whether commercial or public, will have produced them with a view to gathering a particular kind of audience with particular, quite well known, interests and tastes (Meehan, 2005).

We do not, therefore, need to accept the easy conclusion drawn by critics of cultural imperialism that, in effect, it does not matter where programmes are produced since audiences are enormously creative in their consumption of media texts. The fact that the world trade in television programmes and other media artefacts is dominated by products from a small number of countries and that one, the USA, accounts for a huge proportion of that trade, is important. At the very least it means that a particular range of human experiences are examined exhaustively in dramas, in comedy shows, in talk shows and so on, to the exclusion of alternatives. In some cases, the evidence suggests, the result of constant exposure is indeed similar to the strongest claims made by the old imperialist paradigm: people, particularly young people, come to reject the values systems within which they were born and to adopt the ideas and beliefs of other, developed countries.

The next, and perhaps most serious, error of theorists of the imperialism paradigm lay in their emphasis upon the state as the privileged site of resistance to cultural invasion and the guarantor of the vitality of authentic national cultures. Writers critical of this position were entirely correct to point out that there is nowhere a self-evidently national culture shared equally by all members of a society and that there are usually quite sharp conflicts over what kind of culture should be valued and promoted. The official culture of states will tend to reproduce the definitions of the dominant group in a society and to marginalize minority groups. It might perhaps surprise some of the 'Marxist' defenders of 'national cultures' to learn that Lenin put it rather well when he wrote that 'the general "national culture" *is* the culture of the landlords, the clergy and the bourgeoisie' (Lenin, 1913/1964: 24). Any strategy that relies on the state to act as the defender and guarantor of the authenticity of culture will thus be complicit in the imposition of a single cultural vision upon the rich complexities of any society.

The problem with this critique is that while it is essentially correct, it does not provide any alternative mechanisms that might serve to support a plurality of cultures. In media policy debates the traditional polarization of opinion has been between those that defend the role of the state and those that defend the market. It is not at all self-evident that either of these alternatives is comprehensively better than its rival in serving the real diversity of culture life in a given country. States can very often be obliged, by political pressure, to modify their cultural apparatus to allow expression to previously excluded groups: the British state, for example, was pushed in to granting a Welsh-language channel, and subsidizing it heavily, in order to meet the cultural needs of a minority population. Commercial media, for their part, will tend to serve those markets that are profitable for it: so commercial satellite television in the UK provides programming from the Indian sub-continent for diasporic audiences. The limit of the first case is that concessions depend upon political pressure. The limits of the second case are that, usually, provision for minority groups depends upon cheap access to programmes produced elsewhere and that speak to the concerns of their original audiences, and only tangentially to the lives and experiences of the minority audiences. Neither of these strategies is capable of answering the cultural needs of the mass of the population of poor and developing countries, nor of the increasingly diverse populations of the great metropolitan centres.

The final, and closely related, problem with the imperialism paradigm was that although it quite correctly began from as much of a global perspective as do theorists of globalization proper, it divided the world in to centre and periphery, and saw the key issues as being the struggle of the periphery against the centre. It had no sense at all that there were deep divisions within the 'centre' itself, both between states pursuing different national interests and within states between different social classes. It thus closed its eyes to the possibility of there being different ways in which the struggle for the conditions that could lead to free human cultural development could be theorized. In particular, just as contradictions between different versions of 'national culture' were ignored in the developing world, so contradictions within the developed world, and thus the possibility of discovering allies there, were also ignored.

Any viable account of culture in the age of imperialism will thus need to avoid these problems. While it cannot claim that the 'effect' of a diet of US programmes is predetermined for all members of the audience, it can certainly say that a diet of programmes that originate predominantly in other cultures is unlikely to allow the full cultural life of a particular community to flourish. While there may be palliative measures that might alleviate a situation – breaking the stranglehold of a sclerotic state bureaucracy for example, or providing state support for broadcasters serving audiences too small or too poor to provide an attractive market for commercial interests – the only real long term solution lies in a radical recasting of the terms of broadcasting so as to empower the populations of poor countries, and the poor within richer countries, and grant them access to a means of articulating their political and cultural needs.

Is there any such thing as cultural or media imperialism?

There is, however, a more fundamental problem with the theory of cultural imperialism. If we accept the classical Marxist definition of imperialism as the policy of conquest by finance capital, then in what sense is it possible to talk of cultural or media imperialism? The core of imperialism is a grossly coercive exercise of economic, political and military power. In the last resort, the population of one country is forced, one way or another, to accept the will of another country. Cultural or media imperialism, however, would seem to mean something different from this. As has often been noted, this was and is an ill-defined concept, and many writers have adopted contradictory interpretations. We cited Schiller's famous definition in an earlier chapter and we may note that this describes only a 'process', without specifying the agencies or mechanisms through which it was effected (Schiller, 1976: 9). There is a degree of uncertainty in Schiller's definition as to whether the process is one of seduction or coercion. Boyd-Barrett, who offered a narrower and more precise version of media imperialism, articulated a view in which the media of one country exerted 'external pressure' on the media systems of other countries. In his much later defence of his view, he added non-media dimensions to the agencies of pressure

(Boyd-Barrett, 1998: 167–8). Even though we cannot recover from any of these writers a single well-developed view of the nature of cultural and media imperialism it is nevertheless possible to state with some confidence that it was concerned with the ways in which media systems (or perhaps cultures) in powerful, metropolitan societies exert coercion on the media or cultures of other, less powerful, societies. This is not a very good description of the processes by which cultures spread.

The problem can be illustrated very clearly through the example of natural languages. As we saw earlier, language is central to culture, and there is a developed body of opinion that believes that there is something called 'linguistic imperialism', the most important contemporary example of which is the English language. We can readily accept that the dominant powers in the world speak English, that very often English is imposed as the lingua franca of countries or occupations at the expense of the languages spoken by most or many of the people involved. We can accept that this privileging of English as a medium of expression favours particular powerful groups who are either native speakers or who have access to the educational resources necessary for them to gain fluency and confidence in a foreign language (Ostler, 2005: 477–521).

English is certainly deeply imbricated in the power structures of the contemporary world, and thus in imperialist domination, and English is certainly used, consciously or unconsciously, as an instrument of domination, both domestically and as part of an imperial project. It is, however, one thing to say that English is the current language of imperialism (and has been since the nineteenth century) and quite another to say that English is an 'imperialist language'. It is not at all evident how the language, as opposed to the structures of power that use it, acts to dominate and coerce anybody. It is not itself imperialist even if it is the instrument of imperialism (Holborow, 1999).

It is certainly true that many of the structures that sustain the dominance of English – the British Council, the BBC World Service, Voice of America, most scientific associations and so on – are more or less directly instruments of the domination of the elite nations, and of the elite groups within those nations. There have indeed been many examples of political and military powers attempting to impose a language upon a reluctant population, but it is not always true that the learning of English by non-native speakers is experienced as coercion. On the contrary, there is a massive demand for the language, and people make considerable personal sacrifices in order to become fluent in it. They do this not because of the intrinsic attractions of the language but because they seek to use it as a tool for personal advancement inside powerful organizations that use it as the medium of communication. It is the organizations, and not the language, that has the seductive power.

It is possible to argue that the structure of a language imposes certain limitations and definitions on the way in which the world can be thought about and discussed, and if this is generally the case then there is no reason why it should not be true of English. No doubt there are many things that cannot be said in English. On the other hand, the historical reality appears to be that languages, and certainly the English language, have been used for different purposes at different times, and what is in one context the language of the oppressor is in another the language of the oppressed. Whatever the structural limits imposed by the English language, it has frequently been the chosen instrument of those struggling against imperialism. We should remember that one of the great turning points in the long struggle against the Apartheid regime in South Africa was the Soweto Revolt, which was a rising by young blacks protesting against being educated in Afrikaans and demanding to continue their education in English. There appear to be few structural barriers in English that prevent it being used as much to oppose imperialism and domination as to implement it.

If this is the case with language, then it is even more the case with cultural artefacts like news broadcasts and television programmes. There are indeed cases where countries use their power, ultimately their military power, to impose certain cultural and media institutions on other countries. Extreme examples of this are the occupying powers' imposition of broadcasting structures, as the victors did upon Germany and Japan in 1945 (Williams, 1976: 7–12; Smith, 1976: 130–3). A similar process took place later in Kosovo (Berisha, 2002). Iraq, where the funding, planning and many of the personnel were from the dominant countries is another case in point. More generally, USAid is very clear about its own right to control projects it funds for other governments. It forced the removal of all references to the Koran or any other religious elements from school textbooks it funded in Afghanistan and Iraq, according to their spokesman in order to 'bring them into line with the US Constitution', which (quite admirably) insists on the separation of Church and State (Clover, 2003). Less extreme, but still significant, are when the government of a dominant country uses its general political and economic leverage to open a protected market to the import of television programmes. But these are cases where a state uses its economic or military power to achieve cultural ends; they are definitely not cases of one culture coercing another. They are not evidence of cultural or media imperialism as a distinct form of domination. It is difficult to think of any instances whatsoever when cultural or media institutions have acted as independent operators to effect the domination of one country over another. It is thus best to avoid tempting terms like cultural or media imperialism since they obscure the real nature of the problems under consideration.

The cultural consequences of imperialism

The theory of imperialism offers a better explanation of the main features of contemporary society than do the various versions of the globalization paradigm, although the economically based versions of the latter come much closer to an accurate picture of the world than do many of the more culturally inflected versions. The contemporary world is indeed marked by a number of conflicting economic centres, each of which remains quite clearly identified with a particular state. Certainly, there are many companies that operate on a global scale. They have plants in many different countries. They and others move vast sums of money around the world. They sell everywhere on the planet. Their shares may be traded on different stock markets. The vast majority of companies, however, remain distinctly different in major respects, most notably in their identification with different states. General Motors is clearly a US company. Toyota is clearly Japanese. Volkswagen is clearly German.

To say that capital remains organized along national lines is not to say that national states do the immediate bidding of this or that capitalist, but in a more general sense states do attempt to achieve international advantages for what they conceive of as 'the national interest'. That includes a range of activities from peaceful and technical negotiations in the WTO through economic and political pressure right up to outright armed invasion.

The direct use of state power to establish market domination for national media companies is not, however, the everyday norm of domination and imperialism. Rather, the simple economic advantages enjoyed by media production in the advanced countries allow them to exert a mundane domination over the broadcasters of developing countries. The broadcasters of the developed world enjoy production values superior to those of their poorer competitors and thus they are able to sell their wares when their potential competitors are not. This is not 'imperialism' any more than the sale of airplanes or pharmaceuticals is 'imperialism'. It is, however, trade within an imperialist set of power relations and the outcomes act to reinforce the continuation of those relations. It is this structural relationship between grossly disparate markets that ensure the continued domination of the media products of the larger and richer countries, or rather the countries with larger and richer audiences. It is surely not accurate to describe these processes whereby a particular language, or set of cultural values, or range of media artefacts, come to dominate other countries as linguistic, or cultural, or media imperialism. A better description is perhaps that they are the linguistic, or cultural, or media consequences of imperialism. TV programmes do not dominate other TV programmes, still less do they dominate whole countries. They are more widely available, and they are often very enthusiastically consumed. But the condition for them being so widely available and so attractive is the unequal and uneven structures of power in the world, the most important of which is imperialism.

Recognizing the continued centrality of imperialism in explanations of the contemporary world does not imply that we must also accept the theory of cultural imperialism. The original formulations have been heavily, and correctly criticized, and it is neither possible nor desirable to recover the whole theory. The indispensable truth of the theory of cultural imperialism was its recognition that the global circulation of media products was dominated by a few rich countries. This remains as true as it ever was, and this trade imposes important limitations upon the ability of the poor of the world to express themselves and their experiences.

Although this trade in media products maps very closely indeed on to an imperial structure of power, it is a distinct, and illegitimate, step to introduce the concept of cultural or media imperialism. Although media corporations, and in particular trade associations like the MPAA, exert considerable efforts to influence state policy, it cannot be claimed that they act as 'imperialists': that is a term best reserved for politicians and states. Media artefacts very often embody the values of the imperialist states in which they are constructed, including the values of the considerable internal oppositions to imperialism that frequently exist even in the dominant states. Media companies profit from the political and military successes of imperialist states with which they are associated. But they do not act as imperialists in their own right, and neither do the artefacts that they produce.

The limits of participatory communication

The problems with the participatory variant of the development paradigm are much less difficult to confront. Emancipatory strategies from above lead either to repression or paralysis. The insight of the participatory variant, that the impetus towards liberation must come from the people who suffer most directly the shortcomings of the existing order, is surely a correct one. One major component of any synthesis must therefore draw very heavily upon the ideas developed in this tradition.

That is not to say, however, that there are no problems with this paradigm. There has always been a division between those who see participatory communication as a tactic appropriate only in special circumstances and those who see it as an overall strategy for social change. It is only one step from recognizing that participatory communication projects are marginal to the current situation to accepting that they are best considered as a niche activity within a field dominated by one or other descendent of the dominant paradigm funded through the World Bank and the major international development agencies (Servaes, 2000). There is an increasing divergence between this view and the recognition that the condition for effective development communication is that it must 'deal squarely with the problem of the unequal power of people at the grassroots and work to "empower" them' (Melkote and Kandath, 2001: 195). It is not easy to see how it is possible to reconcile a continued acceptance of the kinds of social power relations that are demanded by the World Bank and other agencies with a commitment to participation and genuine popular empowerment. The idea of empowerment – of democracy in the fullest sense – is a radical one that cannot co-exist with the authoritarian relations of the market and the state. It is this idea of participatory communication that forms the starting point for our discussion here.

Who, then, should 'participate'? We saw above that the notion of community upon which these theories tend to rest is an extremely problematical one. All 'communities' have different interests within them, and that is particularly the case of those that have long struggled with the immediate problems of social existence. In practice, an appeal to the will of the community and values of the community is exactly analogous, although on a much smaller scale, to the appeal of the imperialism paradigm to the national state. In both cases, the values and the will that are immediately present and dominant are those of the dominant groups. Listening more closely, one will normally hear conflicting voices, including those from within the community that articulate the problems in a different way and propose different solutions. The condition for action, and it is very much to the credit of the participatory paradigm that it is a theory of action, is that one chooses between these different, potentially contradictory voices, and devotes ones efforts and resources to helping one group or another to give a public communicative expression to its concerns. The problem is: which group to choose? Here the participatory paradigm provides no guidance.

The third major problem with the participatory paradigm lies in its location of the poor. The original dominant paradigm was overwhelmingly concerned with the rural poor. It identified both the productivity of peasant agricultural and the nature of peasant culture as being the major obstacles to development. While the participatory paradigm rejected the notion of the backward peasant trapped with an obsolete, pre-modern culture, it did inherit what we might term the 'rural bias' of the dominant paradigm. There was very good reason for this, in that, twenty years ago, the vast majority of the world's poor lived in the countryside. It was true then, and it remains true today, that however bad conditions are in the slums of the cities, rural poverty is in practice even less attractive. The flight from the countryside to the cities, long a feature of the advanced countries, is today the major form of human displacement in the world. It is entirely true that hundreds of millions still live on the land, and live poorly on the land, throughout the developing world, but the cities are no longer tiny islands isolated in a primarily rural economy and society. This increasing urbanization is likely to continue: it is projected that by 2030 around 60 per cent of the world's population will live in cities (UNCHS, 2001: 7). It follows from this that any strategy that seeks to improve the lot of the poor must today have a substantial, and steadily increasing, urban component. From this perspective, there is an increasing convergence between the kinds of problems, and the kinds of solutions, that are appropriate in the developing world and in the developed world. There has, historically, been a division between discussions of development communication and theories of radical and alternative media in the developed world. As social change transforms the world into a network of great cities, both sides of this division have increasing opportunities to learn from each other.

The fourth problem arises directly from these social changes. Poverty comes in different forms, and in the great cities of the developing world it manifests itself in irregular and casual work or in unemployment, in grotesquely inadequate housing, in crime and drug addiction and in a brutal and repressive police force. The 'community' in the city inevitably confronts forces that have different interests: the exploiters, the armed state, criminal gangs. It is not possible to imagine in the cities that the problems of the urban poor can be addressed through self-help schemes involving small agricultural improvements as they can in the countryside. Their problems are such that they demand concerted political action – for employment and employment protection, for sanitation, for housing and for security. Political action, however, means argument and, more often than not, some form of conflict. Although it provides an indispensable starting point, the participatory paradigm is not really designed to address such questions.

The fifth problem is one of agency. To its credit, the participatory paradigm, at least at the local level, rejects the state as an agent of liberation, but it is less clear that some of its preferred allies form an adequate alternative. Many contemporary versions of the participatory paradigm identify non-governmental organizations (NGOs), or more generally civil society organizations (CSOs), as the key allies, but these are very far from unproblematic and they are very variable in the actual extent of their independence from the state. Many depend heavily on governmental money. According to the OECD, governments committed $1billion directly, and another $1bn indirectly to CSOs internationally. According to another study, now rather dated, NGO income from government sources was growing rapidly and accounted for 40 per cent of total income in 1992. With this funding comes, at least sometimes, pressure to conform to the will of the donor (Rahman, 1995: 26–31). The fact is that in many cases the work of NGOs is necessarily restricted by their donors, but certainly there has been a growing trend in the last few years, particularly with the 'war on terror' (Anon, 2003; Hilton, 2004). Dependence on state funding renders NGOs potentially little more than convenient channels for government policies by other means, and very often they are a mechanism whereby the donor governments in the developed world can exert an indirect influence on the policies of governments in the developing world. According to the US charity grouping InterAction, the head of USAid told them that in fulfilling US government contracts they were acting as 'an arm of the US government' and should highlight their links in the work (Beattie, 2003). Dependence on individual private donors is not a magical solution to these problems, although any organization that depends on a large number of very small donations is likely to have a greater degree of independence than one dependent upon government or a few large corporate donors. As one commentator wrote, 'Development theology holds that NGOs stand outside the establishment. They represent a credible alternative to it. The majority of NGOs are, alas, deeply integrated with the establishment, with government and with the agenda of their funding bodies' (Gupta, 1999: 97).

The participatory project thus needs some substantial modifications if it is to be effective. In situations that demand a choice between alternative visions of the future, it is not possible to sustain the relativism of regarding all views as of equal status and values. It was the strength of the old dominant paradigm that it recognized this. However crudely writers like Lerner might sometimes have expressed the idea, some courses of action lead to stagnation or decline, while others lead to an improvement in the human condition. Secondly, it must recognize that the terrain of liberation is, everywhere, more and more urban, and that the problems facing the poor of the developing world, while vastly worse, are the same in kind as those facing the urban poor in the developed world. Thirdly, the issues that need to be confronted are ever more clearly political issues about who holds power and how they can be obliged to surrender some or all of it. Finally, the resources available for these kinds of radical actions are always going to be limited. Perhaps one may occasionally be so fortunate as to obtain resources without corresponding supervision, but mostly gifts are closely policed by donors. The struggle to improve the lot of the world's poor is, as it has always been, a struggle conducted with the slenderest of resources.

In conclusion: moving ahead

The operational conclusions from this discussion of the available paradigms are relatively simple to outline, although of course they are immensely difficult to implement in practice. The first condition is to begin with an honest and sober assessment of the resources, human and material, available to those who wish to effect a radical change in the world that will be of benefit to the mass of the poor. Such an assessment will, inevitably, come to the conclusion that the resources available are few and poor. There are no magic sources through which an attempt to empower the wretched of the earth will suddenly be endowed with the material and technical riches of the dominant mass media, either state or private. It is essential to be absolutely clear about this poverty of resources. It is not encouraging or hopeful to recognize the limitations within which one is forced to operate, nor is such a situation desirable. It is, however, unavoidable. There are sources from which a movement might gain resources, but most of them are extremely problematic.

We have seen above how the attempt to find allies in positions of political power led the proponents of the imperialism paradigm into unacceptable compromises that in the end contributed greatly to their political defeat. Governments have enormous resources at their disposal, and if they could be released to help the poor find a voice then great achievements would be possible. Unfortunately, governments are rarely, if ever, disposed to hand over resources without retaining a controlling interest in their use. The consequence is that they are, almost by definition, unlikely ever to grant people the untrammelled power to use considerable resources, even communicative resources, in ways that they determine entirely for themselves. We saw that very clearly in the case of the 'continuity variant' of the dominant paradigm. This approach begins with a conscious recognition of the need to work entirely within the framework provided by the existing order, and although it makes claims to responding to the needs of the target population, in practice the campaigning priorities are set centrally. The people are consulted only in so far as it is necessary to design messages better fitted to persuading them to adopt governmental policies. Any more radical project, which will of necessity seek to shift power and resources away from the dominant groups and towards people who are today poor and powerless, cannot build its strategy on the assumption that the state will suddenly recognize the errors of its ways and consciously provide the means to diminish its power.

Corporate donations are another possible source, but they have similar limitations. It is unlikely that this would provide a reliable stream of funding for any strategy for social change that involved a substantial shift in wealth and power. Just as much as the state, large companies are part of the problem rather than the solution. When states, even liberal well-intentioned states, and corporations, even liberal well-intentioned corporations, make substantial donations to a cause, like they did to funding the WSIS meeting in Tunisia, this is because they expect to influence the outcome in directions of which they approve, not because they aim to hand over control to other people entirely.

A different set of problems haunts the attempts by the proponents of the participatory paradigm to rely upon civil society organizations, and in particular on international non-governmental organizations. This is, it is true, a less disabling strategy. While it is hard or impossible to think of any government that does not rest on privilege and rely upon coercion, there are many NGOs that have exemplary records. They do identify wholeheartedly with the poor and devote their energies to helping them. In financial terms, however, various forms of government funding are increasingly important in the world of the international NGO and with that funding, as we saw, comes governmental influence. A realistic appraisal of the quantity of support available through NGO channels that can be directed towards the ends of radical social change is bound to conclude that it is very limited.

The final possible source of resources is to gather them from the people involved in social change themselves. This is extremely difficult, since almost by definition such people tend to be very poor and do not have vast amounts of money to spare from the daily struggle for the necessities of life. At the outset of a struggle, these realities mean that for small movements, modesty as to what can be achieved in the short term is an absolute necessity. As a movement grows, so the resources available become larger, both in terms of the money that can be raised and, perhaps more importantly, in terms of the time and energy and creativity that people give willingly and freely to a cause they believe will make the world a better place. Even then, however, what is available will almost always be dwarfed by the money and material that are available to those who uphold the existing order.

Given the limitations of available resources, it is necessary to make some very difficult initial choices about how they are best to be used. One besetting temptation, which was characteristic of the strategy following from the imperialism paradigm, was to invest energy into trying to influence states and international organizations. Quite apart from the political compromises that this entailed in the struggle for NWICO, such a strategy meant that the time, energy and resources of theorists and activists was directed towards an agenda and a timetable determined by UNESCO and its member states. This, as we saw, is a terrain upon which it is very difficult indeed for radical ideas to find any real purchase. It is not a question, as one prominent writer has argued, of displaying a 'libertarian bias' that leads to a 'demonization of the state' (Nordenstreng, 2001: 159). The state remains, we have argued, central to any political process in the contemporary world. It is rather that a strategic orientation on influencing the state implies a downgrading of the emphasis upon self-organization and self-expression that is central to the participatory paradigm.

In the case of the NWICO debates, it was not only that the strategy involved a series of alliances with some very unsavoury states but that the views and the will of the poor became inaudible. It was Schiller himself, as ever a writer more acute and nuanced than his traducers are prepared to admit, who recognized this most clearly. He wrote:

Acknowledgement must be made of UNESCO's leading role in giving prominence to the need for formulating communications policies; but the preference for experts, professionalism and from the top-down policy making evident in UNESCO papers and documentation on this subject is quite explicit ... At some point a choice has to be made between professionalism and popular participation ... [In an Advisory Panel's suggestions for a national communication policy panel] Where are the working people? Where are the nonprofessionals? How do initiatives in this proposed council originate? From the top, apparently. No feed-in from the bottom is recommended. (Schiller, 1976: 95)

The gap spotted by Schiller was not the result of some accident, or the bad faith of individuals, or a simple oversight: it came about because of the nature of the processes involved. The world of the state and the international organization is the world of the expert, the diplomat, the professional. It is not the world of the working people and the poor.

This strategic issue is not of purely historical importance. As we have seen, the will to find influence with the states and the corporations, and to have a voice and influence in international organizations is exactly what animates the enthusiasts for the WSIS. There is no question that the problems that they raised were and are of great importance, and that these activists had the best of democratic intentions, but the consequences of their choice were that, whatever the outcomes, and they were modest indeed in terms of practical results, the process remained exactly the same kind of 'top-down' activity that was characteristic of the earlier struggles.

The only realistic strategy for the use of the media, whether old traditional printed texts or the resources of cyberspace, is one that begins from an insistence upon a starting point at the bottom. This is, after all, the main conclusion reached by those who have developed the participatory paradigm, in its radical variant at least. In the case in point, the choice between a top down strategy based on the ITU and WSIS must be seen as a clear alternative to a bottom up strategy based on the World Social Forum (WSF). The latter has gathered together a large number of individuals and organizations representing various under-privileged and exploited groups and has provided a forum for exactly the kinds of discussions around how to address development that are central to any radical perspective. It is true that the WSF has been problematic in any number of ways, and may now have reached a point of diminishing returns. It has been riven by quite substantial debates: one influential current, for example, rejects any notion of a struggle over power (Holloway, 2002). It is also true that questions of communication proper, while certainly present, have not been central to the events up until now. Given the open nature of the process, however, this is more an indication of the extent to which radical communication scholars have directed their energies elsewhere than to any conscious downplaying of communication issues on the part of the organizers.

From the point of view of a bottom up strategy, the modesty of available resources is not an insurmountable obstacle. Indeed, one can even make a virtue of this necessity in that modest resources can be best applied to modest projects that begin from addressing the local and small scale problems faced by different groups of the poor. It is obvious that, at least in the short term, the possible achievements will be very modest indeed. An orientation on the grass roots, whether it is in the villages of Uttar Pradesh, the slums of Rio or the suburbs of Paris will confront a terrible shortage of resources. The natural media upon which activists will concentrate will be the small scale newspaper, the micro-local radio station, and perhaps the modest web presence. Everywhere in the world, these voices will not sound loudly against the din of the commercial media, but they will be able to articulate grievances and debate issues that find no reflection in the mainstream.

If the aim is to give the poor a voice in order to articulate their grievances and mobilize to redress them, then it is most unlikely, at least at the outset, that the large-scale media will play any central role. Everywhere in the world, the main broadcasters and newspapers are deeply implicated in the existing power structure. While they may play some role in exposing this or that abuse of the system, they do not habitually lead campaigns for a fundamental transformation of the system. Occasionally, perhaps, the voices of the poor will be heard, but usually as individuals responding to agendas set elsewhere. Very seldom do the under-privileged get the opportunity to set the terms of the debate in the mass media. It is with the small-scale media that there is an initial possibility of relating to genuinely radical movements.

It is often thought that 'small scale' means local, and that the best that can be hoped for is the development of geographically limited media. It is true that financial and physical restraints can often mean that such media are limited in distribution to just such small localities, but it does not follow that they should be so limited in their content and aspirations. On the contrary, it is essential to have a much broader perspective, both as regards the economic and political dimension of change. Political power, with which any movement for serious change must engage, if not actually confront, is overwhelmingly organized at the level of the state. It is further one of the central positive elements that must be retained from the theory of globalization that, at least so far as economic power is concerned, the arena of conflict is world wide. Even though it is essential to begin with the small scale, the perspective must always be far broader than simply the local. The ambition for a global scope that leads scholars and activists to engage with the UN system is not in itself mistaken. The problem is the choice of agency. It is not with the ITU, UNESCO or any of the other places that people have tried to spread a radical message that an international audience eager for social change can be reached. It is much more likely that the chance to generalize from the local and particular to the global and the general will be found in processes like the WSF than amongst the diplomats and consultants who dominate the official forums.

There is a further sense in which no movement that is serious about change can limit itself to the purely local and the small scale. Any lasting and fundamental change to the position of the poor of the world requires far-reaching social and political changes, and will thus ultimately involve large-scale social action. It is characteristic of such movements that, when they reach a significant size, they begin to attract towards them all sorts of groups who are themselves often relatively privileged individuals. Journalists working for the large-scale media are one such group. In periods of social crisis, at least some of these people are likely to break with the ties that bind them to the rich and powerful and to seek to find ways of assisting in social change. Very often, in serious social crises like Portugal in 1974–75 and Poland in 1980–82, almost the entire journalistic workforce will identify with the need for social change. This can entail them having their own conflict with the traditional owners of the media, and in some cases seizing the large scale outlets and running them on behalf of the mass of the population (Downing, 2001: 237–65).

As the most consistently radical proponents of the participatory paradigm recognize, it is only in and through major social crises that large-scale and long-lasting social change can be achieved. It is in such historic moments that the previously silenced and marginalized find the confidence to give expression to their deepest thoughts and hopes, and it is at precisely such moments that the compulsive routines that shackle the major media are most weakened. If it is the aim and ambition of the radical movement to speak to the whole of society, it cannot do that any time or any day. It is only in periods of real social crisis that anything more than a small-scale project becomes at all feasible.

There is a further, important, consequence of this recognition that it is in moments of social crisis that the aim of radical communication can be achieved. The challenge to the existing controllers of the mass media, whether state or commercial, that is implicit in the desire for radicalizing communication is inescapable. A social crisis in which new voices are heard is a social crisis inside all of the power structures of society, including (perhaps especially) the mass media. The expectation must be that, as in the Chilean case analysed by Mattelart, the existing controllers of the media will resist the attempts to change the bias of communication in favour of the poor. What follows from that, however, is the opposite of the conclusion that the media imperialism paradigm wished to draw. If it is only in great social crises that the chances exist for changing communication, and if in those moments it is almost certain that the state and the media owners will resist such a change, then it is a mistake to ally with exactly these people in the struggle against 'imperialism', whether cultural or military or economic.

Imperialism is, we have seen, a real and central force in contemporary politics, and it is certain that human liberation cannot be achieved without overcoming it. The allies of the poor and the powerless in the developing world are not, however, the people who run the media in their own countries. However much the latter may resent their subordination to the rulers of the developed world, they fear and will oppose their own poor even more. Of course, the poor of the developing world need allies. Otherwise they can have few hopes of defeating the enormous wealth and power that lies in the hands of their opponents. But those allies are more likely to be found amongst the poor and the powerless of the developed world than amongst the rich and the powerful of their own countries or of the richer countries themselves.

The long record of research and activism that we have reviewed in this book thus leads to a series of fairly clear conclusions. The strand of thinking that we have labelled the participatory paradigm is, in its radical versions, the analysis that comes closest to grasping the essence of the matter. This line of thought begins, correctly, from the perception that it is only when the poor and the oppressed find their own voices that they will have the power and the confidence to resolve their own problems. The starting point for any better understanding of the way ahead is this fundamental insight. The task is not to replace it but to develop its logical implications.

That logic begins from the 'bottom' and works up, rather than the other way around, but a stress on the popular is not enough to resolve each and every question that presents itself. As we saw, the 'community' is almost always made up of different groups with different ideas and interests, and we need to decide which, if any, of these are likely to lead to positive results. What is more, not every manifestation of popular opinion, even from oppressed groups, necessarily contributes to liberation: in the advanced countries, for example, racism is often found in a particularly virulent form amongst groups who, while not at the very bottom of the social hierarchy, occupy a place just above it. There are, no doubt, other examples from the developing world that demonstrate the same problem.

Effective communication, and effective social changes, thus require judgement about which groups to give voice to, and which objectives to attempt to achieve: in other words, it is irreducibly political. What the detail of those politics should be is not something that we can properly discuss here, but we can at least identify the main issues that it would have to resolve. The first of these is the nature of the 'change agent' in this approach. Media, even the very modest media with which it is necessary to begin, do not arise without planning and organization, and if the task at hand is essentially political, then the kind of organization under discussion must be political as well. The change agents, or the 'committed cadres' as we heard Pradip Thomas call them, are necessarily political activists with a view as to how change can come about.

The second follows directly from the basic propositions of the participatory paradigm: in sharp contrast both to the dominant paradigm and its descendants on the one hand, and the imperialism paradigm on the other, the new approach must of necessity be of the most thoroughgoing democratic kind. This approach has no theoretical space for forcing or obliging people to do what an elite, whether Stalinist, Social-Democratic or Free Market Liberal by persuasion, knows is best for them.

An acceptance of this founding principle together with the recognition of the complexity of popular sentiment implies that persuasion as well as expression will be a central task. If, as is likely, there are contradictory views about what should be done, then a majority view can only be achieved through debate and discussion. The organization that is working for change will unquestionably have views on the best course of action that should be pursued, and these will rightly and properly find expression in the media they are producing. In other words, one of the functions of media designed to effect social change is that they are propagandist, although if they are only propagandist and do not enter into a genuine dialogue with the mass of the population they will fail even in this task.

The fourth problem that will require a resolution is the issue of friends and enemies. It is here that the old alliance with the unreconstructed imperialism paradigm was at its most destructive, but a proper understanding of what imperialism means can lead to a much more positive outcome. The poor of the world whose plight formed the starting point of this entire discussion are both oppressed and exploited. Their natural allies in the world are not governments or businesses but other people who have the same experiences. These are certainly to be found in the developing countries of the world, but they are also to be found in the heartlands of imperialism itself. Conditions of life and labour are enormously better in Detroit or Nagoya or Birmingham or Paris than they are in the cities of the developing world, but the same kinds of divisions between rich and poor, rulers and ruled, exist in both situations. The theory of 'centre and periphery' includes amongst its many faults the fact that it considers the countries of the developed world to be undifferentiated enemies of the poor, and thus turns its back upon millions of potential allies.

The final problem to be mentioned here is deciding upon the nature of social change. It is obvious that the kinds of self-confidence and self-expression that are central to this approach are not, most of the time, mass phenomena. A host of structures exist that, if they are not designed expressly to silence and humiliate, have the effect of doing so in spite of themselves. The moments in which the poor find a voice and find confidence are rare just because of their inherent tendency to generalize. If once villagers have the confidence to stand up to landlords, or if urban workers have the confidence to stand up to their bosses, then that confidence cannot be isolated on the farm or in the factory. It necessarily questions all of the structures, mental and physical, that keep the poor in their places.

The role of communication and media in the effort to improve the lot of the world's poor is therefore one that is integral to building a social movement. On its own, the best communication cannot succeed in changing the situation. Only when the poor are organized and confident can the problems that face them be addressed, and it is social action that gives people confidence and organization. The media have a central role in this process because finding a public voice is one of the ways in which both confidence and organization can be built.

REFERENCES

Ahmad, A. 1995. Globalization and the Nation-State. *Seminar #4: India 1995. A Symposium on the Year that Was,* pp. 43–48.

Albrow, M. 1996. *The Global Age: State and Society beyond Modernity.* Cambridge: Polity Press.

Al Hurra. 2004. *Welcome to Alhurra.* At http://www.alhurra.com/. Accessed 25 February 2004.

Alleyne, M. 1997. *News Revolution: Political and Economic Decisions about Global Information.* Basingstoke, Hants: Macmillan.

Amin, S. 1997. *Capitalism in the Age of Globalization.* London: Zed Books.

Amnesty International. 2003. *People's Republic of China: Continuing abuses under a new leadership – summary of human rights concerns.* 1 October 2003. At http://web.amnesty.org/library/Index/ENGASA170352003. Accessed 23 February 2004.

——— 2004. *Rights for All: Amnesty International's Campaign on the United States of America.* At http://www.amnestyusa.org/rightsforall/prison.html. Accessed 22 February 2004.

Ang, I. 1985. *Watching Dallas: Soap operas and the melodramatic imagination.* London: Methuen.

Ang, P. H. and S. Dalmia. 2000. 'Operational, not theoretical: a critique of the current paradigm in development communication'. *Asian Journal of Communication,* 10 (1): 18–32.

Anonymous. 1967. *Radio and Television in the Service of Education and Development in Asia: Reports and Papers in Mass Communication #49.* Report of a conference held in Bangkok 16–23 May 1966. Paris: UNESCO.

Anonymous. 1970a. *Broadcasting From Space: Reports and Papers in Mass Communication #60.* Paris: UNESCO.

Anonymous. 1970b. *Mass Media in Society: The Need for Research: Reports and Papers in Mass Communication #59.* Paris: UNESCO.

Anonymous. 2003. 'NGOs and UN face pressure over Iraq'. *Reuter's Foundation AlertNe 7 July 2003.* At http://www.alternet.org/thefacts/reliefresources/minearview.htm. Accessed 15 July 2004.

Apfel, F. 1999. Introduction. F. Apfel, ed. *The Pen is as Mighty as the Surgeon's Scalpel: Improving health communication impact.* London: Nuffield Trust/World Health Organisation, pp. 1–3.

Appadurai, A. 1990. 'Disjuncture and difference in the global cultural economy' in M. Featherstone, ed., *Global Culture: Nationalism, Globalization and Modernity.* London: Sage, pp. 295–310.

——— 1996. *Modernity at Large: cultural dimensions of globalization.* Minneapolis, MN: University of Minnesota Press.

Arnst, R. 1996. 'Participation approaches to the research process' in J. Servaes, T. Jacobson and S. White, eds, *Participatory Communication for Social Change.* New Delhi: Sage, pp. 109–22.

Ascroft, J. 1995. 'Participatory decision making: a parable' in S. White, S. Nair and J. Ascroft, eds, *Participatory Communication: Working for Change and Development*. New Delhi: Sage, pp. 247–58.

Ascroft, J. and S. Masilela. 1995. 'Participatory decision making in Third World development' in S. White, S. Nair and J. Ascroft, eds, *Participatory Communication: Working for Change and Development*. New Delhi: Sage. pp. 259–94.

Ashok Kumar, E. 1999. *Social Dimensions of Communication and Rural Development*. Rothak, India: Spellbound Publications.

Askoy, A. and K. Robins. 1992. 'Hollywood for the 21st century: global competition for critical mass in image markets. *Cambridge Journal of Economics*, 16 (1): 1–22.

Awa, 1996. The indigenous farmer and the scientific researcher: issues in participatory research in Africa, in J. Servaes, T. Jacobson and S. White, eds, *Participatory Communication for Social Change*. New Delhi: Sage, pp. 127–49.

Balakrishnan, G. ed. 2003. *Debating Empire*. London: Verso.

Baldwin, K. 1995. 'Montezuma's revenge: reading *Los Ricos También Lloran* in Russia' in R. Allen, ed., *To be Continued: Soap operas around the world*. London: Routledge, pp. 285–300.

Balit, S. 1999. 'Looking toward the year 2000: communication for development in a changing world', in *Journal of Development Communication*, 10 (1): 1–8.

Baran, P. and P. Sweezy. 1966. *Monopoly Capital: an Essay on the American Economic and Social Order*. New York: Monthly Review Press.

Barker, C. 1997. *Global Television: an Introduction*. Oxford: Basil Blackwell.

———— 1999. *Television, Globalization and Cultural Identities*. Buckingham: Open University Press.

Barratt Brown, M. 1974. *The Economics of Imperialism*. London: Penguin.

Bauman, Z. 1998. *Globalization: The Human Consequences*. Cambridge: Polity Press.

Beattie, A. 2003. 'NGOs under pressure on relief funds', *FT.com*. Accessed 15 July 2004.

Beck, U. 2000. *What is Globalization?* Cambridge: Polity Press.

Beltrán, L. 1976. Alien premises, objects and methods in Latin American communication research, in E. Rogers, ed. *Communication and Development: Critical Perspectives*. London: Sage, pp. 15–42.

———— 1988. Foreword, in Fox, E. ed. *Media and Politics in Latin America: The Struggle for Democracy*. London: Sage, pp. 1–5.

———— 1989. Development communication: alternative systems. *International Encyclopaedia of Communication*, 2: 12–17.

Berisha, V. 2002. *Media in Kosova: Struggles in building a public service broadcaster from scratch*. Unpublished MA thesis, University of Westminster.

Berrigan, F. 1981 *Community Communications: The Role of Community Media in Development: Reports and Papers on Mass Communication #90*. Paris: UNESCO.

Bertelsmann. 2002. *Annual Report January 1 through December 31, 2002*. At http://investor.bertelsmann.de/wms/pdf/Geschftsbericht_engl.pdf. Accessed 6 April 2003.

Berwanger, D. 1980. 'The establishment of a new international information order – summary of a world-wide debate' in D. Bielenstein, ed., *Towards and New World Information Order: Consequences for Development Policy*. (2nd edn). Bonn: Institut für Internationale Begegnungen and Friedrich-Ebert-Stiftung, pp. 17–48.

Bessette, G. 1999. 'Educating and communicating for social change: a letter from Aminou'. *Journal of Development Communication*, December 1999, 10 (2): 1–24.

—— 1995. 'Development communication: a conceptual framework', in C. Okigbo, ed., *Media and Sustainable Development*. Nairobi: African Council for Communication Education, pp. 111–32.

—— 2006. 'Facilitating dialogue, learning and participation in natural resources management' in G. Bessette, ed., *People, Land And Water: Participatory Development Communication for Natural Resource Management*. London: Earthscan, pp. 3–32.

Beyer, P. 1994. *Religion and Globalization*. London: Sage.

BHHRG. 2002. *British Helsinki Human Rights Group. The Czech Republic: The Czech Media One Year On*. At http://www.bhhrg.org/Print.asp?ReportID =4&CountryID=8. Accessed 9 March 2004.

Bielby, D. and L. Harrington. 2002. 'Markets and Meanings: The global syndication of television programming' in D. Crane, N. Kawashima and K. Kawasaki, eds, *Global Culture: Arts, Policy and Globalization*. London: Routledge, pp. 215–232.

Bielenstein, D. (ed.). 1980. *Towards and New World Information Order: Consequences for Development Policy*. (2nd edn). Bonn: Institut für Internationale Begegnungen and Friedrich-Ebert-Stiftung.

Bigman, S. (For USIA). 1952/1961. 'Prestige, personal influence, and opinion', in W. Schramm, ed., *The Process and Effects of Mass Communication Research*. Urbana, IL: University of Illinois Press, pp. 402–10.

Boot, M. 2003. 'American imperialism? No need to run away from the label', *USA Today*, May 5 2003. Republished at http://www.benadorassociates.com/ article/368. Accessed 19 June 2004.

Bordenave, J. 1995. 'Participative communication as a part of building participative society', in S. White, S. Nair and J. Ascroft, eds, *Participatory Communication: Working for Change and Development*. New Delhi: Sage, pp. 35–48.

Boron, A. 2005. *Empire and Imperialism: A critical reading of Michael Hardt and Antonio Negri*. London: Zed.

Boyd-Barrett, O. 1977. 'Media imperialism; towards an international framework for the analysis of media systems', in J. Curran, M. Gurevitch and J. Woollacott, eds, *Mass Communication and Society*. London: Edward Arnold, pp. 116–35.

—— 1980. *The International News Agencies* London: Constable.

—— 1997. 'international communication and globalization: contradictions and directions', in Ali Mohammadi, ed., *International Communication and Globalization*. London: Sage, pp. 7–26.

—— 1998. 'Media imperialism reformulated' in D. Thussu, ed., *Electronic Empires: Global Media and Local Resistance*. London: Arnold, pp. 157–76.

Boyd-Barrett, O. and D. Thussu. 1992. *Contraflow in global news: international and regional news exchange mechanisms*. London: John Libbey.

Brennan, S. 2003. 'Chinese television', *The Hollywood Reporter.com*. May 18 2003. At http://www.hollywoodreporter.com/thr/international/feature_display.jsp?vnu_ content_id=1913513. Accessed 26 March 2004.

Brooks, S. and W. Wohlforth. 2002. 'American primacy in perspective', *Foreign Affairs*, 81 (4): 20–33.

Brown, A. 1995. 'Caribbean cultures and mass communication technology: re-examining the cultural dependency thesis' in H. Dunn, ed., *Globalization, Communications and Caribbean Identity*. Kingston, Jamaica: Ian Randle, pp. 40–54.

—— 1997. 'New communication policies and communication technologies in the Caribbean' in M. Bailie and D. Winseck eds, *Democratic Communication:*

Comparative Perspectives on Information and Power. Cresskill, NJ: Hampton, pp. 159–71.

Brown, H. 1995. 'American media impact on Jamaican youth: the cultural dependency thesis', in H. Dunn, ed., *Globalization, Communication and Caribbean Identity.* Kingston, Jamaica: Ian Randle, pp. 40–54.

Brown, W. J., S. Kiruswa and B. P. Fraser. 2003. 'Promoting HIV/AIDS prevention through soap operas: Tanzania's experience with "Maisha"' *Communicare,* 22: 90–111.

BTS. 2002. *Bureau of Transportation Statistics: National Transportation Statistics 2002.* At http://www.bts.gov/publications/national_transportation_statistics/2002/index.html. Accessed 11 February 2004.

Bukharin, N. 1972. *Imperialism and the World Economy.* London: The Merlin Press.

Callinicos, A. 1994. *Marxism and the New Imperialism.* London: Bookmarks.

———— 2003. *The New Mandarins of American Power.* Cambridge: Polity.

Canova-Lamarque, G., M. Perrot and B. López. 1995. 'France: Identity crisis of regional television and expansion of local television in M. Spà and C. Garitaonandia, eds, *Television in the regions and the European audio-visual space.* London: John Libbey, pp. 43–64.

Caute, D. 1978. *The Great Fear: The Anti-Communist Purge Under Truman and Eisenhower.* London: Secker and Warburg.

Chan, J. 1996. 'Television in Greater China: structure, exports and market formation' in J. Sinclair, E. Jacka and S. Cunningham, eds, *New Patterns in Global Television: Peripheral Vision.* Oxford: Oxford University Press, pp. 126–60.

———— 2002. 'Disneyfying and globalizing the Chinese legend mulan: a story of transculturation', in J. Chan and B. McIntyre, eds, *In Search of Boundaries: Communication, Nation-states and Indentities.* Westport, CT: Ablex, pp. 225–48.

Chander, R. and K. Karnik. 1976. *Planning for Satellite Broadcasting: The Indian Instructional Television Experiment: Reports and Papers in Mass Communication #78.* Paris: Unesco.

Chapman, G., J. Johnson and P. Gould. 1986. *International Television Flow in Western Europe.* Cambridge: Development Policy.

Chin Saik Yoon. 1996. 'Participatory communication for development' in G. Bessette and C. V. Rajasunderam, eds, *Participatory development communication: A West African agenda.* Ottawa: IDRC, pp. 37–61.

———— 2000. 'Development communication in Asia' in Jan Servaes, ed., *Walking on the other side of the information highway.* Penang: Southbound, pp. 22–44.

Chu, G. 1994. 'Communication and development: some emerging theoretical perspectives' in A. Moemeka, ed., *Communicating for Development: A New Pan-Disciplinary Perspective.* Albany, NY: SUNY Press, pp. 34–73.

Clover, C. 2003. Education minister hits at USAid over textbook policy. *Ft.com.* Accessed 15 July 2004.

CME. 2004. *Central European Media Enterprises Ltd. Annual Report for the Fiscal Year ended 31 December 2003* (Form 10-K). At http://www.sec.gov/Archives/edgar/data/925645/000101540204000664/body_10k.htm. Accessed 9 March 2004.

Cohen, S. 1996. 'Mobilising communities for participation and empowerment' in J. Servaes, T. Jacobson and S. White, eds, *Participatory Communication for Social Change.* New Delhi: Sage, pp. 223–48

Collins, R. 1993. *Audiovisual and Broadcasting Policy in the European Community.* London: University of North London Press.

Corcoran, F. 2004. *RTÉ and the Globalization of Irish Television*. Bristol, UK: Intellect.

Cruise O'Brien, R. 1976. *Professionalism in Broadcasting: Issues of International Dependence*. Brighton: Institute of Development Studies at the University of Sussex.

Cunningham, S. and E. Jacka. 1996. *Australian Television and International Mediascapes*. Cambridge: Cambridge University Press.

Curran, J. 2002. 'New revisionism in media and cultural studies' in J. Curran *Media and Power*. London: Routledge, pp. 107–26. (Originally published in the *European Journal of Communication* 5: 2–3, 1990.)

Curran, J. and J. Seaton. 2003. *Power with Responsibility: The press and broadcasting in Britain (6th edn)* London: Routledge.

de Moragas Spà, M. and C. Garitaonandia. 1995. *Television in the regions and the European audio-visual space*. London: John Libbey, pp. 5–20.

de Santis, H. 2003. 'Mi programa es su programa: tele/visions of a Spanish-language diaspora in North America' in K. Karim, ed., *The Media of Diaspora*. London: Routledge, pp. 63–75.

de Sola Pool, I. 1966. 'Communication and development' in M. Weiner, ed., *Modernization: The Dynamics of Growth*. New York: Basic Books, pp. 98–109.

———— 1977. 'The governance of mass communication' in M. Terheranian, F. Hakimzadeh and M. Vidale, eds, *Communications Policy for National Development: A Comparative Perpsective*. London: Routledge and Kegan Paul, pp. 130–48.

DCMS. 13 May 2004. Press notices: UK TV exports approach $1 billion for the first time. At http://www.culture.gov.uk/global/press_notices/archive_2004/dcms_release.htm. Accessed 29 July 2005.

Dervin, B. and R. Huesca. 1995. 'The participatory communication for development narrative: an examination of meta-theoretic assumptions and their impacts' in T. Jacobson and J. Servaes, eds, *Theoretical Approaches to Participatory Communication*. Cresskill, NJ: Hampton Press pp. 169–210.

Dirlik, A. 2003. 'Global modernity? Modernity in an age of global capitalism. *European Journal of Social Theory*, 6 (3): 275–92.

Dissanayake, W. 1984. 'A Buddhist approach to development: a Sri Lankan endeavour' in G. Wang and W. Dissanayake, eds, *Continuity and Change in Communication Systems*. Norwood, NJ: Ablix, pp. 39–51.

Dissanayake, W. and B. Belton. 1983. 'Reflections on critical theory and communica-tion research' in W. Dissanayake, and A. Said, eds, *Communications Research and Cultural Values*. Singapore: Asian Media Information and Communication Centre, pp. 127–39.

Dorfman, A. and A. Mattelart. 1975/84. *How to Read Donald Duck: Imperialist Ideology in the Disney Comic*. New York: International General.

Dower, J. 1999. *Embracing Defeat: Japan in the Wake of World War II*. London: Allen Lane, The Penguin Press.

Downing, J. 2001. *Radical Media: Rebellious Communication and Social Movements*. Thousand Oaks, CA: Sage.

Dragon, A. 2001. *Making Waves: Stories of Participatory Communication for Social Change*. New York: Rockefeller Foundation.

Drilik, A. 1996. 'The global in the local' in R. Wilson and W. Dissanayake, eds, *Global/Local: Cultural Production and the Transnational Imaginary*. London: Duke University Press, pp. 21–45.

The Drum Beat. Available at http://www.comminit.com.

Dube, S. 1967. 'A note on communication in economic development' in D. Lerner and W. Schramm, eds, *Communication and Change in the Developing Countries.* Honolulu, Hawaii: East-West Center Press, pp. 93–97.

Duczynska, I. 1978. *Workers in Arms: The Austrian Schutzbund and the Civil War of 1934.* New York: Monthly Review Press.

Eapen, K. 1986. 'Transfer of technology: the Insat experience' in J. Becker, G. Hedebro and L. Paldan, eds, *Communication and Domination: Essays to Honor Hebert I. Schiller.* Norwood, NJ: Ablex, pp. 45–52.

Easlea, B, 1973. *Liberation and the Aims of Science. Obstacles to the Building of Beautiful World.* London: Chatto and Windus (for Sussex University Press).

EIC. 8 May 2003. Written comments of the entertainment industry coalition for free trade on the US – Chile Free Trade Agreement before the International Trade Commission May 8 2003. At http://www.mpaa.org/legislation/index.htm. Accessed 13 February 2004.

Eisenstadt, S. 1966. *Modernization: Protest and Social Change.* Englewood Cliffs, NJ: Prentice-Hall Inc.

——— 1973. *Tradition, change and modernity.* New York: John Wiley and Sons.

El-Oteifi, G. n.d. *Call for a New International Information Order: Preliminary Remarks.* Paris: UNESCO. (Probably 1981.)

Fair, J.E. 1989. '29 years of theory and research on media and development: the dominant paradigm impact'. *Gazette,* 44: 129–50.

Fair, J.E. and H. Shah. 1997. 'Continuities and discontinuities in communication and development research since 1958'. *Journal of International Communication,* 4 (2): 3–23.

Farn, A.C., K. Witte, K. Jarato and T. Menard. 2005. 'The effectiveness of media use in health education: Evaluation of an HIV/AIDS television campaign in Ethiopia'. *Journal of Health Communication,* 10 (3): 225–236.

Fascell, D. 1979. 'Introduction' in D. Fascell, ed., *International News Under Attack.* London: Sage, pp. 1–14.

——— 1986. *International Communication Policy: Preparing for the Future.* Washington, DC: Center for Strategic and International Studies, Georgetown University.

Featherstone, M. 1996. *Undoing Culture: Globalization, Postmodernism and Identity.* London: Sage.

Ferguson, M. 1992. 'The mythology about globalization. *European Journal of Communication,* 7 (1992): 69–93.

Ferguson, N. 2003. *Empire: How Britain made the Modern World.* London: Allen Lane.

——— 2004. *Colossus: The Rise and Fall of the American Empire.* London: Allen Lane.

Financial Times. 12 February 2004. Leader: Sweet Deal. At http://search.ft.com/search/article.html?id=040212001352&query=sugar&vsc_appId=totalSearch&state=Form. Accessed 13 February 2004.

Flor, A. 1991. 'Development communication and the policy sciences'. *Journal of Communication Development,* December 1991 2 (2): 74–81.

Flournoy, D. 1992. *CNN World Report: Ted Turner's International News Coup.* London: John Libbey.

Flournoy, D. and R. Stewart. 1997. *CNN: Making News in the Global Market.* Luton: University of Luton Press/John Libbey Media.

Fox, E. 1988. 'Media politics in Latin America' in Fox, E., ed., *Media Politics in Latin America: the struggle for democracy.* London: Sage, pp. 6–35.

———— 1997. *Latin American Broadcasting: From Tango to Telenovela*. Luton: John Libbey Media.

Frank, A.G. 1967. *Capitalism and Underdevelopment in Latin America*. New York: Monthly Review Press.

———— 1972. *Lumpenbourgeoisie: Lumpenproletariat. Dependency, Class and Politics in Latin America*. New York: Monthly Review Press.

Friedman, J. 1990. 'Being in the world: Globalization and localization. 1990'. *Theory, culture and Society*, 7 (2), 1990: 311–28.

———— 1994. *Cultural Identity and Global Process*. London: Sage.

———— 2002 'Globalization and the making of a global imaginary' in G. Stald and T. Tufte, eds, *Global Encounters: Media and Cultural Transformation*. Luton: University of Luton Press, pp. 13–31.

French, D. and M. Richards. 1996. 'From global development to global culture' in D. French and M. Richards, eds, *Contemporary Television: Eastern Perspectives*. London: Sage, pp. 22–48.

Frith, S. 2000. 'The discourse of world music' in G. Born and D. Hesmondhalgh, eds, *Western Music and its Others: Difference, Representation and Appropriation in Music*. Berkely, CA: University of California Press, pp. 305–22.

FT.com. 2004. *Investing data tools*. At http://briefings.ft.com/company. Accessed 28 February 2004.

Galtung, J. and Vincent, R. 1992. *Global Glasnost: Toward a New World Information and Communication Order?* Cresskill, N.J.: Hampton Press.

Garitaonandiá, C. 1993. 'Regional television in Europe'. *European Journal of Communication*, 8 (4): 277–94.

Geras, N. 1990. 'Seven types of obloquy: Travesties of Marxism' *The retreat of the intellectuals: Socialist Register 1990*. London: Merlin, pp. 1–34.

Gerbner, G., H. Mowlana and K. Nordenstreng, eds, 1993. *The Global Media Debate: Its Rise, Fall and Renewal*. Norwood, N.J.: Ablex.

Gerth, H. and W. Mills. 1958. *From Max Weber: Essays in Sociology*. New York: Oxford University Press.

Giddens, A. 1990. *The Consequences of Modernity*. Cambridge: Polity Press.

———— 2002. *Runaway World: How Globalization is Reshaping our Lives*, (2nd edn). London: Profile.

Gillespie, M. 1995. *Television, Ethnicity and Cultural Change*. London: Routledge.

Gilpin, R. 2000. *The Challenge of Global Capitalism: The World Economy in the 21st Century*. Princeton, NJ: Princeton University Press.

Gleick, E. 1998. 'The Murdoch chill factor'. *Time*, March 9 1998, 151 (10). At http://www.time.com/time/magazine/1998/int/980309/business.the_murdoch_chi9.html. Accessed 11 July 2003.

Global Policy Forum. 2004. *Funding For NGOs*. At http://www.globalpolicy.org/ngos/role/fundindx.htm. Accessed 27 July 2004.

Golding, P. 1974. 'Media role in national development: critique of a theoretical orthodoxy'. *Journal of Communication*, 24 (3): 39–53.

———— 1977. 'Media professionalism in the Third World: the transfer of an ideology' in J. Curran, M. Gurevitch and J. Woollacott, eds, *Mass Communication and Society*. London: Edward Arnold, pp. 291–314.

Golding, P. and P. Eliot. 1979. *Making the News*. London: Longman.

Gomez, R. 1999. Facilitating participatory action research: looking into the future with Orlando Fals Burda' in S. White, ed., *The Art of Facilitating Participation: Releasing the Power of Grassroots Communication*. New Delhi: Sage, pp. 151–59.

Gonzales Manet, E. 1986. 'Issues and developments' in K. Nordenstreng, E. Gonzales Manet and W. Kleinwächter, eds, *New International Information and Communication Order Sourcebook*. Prague: International Organisation of Journalists, pp. 43–60.

Gore, M. 1983. *The Site Experience: Reports and Papers in Mass Communication #91*. Paris: UNESCO.

Gould, P., J. Johnson and G. Chapman. 1984. *The Structure of Television/Television: The World of Structure*. London: Pion.

Grantham, B. 2000. *Some Big Bourgeois Brothel: Contexts for France's Culture Wars with Hollywood*. Luton: University of Luton Press.

Griffiths, A. 1993. '*Pobol y Cwm*: The construction of national and cultural identity in a Welsh-language soap opera' in P. Drummond, R. Patterson and J. Willis, eds, *National Identity in Europe*. London: British Film Institute, pp. 9–24.

Guback, T. and T. Varis. 1982. *Transnational Communication and Cultural Industries: Reports and Papers in Mass Communication #92*. Paris: UNESCO.

Guevara, J. 1995. 'El Salvadorean women: empowerment through sustained economic and community development in D. Newsom and B. Carrel, eds, *Silent Voices*. Lantham, MA: University Press of America, pp. 17–29.

Gumucio-Dagron, A. and T. Tufte, eds. 2006. *Communication for social change Anthology: Historical and contemporary readings*. South Orange, NJ: Communication for Social Change Consortium.

Gupta, V. 1999. *Communication Technology, Media Policy and National Development*. New Delhi: Concept Publishing.

Hachten, W. 1971. *Muffled Drums: The News Media in Africa*. Ames, Iowa: University of Iowa Press.

Hafez, K. 2007. *The myth of media globalization*. Cambridge: Polity.

Hall, S. 1991. 'The local and the global: Globalization and ethnicity' in A. King, ed., *Culture, Globalization and World-System*. Basingstoke: Macmillan, pp. 19–40.

——— 1992. 'The question of cultural identity' in S. Hall, D. Held and T. McGrew, eds, *Modernity and its Futures*. Cambridge: Polity, pp. 273–326.

Hamelink, C. 1977. *The Corporate Village*. Rome: IDOC. (*Dossier #4*.)

——— 1984. *Transnational Data Flows in the Information Age*. Lund, Sweden: Studentlitterartur.

——— 1994. *The Politics of World Communication: A Human Rights Perspective*. London: Sage.

——— 1997. 'World communication: business as usual?' in M. Baillie and D. Winseck, eds, *Democratising Communication: Comparative Perspectives in Information and Power*. Cresskill, NJ: Hampton, pp. 407–25.

——— 2006. 'Could the WSIS have been different?' *IAMCR Newsletter*, 16 (1), April 2006: 7–8.

Hannerz, U. 1990. 'Cosmopolitans and locals in world culture' in M. Featherstone, ed., *Global Culture: Nationalism, Globalization and Modernity*. London: Sage. pp. 237–51.

——— 1996. *Transnational Connections: Culture, People, Places*. London: Routledge.

Hardt, M. and A. Negri. 2000. *Empire*. Cambridge, MA: Harvard University Press.

Harman, C. 1983. *Class Struggles in Eastern Europe 1945-83*. London: Pluto Press.

——— 1988. *The Fire Last Time: 1968 and After*. London: Bookmarks.

——— 2003. 'Analysing imperialism'. *International Socialism*, 2 (99): 3–81.

Harris, N. 1971. *Beliefs in Society: The Problem of Ideology*. London: Penguin.

Harrison, P. and A. Beck. 2003. *USA Prisoners in 2002*. At http://www.prisonersbiblecrusade.org/Reports%20&%20Stats/usa_prisoners_2002.htm. Accessed 22 February 2004.

Hart-Landsberg, M. and P. Burkett. 2005. *China and Socialism: Market reforms and class struggle*. New York: Monthly Review Press.

Hartmann, P., B. Patil and A. Dighe. 1989. *The Mass Media and Village Life: An Indian Study*. New Delhi: Sage.

Harvey, D. 2003. *The New Imperialism*. Oxford: Oxford University Press.

Hasanpour, A. 2003. 'Diaspora, homeland and communication technologies' in K. Karim, ed., *The Media of Diaspora*. London: Routledge, pp. 76–88.

Hedebro, G. 1982. *Communication and Social Change in Developing Nations: A Critical View*. Ames, Iowa: Iowa State University Press.

Held, D. and A. McGrew. 2002. *Globalization/Anti-Globalization*. Cambridge: Polity Press.

Held, D., A. McGrew, D. Goldblatt and J. Perraton. 1999. *Global Transformations: Politics, Economics and Culture*. Cambridge. Polity Press.

Hepworth, M. 1994 'The information economy in a spatial context: city states in a global village' in R. Babe, ed., *Information and Communication in Economics*. London: Kluwer Academic, pp. 211–28.

Herman, E. and R. McChesney. 1997. *The global media: the new missionaries of global capitalism*. London: Cassell.

Hernández-Ramos, P. and W. Schramm. 1989. 'Development communication: I history and theories'. In *International Encyclopaedia of Communication*, vol. 2. New York: Oxford University Press, pp. 9–12.

Hesmondhalgh, D. 1998. 'Globalisation and cultural imperialism: a case study of the music industry' in R. Keily and P. Marfleet, eds, *Globalization and the Third World*. London: Routledge, pp. 163–83.

———— 2002. *The Cultural Industries*. London: Sage.

Hewavitharana, S. 1995. 'Some thoughts concerning participation in development. *Journal of Development Communication*, 6 (1): 38–45.

Hilton, I. 2004. 'Comment and analysis: hearts and minds at any cost'. *Guardian Unlimited 13 July 2004*. At http://www.guardian.co.uk/comment/story/0,3604,1259859,00.html. Accessed 15 July 2004.

Hirst, P. and G. Thompson. 1996. *Globalization in question: The International Economy and the Possibilities Of Governance*. Cambridge: Polity.

Hjarvard, S. 2002. 'Mediated encounters: an essay on the role of communication media in the creation of trust in the 'global metropolis' in G. Stald and T. Tufte, eds, *Global Encounters: Media and Cultural Transformation*. Luton: University of Luton Press, pp. 69–84.

Hobsbawm, E. 1968. *Industry and Empire: An economic history of Britain since 1750*. London: Weidenfeld and Nicolson.

Hobson, J. 1902/1938. *Imperialism: A study*. London: George Allen & Unwin.

Holborow, M. 1999. *The Politics of English*. London: Sage.

Hollifield, C.A. 2004. 'The economics of international media' in A. Alexander, J. Owers, R. Carveth, C.A. Hollifield and A. Greco, eds, *Media Economics: Theory and Practice*. Mahwah, NJ.: Lawrence Erlbaum, pp. 85–106.

Holloway, J. 2002. *Change the world without taking power*. London: Pluto.

Hornik, R. 1988. *Development Communication: Information, Agriculture, and Nutrition in the Third World*. New York: Longman.

———— 1989. 'Development communication: Projects' in *International Encyclopaedia of Communication*, volume 2. New York: Oxford University Press, pp. 17–22.

———— 2002. 'Public health communication: Making sense of contradictory evidence' in R. Hornik, ed., *Public health communication: Evidence for behavior change*. Mahwah, NJ: Lawrence Erlbaum Associates, pp. 1–19.

Hoskins, C., S. McFadyen and A. Finn. 1997. *Global Television and Film: An Introduction to the Economics of the Business*. Oxford: Oxford University Press.

IATA. 2003. *International Air Transport Authority Annual Report 2003*. At http://www.iata.org/NR/ContentConnector/CS2000/SiteInterface/sites/about/file/ar2003web.pdf. Accessed 11 February 2004.

IMF. 2003. *International Monetary Fund Global Financial Stability Report 2003: Statistical Appendix*. At http://www.imf.org/external/pubs/ft/GFSR/2003/02/pdf/statappx.pdf Accessed 11 February 2004. Table One.

Inayatullah. 1967. 'Towards a non-western model of development' in D. Lerner and W. Schramm, eds, *Communication and Change in the Developing Countries*. Honolulu, Hawaii: East-West Center Press, pp. 99–102.

Inkeles, A. 1966. 'The modernization of man' in M. Weiner, ed., *Modernization: The Dynamics of Growth*. New York: Basic Books, pp. 138–50.

Inkeles, A. and D. Smith. 1974. *Becoming Modern: Individual Change in Six Developing Countries*. London: Heinemann.

Innis, H. 2004. *Changing Concepts of Time*. Lanham, MA: Rowman and Littlefield.

Institute of Medicine (of the National Academies of Science). 2002. *Shaping the future for health*. Washington DC: National Academies Press.

International Organization of Journalists. 1988. *NAM and NIICO: Documents of the Non-Aligned Movement on the New International Information and Communication Order (1986–1987)*. Prague: International Organization of Journalists.

Isaacs, H. 1951. *The Tragedy of the Chinese Revolution*, (2nd edn) Stanford, CA: Stanford University Press.

ITC. n.d. (but probably c.1999) *ITC Notes: 'Adult' Services*. At http://www.itc.org.uk/itc_publications/itc_notes/view_note.asp?itc_note_id=49. Accessed 11 July 2003.

Ito, Y. 1993. 'How Japan modernized earlier and faster than other non-western countries: an information sociology approach'. *Journal of Development Communication*, 4 (2): 60–78.

———— 1997. *Johoha* (Informatization) and Modernization. *Journal of Development Communication*, 8 (2): 42–53.

ITU. 2000. *ITU Telecommunication Indicators Update July–September 2000*. At http://www.itu.int/itu-d/ict/update/pdf/update_2.pdf. Accessed 11 February 2004.

———— 2001. *ITU Telecommunication Indicators Update January–March*. At http://www.itu.int/itu-d/ict/update/pdf/update_1_01.pdf. Accessed 11 February 2004.

———— 2005. *World Summit on the Information Society. Second Phase – Tunis: Funding of WSIS 2005*. At http://www.itu.int/wsis/funding/contributors2.html. Accessed 14 March 2006.

Iwabuchi, K. 2002. 'From western gaze to global gaze: Japanese cultural production in Asia' in D. Crane, N. Kawashima and K. Kawasaki, eds,. *Global Culture: Media, Arts, Policy and Globalization*. London: Routledge, pp. 256–73.

Jacobson, T. 1995. 'Modernization and postmodernization approaches to participatory communication for development' in S. White, S. Nair and J. Ascroft, eds, *Participatory Communication: Working for Change and Development*. New Delhi: Sage, pp. 60–75.

Jacobson, T. 1996a. 'Conclusion: prospects for theoretical development' in J. Servaes, T. Jacobson and S. White, eds, *Participatory Communication for Social Change*. New Delhi: Sage, pp. 266–77.

———— 1996b. 'Development communication in the "wake" of positivism' in J. Servaes, T. Jacobson and S. White, eds, *Participatory Communication for Social Change*. New Delhi: Sage, pp. 67–81.

Jacobson, T. and S. Kolluri. 1999. 'Participatory communication as communicative action' in T. Jacobson and J. Servaes, eds, *Theoretical Approaches to Participatory Communication*. Cresskill, NJ: Hampton Press, pp. 265–80.

James, S. 1995. 'Facilitating communication within rural and marginal communities' in S. White, S. Nair and J. Ascroft, eds, *Participatory Communication: Working for Change and Development*. New Delhi: Sage, pp. 329–41.

Jauert, P. and O. Prehn. 1997. 'Local Television and Local News'. *Communications* (22): 31–56.

Jeffrey, R. 2000. *India's Newspaper Revolution: Capitalism, Politics and the Indian-language Press 1977–1999*. London: Hurst and Company.

Joseph, J. 1997. *Mass Media and Rural Development*. Jaipur, India: Rawat.

Kantowsky, D. 1980. *Sarvodaya: the Other Development*. New Delhi: Vikas Publishing House.

Kar, S. R., Alcalay and S. Alex. 2001. 'Communicating with multicultural populations: a theoretical framework' in S. Kar, R. Alcalay and S. Alex, eds, *Health communication: A multicultural perspective*. London: Sage, pp. 109–137.

Katz, E. 1973. 'Television as horseless carriage' in G. Gerbner, L. Gross, and W. Melody, eds. Communication Technologies and Social Policy. London: Wiley-Interscience, 382–92.

Katz, E., J. Blumler and M. Gurevitch. 1974. 'Utilization of mass communication by the individual' in J. Blumler and E. Katz, eds, *The Uses of Mass Communications*. London: Sage, pp. 9–32.

Katz, E. and G. Wedell. 1978. *Broadcasting in the Third World: Promise and Performance*. London: Macmillan.

Kautsky, K. 1983. *Selected Political Writings*, edited and translated by Patrick Goode. London: Macmillan.

Keever, B. 1991. 'A biographical sketch of Wilbur Schramm'. *Mass Comm Review*, 1991, 18 (1–2): 4–9.

Keily, R. 1998a. 'Globalisastion, (post-)modernism and the Third World' in R. Keily and P. Marfleet, eds, *Globalization and the Third World*. London: Routledge, pp. 1–22.

———— 1998b. 'The crisis of global development' in R. Keily and P. Marfleet, eds, *Globalization and the Third World*. London: Routledge, pp. 23–43.

Kemp, T. 1967. *Theories of Imperialism*. London: Dennis Dobson.

———— 1972. 'The Marxist theory of imperialism' in R. Owen and B. Sutcliffe, eds, *Studies in the theory of imperialism*. London: Longman, pp. 15–33.

Kennedy, P. 1989. *The Rise and Fall of the Great Powers: Economic Change and Military Conflict from 1500 to 2000*. London: Fontana.

Kleinsteuber, H. and B. Thomass. 1995. 'Germany : the initiative in the hands of the Länder' in M. de Moragas Spà and C. Garitaonandia, *Television in the regions and the European audio-visual space*. London: John Libbey, 65–81.

Kleinwächter, W. 1993. 'Three waves of the debate' in G. Gerbner, H. Mowlana and K. Nordenstreng, eds, *The Global Media Debate: Its Rise, Fall and Renewal*. Norwood, N.J.: Ablex, pp. 13–20.

—— 1999. 'The cyberight to communicate' in R. Vincent, K. Nordestreng and M. Traber, eds, *Towards Equity in Global Communication: MacBride Update*. Cresskill, NJ. Hampton, pp. 91–101.

Knight Lapinski, M. and K. Witte. 1998. 'Health communication campaigns' in L. Jackson and B. Duffy, eds, *Health communication research: A guide to developments and directions*. Westport, CT: Greenwood Press, pp. 139–61.

Kolko, G. 1990/1968. *The Politics of War: The World and United States Foreign Policy 1943–1945*. New York: Pantheon Books.

Koven, R. 2003. 'A new opening for press controllers'. Freedom House *Freedom of the Press 2003*. Lanham, MD: Rowman and Littlefield, pp. 31–9.

Kraidy, M. 2003. Glocalization: An international communication framework? *Journal of International Communication*, 9 (2): 29–49.

Kuhn, T. 1962. *The Structure of Scientific Revolutions*. Chicago, IL: University of Chicago Press.

Kuisel, R. 1993. *Seducing the French: The Dilemma of Americanization*. Berkley, CA: University of California Press.

Kumar, K. 1995. 'Communication approaches to participation and development: challenging the assumptions and perspectives' in S. White, S. Nair and J. Ashcroft, eds, *Participatory Communication: Working for Change and Development*. New Delhi: Sage, pp. 76–92.

—— 1996. 'International news on Indian television: a critical analysis of *The World This Week*' in D. French and M. Richards, eds, *Contemporary Television: Eastern Perspectives*. London: Sage, pp. 282–301.

Lashley, L. 1995. 'Television and the Americanization of Trinbagonian youth: A study of six secondary schools' in H. Dunn, ed., *Globalization, Communication and Caribbean Identity*. Kingston, Jamaica: Ian Randle Publishers, pp. 83–97.

Le Sueur Stewart, M. 1991. *To See the World: The Global Dimension in International Direct Television Broadcasting by Satellite*. Dordrecht, The Netherlands: Martinus Nijhoff.

Lee, Chin-Chuan. 1980. *Media Imperialism Reconsidered: The Homogenizing of Television Culture*. London: Sage.

Legrain, P. 2002. *Open world: The truth about globalization*. London: Abacus.

Lenin, V. 1913/1964. 'Critical remarks on the national question' in V. Lenin *Collected Works*, volume 20. Moscow: Progress, pp. 17–51

—— 1917/1964. 'Imperialism, the highest stage of capitalism' in V. Lenin *Collected Works*, volume 22. Moscow: Progress, pp. 185–304.

Lent, J. 1995. *A Different Road Taken: Profiles in Critical Communication*. Boulder, CO: Westview.

Lerner, D. 1958. *The Passing of Traditional Society*. Glencoe, Il.: The Free Press.

—— 1963. 'Toward a communication theory of modernization' in L. Pye, ed., *Communication and Political Development*. Princeton, NJ: Princeton University Press, pp. 327–50.

—— 1967a. 'The coercive ideologists in perspective' in H. Lasswell and D. Lerner, eds, *World Revolutionary Elites: Studies in Coercive Ideological Movements*. Cambridge, MA: MIT Press.

—— 1967b. 'International cooperation and communication in national development' in D. Lerner and W. Schramm, eds, *Communication and Change in the Developing Countries*. Honolulu, Hawaii: East-West Center Press, pp. 104–25.

Lerner, D. and M. Gorden. 1969. *Euratlantica: Changing Perspectives of the European Elites*. Cambridge, MA: MIT Press.

Lerner, D. and W. Schramm. 1967. 'Preface' in D. Lerner and W. Schramm, eds, *Communication and Change in the Developing Countries*. Honolulu, Hawii: East-West Center Press, pp. i–xi.

Lerner, D. I., de Sola Pool, and G. Schueller. 1951. *The Nazi Elite. Hoover Institute Studies Series B: Elite Studies*, no.3, August 1951. New York: Stanford University Press.

Leys, C. 1996. *The Rise and Fall of Development Theory*. London: Currey.

Liebes, T. and E. Katz. 1990. *The export of meaning: Cross cultural readings of 'Dallas'*. Oxford: Oxford University Press.

Litman, B. and S. Sochay. 1994. 'The emerging mass media environment' in R. Babe, ed., *Information and Communication in Economics*. London: Kluwer Academic Publishers, pp. 233–68.

Liu, C. 2002. *The Call of the Chinese Market: Keynote Speech to the CAASBA Convention 2002*. Delivered 4 December 2002. At http://www.casbaa.com/doc/Speech_Liu%20Changle.pdf. Accessed 6 April 2003.

Lozare, B. 1995. 'Power and conflict: hidden dimensions of communication, participative planning, and action. the catalyst communicator: facilitating without fear' in S. White, ed., *The Art of Facilitating Participation: Releasing the Power of Grassroots Communication*. New Delhi: Sage, pp. 229–44.

Lull, J. (ed.) 1988. *World families watch television*. London: Sage.

———— 1990. *Inside Family Viewing: Ethnographic research on television audiences*. London: Routledge.

———— 2001. 'Superculture for the communication age' in J. Lull, ed., *Culture in the Communication Age*. London: Routledge, pp. 132–63.

Lusi, G. and F. Batundi. 2002. 'Health promotion and the myth of community' in A. Alali and B.A. Jinadu, eds, *Health Communication in Africa*. Lanham, MA: University Press of America, pp. 109–117.

MacBride, S. 1980. *Many Voices, One World: Toward a new more just and more efficient world information and communication order*. London: Kogan Page.

McChesney, R. 1998. 'The political economy of global communication' in R. McChesney, E. Meiksins Wood, and J. Bellamy Foster, eds, *Capitalism in the Information Age: The Political Economy of the Global Communication Revolution*. New York: Monthly Review Press, pp. 1–26.

———— 1999. *Rich Media, Poor Democracy. Communication Politics in Dubious Times*. Urbana, IL: University of Illinois Press.

McPhail, T. 1981. *Electronic colonialism: The future of international broadcasting and communication*. London: Sage.

Magdoff, H. 1972. 'Imperialism without colonies' in R. Owen and B. Sutcliffe, eds, *Studies in the Theory of Imperialism*. London: Longman, pp. 144–70.

———— 2003. *Imperialism without colonies*. New York: Monthly Review.

Mallaby, S. 2002. 'The reluctant imperialist: Terrorism, failed states, and the case for an American empire'. *Foreign Affairs*, March/April 2002. At http://www.foreignaffairs.org/20020301facomment7967-p20/sebastian-mallaby/the-reluctant-imperialist-terrorism-failed-states-and-the-case-for-american-empire.html. Accessed 20 July 2004.

Mann, M. 2003. *Incoherent Empire*. London: Verso.

Mankekar, D. 1978. *One Way Free Flow: Neo-Colonialism via News Media*. Delhi: Clarion Books.

Marx, K. and F. Engels. 1848/1976. *Manifesto of the Communist Party*. K. Marx and F. Engels *Collected Works*, volume 6. London: Lawrence and Wishart, pp. 481–519.

Masmoudi, M. 1986. *Voie Libre Pour Mond Multiple*. Dar El Amal, Tunisia: Economika.

Mastrini, G. and D. de Charras. 2005. 'Twenty years mean nothing'. *Global Media and Communication*, December 2005 1 (3): 273–88.

Mato, D. 1999. 'Problems of social participation in "Latin" America in the age of globalization: theoretical and case-based considerations for practitioners and researchers' in T. Jacobson and J. Servaes, eds, *Theoretical Approaches to Participatory Communication*. Creskill, NJ: Hampton Press, pp. 51–75.

Mattelart, A. 1979. *Multinational Corporations and the Control of Culture: the ideological apparatuses of imperialism*. Brighton, Sussex: The Harvester Press.

———— 1980. *Mass Media, Ideologies, and the Revolutionary Movement*. Brighton, Sussex: The Harvester Press.

Maxwell, R. 2003. *Herbert Schiller*. Lanham, MD: Rowman and Littlefield.

Meehan, E. 2005. *Why TV is not our faulty: Television Programming, viewers and who's really in control*. Lanham, MD: Rowman and Littlefield.

Melkote, S. 1991. *Communication for National Development in the Third World: Theory and Practice*. London: Sage.

Melkote, S. and K. Kandath. 2001. 'Barking up the wrong tree? An inward look at the discipline and practice of development communication' in S. Melkote and S. Rao, eds, *Critical issues in communication: Looking inward for answers*. New Delhi: Sage, pp. 188–204.

Melkote, S. and D. Mudpidi. 1999. 'Aids communication: role of knowledge factors on perceptions of risk. *Journal of Development Communication*, 10 (2): 16–26.

Melkote, S. and H.L. Steevers. 2001. *Communication for development in the third world: Theory and practice for empowerment* (2nd edn) New Delhi: Sage.

Merton, R. and D. Lerner. 1951. 'Social scientists and research policy' in D. Lerner and H. Lasswell, eds, *The Policy Sciences*. New York: Stanford University Press, pp. 282–307.

Mezzana, D. 1996. 'Grass roots communication in West Africa' in J. Servaes, T. Jacobson and S. White, eds, *Participatory Communication for Social Change*. New Delhi: Sage, pp. 183–96.

Midgley, J. 1986. *Community Participation, Social Development and the State*. London: Methuen.

Miller, D. 1995. 'The consumption of soap opera: *The Young and the Restless* and mass consumption in Trinidad' in R. Allen, ed., *To be Continued ... Soap operas around the world*. London: Routledge, pp. 213–33.

Mody, B. 1991. *Designing Messages for Development Communication: An Audience Participation Based Approach*. New Delhi: Sage.

Mody, B. and J. Borrego. 1991. 'Mexico's Morelos Satellite: Reaching for Autonomy' in G. Sussman, and J. Lent, eds, *Transnational Communication: Wiring the Third World*. London: Sage, pp. 150–64.

Moemeka, A. 1981. *Local Radio: Community Education for Development*. Zaria, Nigeria: Ahmadu Bell University Press.

———— 1994. 'Development communication: a historical and conceptual overview' in A. Moemaka, ed., *Communicating For Development: A New Pan-disciplinary Perspective*. Albany, NY: State University of New York Press, pp. 3–22.

———— 1995. 'Mass media and rural development' in C. Okgibo, ed., *Media and Sustainable Development*. Nairobi: African Council for Communication Education, pp. 324–62.

Mohammadi, A. and M. Ahsan. 2002. *Globalization or Recolonization: The Muslim World in the 21st Century*. London: Ta-Ha Publishers.

Moore, W. 1963. *Social Change*. Englewood Cliffs, NJ: Prentice-Hall.

Morley, D. and K. Robbins. 1995. *Spaces of Identity: Global Media, Electronic Landscapes and Cultural Boundaries*. London: Routledge.

Mowlana, H. 1985. *International Flows of Information: A Global Report and Analysis: Reports and Papers in Mass Communication #99*. Paris: UNESCO.

———— 1996. *Global Communication in Transition: The End of Diversity?* London: Sage.

———— 2001. 'Communication and development: theoretical and methodological problems and prospects' in S. Melkote and S. Rao, eds, *Critical Issues in Communication: Looking inwards for answers*. New Delhi: Sage, pp. 179–87.

Mowlana, H. and L. Wilson. 1990. *The Passing of Modernity*. New York: Longman.

MPAA. 2000–2003. *Press Release Archive: Legislation 2000–2003*. At http://www.mpaa.org/legislation/index.htm. Accessed 13 February 2004.

———— 9 February 2004. *MPAA Statement on the US-Australia Free Trade Agreement*. At http://www.mpaa.org/legislation/index.htm. Accessed 13 February 2004.

Muturi, N. 2005. 'Communication for HIV/AIDS prevention in Kenya: Social-cultural considerations'. *Journal of Health Communication*, 10 (1): 77– 98.

Nair, S. and S. White. 1995. 'Participatory development communication as cultural renewal' in S. White, S. Nair and J. Ascroft, eds, *Participatory Communication: Working for Change and Development*. New Delhi: Sage, pp. 138–93.

Narula, V. and W. Barnett Pearce. 1986. *Development as Communication: A Perspective on India*. Carbondale, IL: Southern Illinois University Press.

National Statistics. 2004. *Migration: 1991 to 2000, Total international migration: time series, age and sex*. At http://www.statistics.gov.uk/statbase/Product.asp?vlnk=9069&image.x=14&image.y=7. Accessed 25 February 2004.

Negrine, R. and S. Papathanassopoulos. 1990. *The Internationalisation of Television*. London: Pinter.

Neuwirth, R. 2002. 'The cultural industries and the legacy of article iv gatt: rethinking the relation of culture and trade in light of the new WTO round'. Paper presented to the conference *Cultural Traffic: Policy, Culture, and the New Technologies in the European Union and Canada* (Carleton University, November 22–23, 2002). Available at: http://www.carleton.ca/ces/papers/november02/Neuwirth.pdf. Accessed 15 January 2004.

News Corporation. 2002. *Form F20: 2002*. At http://www.sec.gov/edgar.shtml. Accessed 6 April 2003.

Ngidang, D. 1994. 'Building grassroots institutions: lessons from the Comilla experiment'. *Journal of Development Communication*, 5 (1): 1–11.

Nordenstreng, K. 1984. *The Mass Media Declaration of UNESCO*. Norwood, NJ: Ablex with L. Hannikainen.

———— 1993. 'New information order and communication scholarship: reflections on a delicate relationship' in J. Wasko, V. Mosco and M. Pendakur, eds, *Illuminating the Blindspots: Essays Honoring Dallas W. Smythe*. Norwood, NJ: Ablex, pp. 251–73.

———— 1993. 'The story and lesson of a symposium' in G. Gerbner, H. Mowlana and K. Nordenstreng, eds, *The Global Media Debate: Its Rise, Fall and Renewal*. Norwood, N.J.: Ablex, pp. 99–107.

———— 1999. 'The context: the great media debate' in R. Vincent, K. Nordenstreng and M. Traber, eds, *Towards Equity in Global Communication: MacBride Update*. Cresskill, NJ. Hampton, pp. 235–68.

—————— 2001. 'Epilogue' in N. Morris and S. Waisbord, eds, *Media and Globalization: Why the state matters*. Lanham, MD: Rowman and Littlefield, pp. 155–60.

Nordenstreng, K. and T. Varis. 1973. 'The non-homogeneity of the national state and the international flow of communication' in G. Gerbner, L. Gross and B. Melody, eds, *Communications Technology and Social Policy*. New York: John Wiley, pp. 393–412.

—————— 1974. *Television Traffic – A One-way Street? Reports and Papers on Mass Communication #70*. Paris: UNESCO.

Nwafo Nwanko, R. 1995. 'Sustainability as an African communication concept: some theory and practice issues in C. Okgibo, ed., *Media and Sustainable Development*. Nairobi: African Council for Communication Education, pp. 56–110.

Ó Siochrú, S. and B. Girard with A. Mahan. 2002. *Global Media Governance: A Beginner's Guide*. Lanham, MD: Rowman and Littlefield.

Ohmae, K. 1995. *The End of the Nation State: The Rise of the Regional Economies*. London: Harper Collins.

Okigbo, C. 1995. 'Media and sustainable development: a prologue' in C. Okgibo, ed., *Media and Sustainable Development*. Nairobi: African Council for Communication Education, pp. 2–24.

Ostler, N. 2005. *Empires of the word: A language history of the world*. London: Harper Perennial.

Otake, A. and S. Hosokawa. 1998. 'Karaoke in East Asia: Modernization, Japanization, or Asianization?' in T. Mitsui and S. Hosokawa, eds, *Karaoke Around the World: Global Technology, Local Singing*. London: Routledge, pp. 178–201.

Overseas Development Institute. 1995. *ODI Briefing Papers 95 (4). NGOs and Official Donors*. At http://www.odi.org.uk/publications/briefing/odi_ngos.html. Accessed 27 July 2004.

Padovani, C. 2005. 'Debating communication imbalances from the McBride Report to the World Summit on the Information Society'. *Global Media and Communication*, December 2005 1 (3): 316–38.

Page, D. and W. Crawley. 2001. *Satellites over South Asia: Broadcasting, Culture and the Public Interest*. New Delhi: Sage.

Panitch, L. and S. Gindin. 2004. *Global Capitalism and American Empire*. London: Merlin Press.

—————— 2006. 'Imperialism: a reply to Callinicos'. *International Socialism 109*. Winter 2006: 194–99.

Park, R. 1922. *The Immigrant Press and its Control*. New York: Harper and Brothers.

Passavant, P. and J. Dean, eds. 2004. *Empire's new clothes: Reading Hardt and Negri*. London: Routledge.

Peckham, N. and J. Chaffin. 2004. 'The Americas: Iraqi threat to US broadcasting contract'. *Ft.com 10 January 2004*. Accessed 15 July 2004.

Peel, Q. 2004. 'Keep humanitarian aid neutral' *Financial Times*, August 5 2004: 17.

Pendakaur, M. 1990. *Canadian dreams and American control: The political economy of the Canadian film industry*. Detroit, MI.: Wayne State University Press.

Pendakur, M. and J. Kapur. 1997. 'Think globally, program locally: privatization of Indian National Television' in M. Bailie and D. Winseck, eds, *Democratizing Communication: Comparative perspectives on information and power*. Cresskill NJ: Hampton Press, pp. 195–217.

Peruzzo, C. 1996. 'Participation in community communication' in J. Servaes, T. Jacobson and S. White, eds, *Participatory Communication for Social Change*. New Delhi: Sage, pp. 169–79.

Phillipson, R. 1992. *Linguistic Imperialism*. Oxford: Oxford University Press.

Pieterse, J. 2000. 'Shaping globalization' in J. Pieterse, ed. *Global Futures: Shaping Globalization*. London: Zed, pp. 1–19.

Pilsbury, B. and D. Mayer. 2005. '*Women Connect!* Strengthening communication to meet sexual and reproductive health challenges'. *Journal of Health Communication*, 10 (4): 361–71.

Piotrow, P., D.L. Kincaid, J. Rimon and W. Rinehart. 1997. *Health Communication: Lessons from Family Planning and Reproductive Health*. Westport, CT: Praeger.

Pollard, M. 2003. *International Service Transactions of the Film and Television Industries, 2002*. London: Office of National Statistics. October 2003.

Porter, R. 1997. *The Greatest Benefit to Mankind: A Medical History of Humanity from Anitquity to the Present*. London: Harper Collins.

Preston, P. 2005. 'Systematic learnings and forgetting in an "Information Society"'. *Javnost/The Public*, xii (3): 31–46.

Price, M. 2002. *Media and Sovereignty: The Global Information Revolution and its Challenge to State Power*. Cambridge, MA: The MIT Press.

Raboy, M. 2006. 'WSIS is over, long live WSIS?' *IAMCR Bulletin*, April 2006 16 (1): 9 & 21.

Rahim, S. 1994. 'Participatory development communication as a dialogical process' in S. White, S. Nair and J. Ascroft, eds, *Participatory Communication: Working for Change and Development*. New Delhi: Sage, pp. 117–37.

Rahman, M.A. 1995. 'Participatory development towards liberation of co-option?' G. Craig and M. Mayo, eds, *Community empowerment: A reader*. London: Zed, pp. 24–32.

Rantanen, T. 1992. 'Mr. Howard goes to South America: The United Press Associations and foreign expansion'. *Roy W. Howard Monographs in Journalism and Mass Communication Number 2*. Bloomington, IN: Indiana University School of Journalism.

——— 1993. 'Howard interviews Stalin: How AP, UP and TASS smashed the International News cartel'. *Roy W. Howard Monographs in Journalism and Mass Communication Number 3*. Bloomington, IN: Indiana University School of Journalism.

——— 2003. 'The New Sense of Place in 19th-Century News'. *Media, Culture & Society*, 25 (4): 435–449.

Rao, V. 1997. *A Curve in the Hills: Communication and Development*. Shimla: Indian Institute of Advanced Study.

Rees, J. 2001. 'Imperialism: Globalization, the state and war'. *International Socialism*, 2nd series (93): 3–30.

Righter, R. 1978. *Whose News? Politics, the Press and the Third World*. London: Burnett Books/Andre Deutsch.

Riley, J. and W. Schramm. 1951. *The Reds Take a City: The Communist Occupation of Seoul*. New Brunswick, NJ: Rutgers University Press.

Ritzer, G. 1993. *The McDonaldization of Society*. Thousand Oaks, CA: Pine Forge Press.

Roach, C. 1992. 'Anti-communism, UNESCO and International Communication' in L. Alexandre, ed., *The Ideology of International Communications*. New York: Institute for Media Analysis. Monograph #4.

——— 1993. 'Dallas Smythe and the NWICO' in J. Wasko, V. Mosco and M. Pendakur, eds, *Illuminating the Blindspots: Essays Honoring Dallas W. Smythe*. Norwood, NJ: Ablex, pp. 274–301.

Robertson, R. 1992. *Globalization: Social Theory and Global Culture*. London: Sage.

———— 1994. 'Globalization or Glocalization?' *The Journal of International Communication*, 1 (1): 33–52.

Robins, K. 1991. 'Tradition and translation: national culture in its global context', in J. Corner and S. Harvey, eds, *Enterprise and Heritage*. London: Routledge, pp. 1–44.

Robinson, G. 1969/1981. 'Tanjug's complementary role in international communication', in G. Robinson *News Agencies and World News in Canada, the United States and Yugoslavia: Methods and Data*. Friborg, Switzerland: University Press of Friborg, pp. 13–36.

———— 1974/1981. 'Social stratification of international news flow' in G. Robinson *News Agencies and World News in Canada, the United States and Yugoslavia: Methods and Data*. Friborg, Switzerland: University Press of Friborg, pp. 99–119.

Rodrigues Dias, M., J. Lee, K. Nordenstreng and O. Wiio. 1979. *National Communication Policy Councils: Principles and Experiences: Reports and Papers on Mass Communication #83*. Paris: UNESCO.

Rogers, E. 1969. *Modernization among Peasants: The Impact of Communication*, with L. Svenning. New York: Holt, Rinehart and Winston.

———— 1973. *Communication Strategies for Family Planning*. New York: The Free Press.

———— 1976. 'Communication and development: the passing of the dominant paradigm' in E. Rogers, ed., *Communication and Development Critical Perspectives*. London: Sage, pp. 121–48.

———— 1989. 'Inquiry in development communication' in M. Asante and W. Gundykunst, eds, *Handbook of International and Intercultural Communication*. London: Sage, pp. 67–86.

———— 1992. *The Diffusion of Innovations*, (4th edn). New York: The Free Press.

Rosenblum, M. 1981. 'Reporting from the Third World' in J. Richstad and M. Anderson, eds, *Crisis in International News: Policies and Prospects*. New York: Columbia University Press, pp. 221–41.

Rostow, W. 1953. *The Process of Economic Growth*. Oxford: Oxford University Press.

Sabry, T. 2003. 'Exploring symbolic dimensions of emigration: communication, mental and physical emigrations' Unpublished thesis presented for the degree of DPhil, University of Westminster.

Sakr, N. 2001. *Satellite Realms: Transnational Television, Globalization and the Middle East*. London: I.B. Tauris.

———— 2006. 'Media policy in the Middle East: A reappraisal' in J. Curran and M. Gurevitch, eds, *Mass Media and Society*, (4th edn). London: Hodder Arnold, pp. 234–50.

Salinas, R. and L. Paldán. 1979. 'Culture in the process of dependent development: theoretical perspectives' in K. Nordenstreng and H. Schiller, eds, *National Sovereignty and International Communication*. Norwood, NJ: Ablex, pp. 99–111.

Salmon, C. and C. Atkin. 2003. 'Using media campaigns for health promotion' in T. Thompson, A. Dorsey, K. Miker and R. Parrott, eds, *Handbook of Health Communication*. Mahwah, NJ: Lawrence Erlbaum Associates, pp. 449–72.

Salvadori, M. 1979. *Karl Kautsky and the Socialist Revolution: 1880–1938*. London: New Left Books.

Samarjiwa, R. 1987. 'The murky beginnings of the communication and development field: Voice of America and "The Passing of Traditional Society"' in N. Jayaweera and S. Amunugama, eds, *Rethinking Development Communication*. Singapore: Asian Mass Communication Research Centre.

Schiller, H. 1970. *Mass Communication and American Empire*. New York: Augustus M. Kelley.

——— 1973. *The Mind Managers*. Boston, MA: Beacon Press.

——— 1975. 'The appearance of national communication policies: a new arena for social struggle'. *Gazette*, xxi (2): 82–89.

——— 1976. *Communication and Cultural Domination*. White Planes, NY: International Arts and Sciences Press.

——— 1982. 'Sources of opposition to US information supremacy' in J. Schement, F. Guitterrz and M. Sirbu, eds, *Telecommunications Policy Handbook*. New York: Praeger, pp. 258–71.

——— 1989. *Culture, Inc: The Corporate Takeover of Public Expression*. Oxford: Oxford University Press.

——— 1993. 'Not yet the post-imperialist era' in C. Roach, ed., *Communication and Culture in War and Peace*. Newbury Park, CA: Sage, pp. 97–116.

——— 1995. 'The global information highway: project for an ungovernable world' in J. Brook, and I. Boal, eds, *Resisting the Virtual Life*. San Francisco: City Lights, pp. 17–34.

——— 1996. *Information Inequality: The Deepening Social Crisis in America*. London: Routledge.

——— 1998. 'Striving for communication dominance: a half-century review' in D. Thussu, ed., *Electronic Empires: Global Media and Local Resistance*. London: Arnold, pp. 17–26.

Schiller, H. and J. Phillips. 1970. *Super-State: Readings in the Military-Industrial Complex*. Urbana, IL: University of Illinois Press.

Schmitt, D. 2005. 'Who wants to be a millionaire?' *Screen Digest*, 12 April 2005. At http://www.screendigest.com/reports/gttf05/press_relaeases_12_04_2005-n/view.html. Accessed 29 July 2005.

Schramm, W., ed. 1954. *The Processes and Effects of Mass Communication*. Urbana, IL: University of Illinois Press.

——— 1963. 'Communication development and the development process' in L. Pye, ed., *Communications and Political Developments*. Princeton, NJ: Princeton University Press, pp. 30–57.

——— 1964. *Mass Media and National Development: The Role of Information in the Developing Countries*. Paolo Alto, CA: Stanford University Press.

——— 1967. 'Communication and change' in D. Lerner and W. Schramm, eds, Communication and Change in the Developing Countries. Honolulu: East-West Centre Press.

——— 1968. *Communication Satellites for Education, Science and Culture: Reports and Papers in Mass Communication #53*. Paris: UNESCO.

——— 1977. *Big Media, Little Media: Tools and Technologies for Instruction*. London: Sage.

Schrecker, E. 1986. *No Ivory Tower: McCarthyism and the Universities*. New York: Oxford University Press.

Schumacher, A. 2005. 'Water for all: Moving towards access to fresh drinking water and sanitation'. *UN Chronicle Online Edition*. At http://www.un.org/Pubs/chronicle/2005/issue2/0205p20.html. Accessed 17 March 2006.

Schumpeter, J. 1919/1951. *Imperialism and Social Classes*. Oxford: Basil Blackwell.

Schutte, P. 2003. 'Tswana-speaking students' perceptions of HIV/AIDS and poverty: implications for communication'. *Communicare*, December 2003 22 (2): 25–44.

Screen Digest. July 2003. 'Profile: global film production and distribution'. *Screen Digest*, July 2003, pp. 201–208.

Seattle Times Company. 2003. *Circulation and Audience*. At http://www.seattle timescompany.com/advertise/circAudienceDMA.htm. Accessed 25 February 2004.

Seibert, F., T. Peterson, and W. Schramm. 1963/1956. *Four Theories of the Press*. Urbana, IL: University of Illinois Press.

Sepstrup, P. 1990 *The Transnationalization of Television in Western Europe*. London: John Libbey.

Servaes, J. 1989. *One World, Multiple Cultures. A New Paradigm on Communication for Development*. Leuven/Amersfoort: Acco.

—— 1996a. 'Participatory communication research with new social movements: a realistic Utopia' in J. Servaes, T. Jacobson and S. White, eds, *Participatory Communication for Social Change*. New Delhi: Sage, pp. 82–108.

—— 1996b. 'Introduction: participatory communication and research in development settings' in J. Servaes, T. Jacobson and S. White, eds, *Participatory Communication for Social Change*. New Delhi: Sage, pp. 13–25.

—— 1996c. 'Linking theoretical perspectives to policy' in J. Servaes, T. Jacobson and S. White, eds, *Participatory Communication for Social Change*. New Delhi: Sage, pp. 29–43.

—— 1997. 'Participatory methodologies for development communication'. *Journal of Development Communication*, 8 (2): 99–106.

—— 1999. *Communication for Development: One World, Multiple Cultures*. Cresskill, NJ: Hampton Press.

—— 2000. 'Communication for development in global perspective: The role of governmental and non-governmental agencies' in J. Servaes, ed., *Walking on the other side of the information highway*. Penang: Southbound, pp. 47–60.

Servaes, J. and P. Malikhao. 1994. 'Concepts: the theoretical underpinnings of the approaches to development communication' in J. Mayo and J. Servaes, eds, *Approaches to Development Communication*. Paris: UNESCO.

Shaw, M. 1994. *Global Society and International Relations*. Cambridge: Polity.

Sherry, J. 1997. 'Prosocial soap operas for development: a review of research and theory'. *Journal of International Communication*, 4 (2): 75–101.

Shew, W. 1992. 'Trends in the organization of programme production' in T. Congdon, B. Sturgess, N. E. R. A., W. Shew, A. Graham and G. Davies, eds, *Paying for Broadcasting: The Handbook*. London: Routledge, pp. 64–91.

Shingi, P. and B. Mody. 1974. *Farmers' Ignorance and the Role of Television*. Ahmedabad: Indian Institute of Management.

Shore, L. 1980. 'Mass media for development: a re-examination of access, exposure and impact' in E. McAnany, ed., *Communications in the Rural Third World*. New York: Praeger Scientific, pp. 19–45.

Silj, A. 1988. *East of Dallas*. London: British Film Institute.

—— 1992. 'Domestic markets and the European market' in A. Silj, ed., *The New Television in Europe*. London: John Libbey, pp. 15–48.

Simes, D. 2003. 'America's imperial dilemma'. *Foreign Affairs*, November-December 2003. At http://www.foreignaffairs.org/20031101faessay82609/dimitri-k-simes/america-s-imperial-dilemma.html. Accessed 22 June 2004.

Simpson, C. 1994. *Science of Coercion: Communication Research and Psychological Warfare*. New York: Oxford University Press.

Sinclair, J., E. Jacka and S. Cunningham, eds. 1996. *New Patterns in Global Television: Peripheral Vision*. Oxford: Oxford University Press.

Singhal, A. and S. Law. 1997. 'Past, present and future of development communication: a conversation with Everett M. Rogers'. *Journal of Development Communication*, 8 (2): 107–116.

Sinha, M. 1983. *Modernization and Community Power: A Comparative Study of Two Villages in India*. New Delhi: Vikas Publishing House.

SIPRI. 2003. *Stockholm Institute for Peace Research Yearbook 2003*. Chapter 10. Military expenditure by E. Sköns, W. Omitoogun, S. Perlo-Freeman and P. Stålenheim *Chapter summary from the SIPRI Yearbook 2003: Armaments, Disarmament and International Security (Oxford: Oxford University Press, 2003)*. At http://editors.sipri.org/pubs/yb03/ch10.html. Accessed 23 February 2004.

Skutnabb-Kangas, J. and R. Phillipson. 1997. 'Linguistic human rights and development' in C. Hamelink, ed., *Ethics and Development*. Kampen, The Netherlands: Uitgeverij Kok-Kampen, pp. 56–69.

Smith, A. 1976. *The shadow in the cave: The broadcaster, the audience and the state*. London: Quartet.

——— 1980. *The Geopolitics of Information*. London: Faber and Faber.

Smith, A. D. 1990. 'Towards a global culture?' in M. Featherstone, ed., *Global Culture: Nationalism, Globalization and Modernity*. London: Sage, pp. 171–91.

Smith, B. 1952/61. 'Communication research on non-industrial countries' in W. Schramm, ed., *The Process and Effects of Mass Communication Research*. Urbana, IL: University of Illinois Press, pp. 170–79.

Smith, D. 14 April 2005. Press release: 'The global trade in television formats'. At http://www.screendigest.com/reports/gttf05/press_releases_12_04_2005-n/view.html. Accessed 29 July 2005.

Smythe, D. 1981. *Dependency Road: Communications, Capitalism, Consciousness and Canada*. Norwood, N.J.: Ablex.

——— 1990. Foreword. M. Pendakur *Canadian Dreams and American Control: The Political Economy of the Canadian Film Industry*. Detroit, MI: Wayne State University Press, pp. 15–25.

Sondhi, K. 1980. *Problems of Communication in Developing Countries*. New Delhi: Vision Books.

——— 1983. *Communication, Growth and Public Policy*. New Delhi: Breakthrough.

——— 1985. *Communication and Values*. Bombay: Somaiya Publications.

Soros, G. 2002. *On Globalization*. Oxford: Public Affairs.

Sparks, C. 1995. 'The current crisis of public service broadcasting in Britain'. *Critical Studies in Mass Communication*, September 1995, 12 (3): 325–41.

——— 1998a. *Capitalism, Communism and the Mass Media*. London: Sage (with Anna Reading).

——— 1998b. *From the Hundred Aker Wood to the Magic Kingdom*. London: University of Westminster Professorial Lecture Series.

——— 1999. 'CME and broadcasting in the former communist countries'. *Javnost/The Public*, 1999, vi (2): 25–44.

Sreberny-Mohammadi, A. 1991. 'The global and the local in international communications' in J. Curran and M. Gurevitch, eds, *Mass Media and Society*, (1st edn) London: Edward Arnold, pp. 118–38.

Stevenson, R. 1993. *Communication, Development, and the Third World*. Lantham, MA: University Press of America.

Strange, S. 1996. *The Retreat of the State: Cambridge studies in international relations: 49*. Cambridge: Cambridge University Press.

Straubhaar, J. 1991. 'Beyond media imperialism: assymetrical interdependence and cultural proximity'. *Critical Studies in Mass Communication*, March 1991, 8 (1): 39–59.

Sussman, G. 1981. *Telecommunications Transfers: Transnational Corporations, the Philippines and Structures of Domination*. (*Third World Studies, Dependency Papers Series #35.*) Manila: University of the Philippines.

Sussman, G. and Lent, J. 1991. 'Introduction: critical perspectives on communication and third world development' in G. Sussman and J. Lent, eds, *Transnational Communication: Wiring the Third World*. London: Sage, pp. 1–26.

Sussman, L. 1983. *Warning of a Bloodless Dialect: Glossary for International Communications*. Washington, DC: The Media Institute.

——— 1977. *Mass News Media and the Third World Challenge*. (*The Washington Papers #46.*) London: Sage.

Sweezy, P. 1942/1968. *The Theory of Capitalist Development*. New York: Monthly Review Press.

Terhranian, M. 1984. 'Dependency and communication dualism in the Third World' in G. Wang and W. Dissayanake, eds, *Continuity and Change in Communication Systems: An Asian Perspective*. Norwood, NJ: Ablex, pp. 145–67.

Terhranian, M., F. Hakimzadeh and M. Vidale. (1977). 'Preface' in M. Terheranian, F. Hakimzadeh and M. Vidale, eds, *Communications Policy for National Development: A Comparative Perspective*. London: Routledge and Kegan Paul, pp. 1–14.

Teschke, B. 2002. 'Theorizing the Westphalian system of states: International relations from absolutism to capitalism'. *European Journal of International Relations*, 8 (1): 5–48.

Thomas, P. 1995a. Traditional communication and democratization: practical considerations in P. Lee, ed., *The Democratisation of Communication*. Cardiff: University of Wales Press, pp. 148–64.

——— 1995b. 'Participatory development communication: philosophical premises' in S. White, S. Nair and J. Ascroft, eds, *Participatory Communication: Working for Change and Development*. New Delhi: Sage, pp. 49–59.

——— 1996. 'Popular theatre in sickness and health: Observations from India' in J. Servaes, T. Jacobson and S. White, eds, *Participatory communication for social change*. New Delhi: Sage, pp. 213–22.

Thomas, R. 2006. *Health Communication*. New York, NY: Springer.

Thompson, J. 1995. *The Media and Modernity: A Social Theory of the Media*. Cambridge: Polity Press.

Thwaite, A. 1990. *A.A. Milne: His Life*. London: Faber and Faber.

——— 1992. *The Brilliant Career of Winnie-the-Pooh*. London: Methuen.

Tomlinson, J. 1991. *Cultural Imperialism: A Critical Introduction*. London: Pinter.

——— 1997. 'Cultural globalization and the control of difference in A. Mohammadi, ed., *International Communication and Globalization*. London: Sage, pp. 170–190.

——— 1999. *Globalization and Culture*. Cambridge: Polity Press.

Tracey, M. 1985. 'The poisoned challice? international television and the idea of domination'. *Daedalus*. Fall 1985 114 (4): 17–56.

Tran Van Dinh 1987. *Independence, Liberation, Revolution*. Norwood, NJ: Ablex.

Tsatsoulis-Bonnekessen, B. 1995. 'Good women don't drink beer: behavior and integration of female development volunteers' in D. Newsom and B. Carrel, eds, *Silent Voices*. Lantham, MA: University Press of America, pp. 75–94.

Tunstall, J. 1977. *The Media are American*. London: Constable.

UIS. 2005. *International Literacy Day 2005: Women still left behind in efforts to achieve global literacy*. UNESCO Institute for Statistics Fact Sheet

September 2005, Number 06. At http://www.uis.unesco.org/file_download.php?URL_ID=6264&filename=11287105911UIS_factsheet_06_EN.pdf&filetype=application%2Fpdf&filesize=38892&name=UIS_factsheet_06_EN.pdf&location=user-S/. Accessed 17 March 2006.

UNCHS. 2001. *The state of the world's cities 2001*. Nairobi, Kenya: United Nations Commission for Human Settlements.

UNDP. 1999. *United Nations Development Programme: Human Development Report*. New York: Oxford University Press.

UNESCO. 1996. *Basic Texts in Communication: 1989–95*. Paris: UNESCO.

UNHCR. 2003. *United Nations High Commission for Refugees: Refugees by Number*. At http://www.unhcr.ch/cgi-bin/texis/vtx/basics/+WwwBmweF5xpwwwwrwwww wwwmFqtFElfglhFqoUflfRZ2ItFqtxw5oq5zFqtFElfglAFqoUflfRZ2IDzmxwww wwww1FqtFElfgl/opendoc.pdf. Accessed 11 February 2004.

Vargas, L. 1995. *Social Uses and Radio Practices*. Boulder, CO: Westview.

Variety. 2004a. 125 Top Grossing Films Worldwide of 2001. At: http://www.variety.com/index.asp?layout=chart_pass&charttype=chart_top125_01&dept=Film. Accessed 16 March 2004.

——— 2004b. 125 Top Grossing Films Worldwide of 2002. At: http://www.variety.com/index.asp?layout=chart_pass&charttype=chart_top125_02&dept=Film. Accessed 16 March 2004.

——— 2004c. Foreign Box Office. At http://www.variety.com/index.asp?layout=b_o_foreign&dept=Film&date=12%2F31%2F2002&boxmonth=12&boxday=31&boxyear=2002. Accessed 16 March 2004.

Varis, T. 1975. *The impact of transnational corporations on communication*. Research Report #10. Tampere: Tampere Peace Research Institute.

——— 1985. *International Flow of Television Programmes: Reports and Papers in Mass Communication #100*. Paris: UNESCO.

Venturelli, S. 1998. *Liberalizing the European Media: Politics, Regulation and the Public Sphere*. New York: Oxford University Press.

Vilanilam, J. 1996. 'The socio-cultural dynamics of Indian television: from site to insight to privatization' in D. French and M. Richards, eds, *Contemporary Television: Eastern Perspectives*. London: Sage, pp. 61–90.

Vincent, R., K. Nordenstreng and M. Traber. 1999. Preface to their (ed.) *Towards Equity in Global Communication: MacBride Update*. Cresskill, NJ: Hampton Press, pp. vii–x.

Volkmer, I. 1999. *CNN: News in the Global Sphere. A study of CNN and its impact on global communication*. Luton: University of Luton Press.

Wang, G. and W. Dissanayake. 1984. 'Culture, development and change: some explorative observations' in G. Wang and W. Dissanayake, eds, *Continuity and Change in Communication Systems: An Asian Perspective*. Norwood, NJ: Ablex, pp. 3–20.

Ward, D. 2002. *The European Union Democratic Deficit and the Public Sphere: An evaluation of EU media policy*. Amsterdam: IOS Press.

Wasko, J. 2003. *How Hollywood Works*. London: Sage.

Waters, M. 1995. *Globalization*, (1st edn). London: Routledge.

Weber, M. 1918/46. 'Politics as vocation' in H. Gerth and C. Wright Mills trans. and eds. *From Max Weber: Essays in Sociology*. New York: Oxford University Press, pp. 77–128.

——— 1968. *The Protestant Ethic and the Spirit of Capitalism*. London: Unwin University Books.

Wei, W. 1998. 'Dominant or alternative paradigm? a meta-research of mass communication and development studies in Asia in the 1990s'. *Journal of Development Communication*, 9 (2): 31–44.

Wells, C. 1987. *The UN, UNESCO and the Politics of Knowledge*. London: Macmillan.

White, K. 1999. 'The importance of sensitivity to culture in development work' in T. Jacobson and J. Servaes, eds, *Theoretical Approaches to Participatory Communication*. Cresskill, NJ: Hampton Press, pp. 17–49.

White, R. 1995a. 'Participatory development communication as a social-cultural process' in S. White, S. Nair and J. Ascroft, eds, *Participatory Communication: Working for Change and Development*. New Delhi: Sage, pp. 95–116.

―――― 1995b. 'The need for new strategies of research on the democratisation of communication' in T. Jacobson and J. Servaes, eds, *Theoretical Approaches to Participatory Communication*. Cresskill, NJ: Hampton Press, pp. 229–60.

White, S. 1994. 'Introduction' in S. White, S. Nair and J. Ascroft, eds, *Participatory Communication: Working for Change and Development*. New Delhi: Sage, pp. 15–32.

White, S. and S. Nair. 1999. 'The catalyst communicator: facilitating without fear' in S. White, ed., *The Art of Facilitating Participation: Releasing the Power of Grassroots Communication*. New Delhi: Sage, pp. 35–51.

Williams, A. 1976. *Broadcasting and democracy in West Germany*. Bradford, Yorks: Bradford University Press.

Williams, R. 1983. *Towards 2000*. London: Penguin.

Williams, R. 2003. 'Flood of emotion and anger that rose to wash away years of dismay'. *The Guardian*, main section, 15 February 2003: 3.

Wilson, R. and W. Dissanayake. 1996. 'Introduction: Tracking the global/local' in R. Wilson and W. Dissanayake, eds, *Global/Local: Cultural Production and the Transnational Imaginary*. London: Duke University Press, pp. 1–18.

WIPO. 2004. *World Intellectual Property Organisation Convention*. At http://www.wipo.org/about-wipo/en/members/index.html. Accessed 22 February 2004.

World Association of Newspapers. 2001. *World Press Trends 2001*. Paris: World Association of Newspapers.

World Bank. 2002a. *World Development Indicators 2002: Economy*. At http://www.worldbank.org/data/wdi2002/economy.pdf. Accessed 8 July 2002.

―――― 2002b. *World Development Indicators 2002: People*. At http://www.worldbank.org/data.wdi2002/people.pdf. Accessed 8 July 2002.

―――― 2002c. *World Development Indicators 2002: States and Markets*. At http://www.worldbank.org/data.wdi2002/statesmkts.htm. Accessed 8 July 2002.

―――― 2003. *World Development Indicators 2003: Urbanization*. At http://www.worldbank.org/data/wdi2003/pdfs/table%203-10.pdf. Accessed 25 February 2004.

―――― 2004. *World Development Indicators 2003: Data Query*. At http://devdata.worldbank.org/data-query. Accessed 2 March 2004.

World Energy Outlook. 2002. *World Energy Outlook 2002. Executive Summary*. At http://www.worldenergyoutlook.org/weo/pubs/weo2002/WEO20021sum.pdf. Accessed 8 July 2003.

World Tourist Organisation. 2000. *Tourism 2020 Vision*. At http://www.world-tourism.org/market_research/facts/market_trends.htm. Accessed 11 February 2004.

WTO. 1998. *Audiovisual Services: Background note by the Secretariat*. World Trade Organisation Council for Trade in Service. Available at: http://docsonline.wto.org. Accessed 23 September 2004.

Zhao, Yuezhi. 1998. *Media, Market and Democracy in China: Between the Party Line and the Bottom Line*. Urbana, IL: University of Illinois Press.

INDEX

Hobson, J. 200, 202
Hornik, R. 68
Hoskins, C. 141
Hosokawa, S. 143
human rights 124, 161

imagined communities 136
imperialism
 contemporary debates on 204–7
 cultural consequences of 214–16
 definition of 199–201, 204, 212, 226
 old and new forms of 87
 theory of 200–4, 207–8, 214–15
imperialism paradigm 3–4, 7, 12, 16,
 48, 82–5, 92, 101, 105–7, 111–15,
 121–5, 130, 140–7, 189, 193–9,
 203, 210–11, 217, 220–1, 225–6
 end of 111–12
 internal contradictions of 112–15
 persistence of 122–5
Independent Television Commission
 (ITC) 163–4
India 13, 39, 42, 45, 62–3, 98, 115–16,
 119–20, 154, 162, 166–76, 191,
 206, 211
indigenous knowledge systems (IKSs)
 60–4
Innis, H. 202
Instituto Nacional Indigenista 74
intellectual property 153, 160
InterAction 218
International Association for Mass
 Communication Research 109
International Association for Media and
 Communication Research 97
International Monetary Fund (IMF)
 3, 8, 159
International Organization of Journalists
 (IOJ) 109–13
International Program for the
 Development of Communication
 (IPDC) 110
International Telecommunications Union
 (ITU) 125, 136, 198, 222–3
internet resources 125, 134–5, 149–50,
 191, 198
Iran 43–4
Iraq 192, 208–9, 214
Ireland 178, 202
Islam 45
Israel 113, 117
Italy 167, 197
Iwabuchi, K. 146

Jacka, E. 144
Jacobson, T. 57, 61, 63

Japan 10, 45, 83–4, 143, 146, 170–4,
 203, 214
Johnson, Lyndon B. 7
Joseph, J. 28–9, 43

Kandath, K. 216
'KAP gap' 40
Katz, E. 99
Kautsky, K. 201
Keynesianism 156
King Lear 209
knowledge, definition of 24
Kosovo 214
Koven, R. 125
Kuhn, Thomas S. 15, 132
Kumar, Ashok 42
Kumar, K. 115

Lang, Jack 123
language issues 96–7, 137, 213–15
Lauder, Ronald S. 183–4
Lebanon 113
Lee, Chin-Chuan 97
Legrain, P. 158
Lenin, V.I. 200, 211
Lerner, Daniel 6, 21–32, 38, 44–50, 85,
 127, 219
Liu Chang Le 164–5
Lloyd George, David 202
London 138–9
Los Ricos También Lloran 142
Lull, James 116, 143–6

McBride, Sean (and McBride
 Commission) 109–10, 124
McChesney, Robert 125, 127, 135, 191
McGrew, A. 144
McNamara, Robert 56
Magdoff, H. 202
'mainstreaming' 209–10
Malaysia 162
Mallaby, Sebastian 192
Mankekar, D. 103
Marx, Karl 152
Marxism 9–10, 14, 21, 84, 90, 106, 125,
 129–30, 152, 200–2, 205, 211–12
Masilela, S. 59
Masmoudi, M. 12
mass communication, role of 24–8
Mato, D. 78
Mattelart, A. 200, 224
Maxwell, Richard 90
media corporations 157, 172, 174,
 184–5, 208, 215–16
Media Development (journal) 124